BOOKS BY HAROLD C. LIVESAY

MERCHANTS AND MANUFACTURERS:
STUDIES IN THE CHANGING PATTERNS OF
NINETEENTH CENTURY DISTRIBUTION

ANDREW CARNEGIE AND THE RISE OF BIG BUSINESS

SAMUEL GOMPERS AND AMERICAN LABOR

AMERICAN MADE: MEN WHO SHAPED THE AMERICAN ECONOMY

American Made

American Made

Men Who Shaped the
American Economy

by HAROLD C. LIVESAY

HarperCollins*Publishers*

Library of Congress Catalog Card No. 79–15971

ISBN 0-316-52874-9

MV

Published simultaneously in Canada
by Little, Brown & Company (Canada) Limited

PRINTED IN THE UNITED STATES OF AMERICA

Dedication

TO MY FATHER, WHO TOLD ME

*Horace Heidt's Pot of Gold may call and give you a
thousand dollars, but if I were you, I wouldn't count on it.
(I didn't, Pop, and you were right: Horace didn't call.)*

TO MY MOTHER, WHO WARNED

*When you get right down to it, life is just a question of
"Root hawg, or die!"
(Don't worry, Mother, I'm steady rootin'.)*

TO MY GRANDMOTHER, WHO DEMANDED

*Enough of this dithering. What is to be done?
(Get tenure, Mom, and try to stay human.)*

TO MY GRANDFATHER, WHO SAID

*Son, one of the nice things about getting old is that
you can remember things any way you want, so you
might as well remember them happy.
(I'm looking forward to it, Mr. Brown. I'll try not to start too soon.)*

Acknowledgments

WITHOUT the encouragement of Marian Ferguson at Little, Brown, this project might have remained an idea. Without Professor Alfred D. Chandler, Jr., my mentor and friend, I wouldn't be writing history in any case. My deepest debt, however, is to my colleague Professor Charles B. Forcey, who took the time and care to read the manuscript with scrupulous attention to every line. That kind of editing can be hard, unrewarding work. I hope the extent to which I have heeded his advice expresses my respect and gratitude for his efforts.

I am also obligated to Ken Dowling of the Ford Motor Company for facilitating my research over several years.

Portions of the research for this book received the generous support of the Carnegie Endowment for International Peace and the National Endowment for the Humanities. Their aid was crucial and I am pleased to acknowledge their support.

Contents

American Made

1

Introduction

THIS is a book about some businessmen, their impact on America, and America's influence upon them. From the host of actors who have played the businessman's role in America's past, I have chosen this particular cast because of a common trait. All these men manufactured things; moreover, the things they made, or the way they made them, became part of the kit of tools used to carve American civilization out of the continent's wilderness.

That business shaped America past and present can be easily and literally seen. In the seventeenth and eighteenth centuries, churches and steeples dominated the city skylines; in the nineteenth century, the horizon silhouetted mills and smokestacks; in the twentieth century, corporate skyscrapers reign. This visible progression of business dominance cannot be claimed as uniquely American, but surely it enveloped American society completely, sooner than elsewhere. In American cities, business shouldered aside the past to make room for its symbols of present power, spiking itself deep in the earth and high in the sky from coast to coast. With the John Hancock Building in Boston, the World Trade Center in New York, the Sears Building in Chicago, the Superdome in New Orleans, the Transamerica Tower in San Francisco, business memorializes not only its own achievements, but also the values of a society that finds such power congenial and reassuring.

In other societies, business, retarded by the state of economic development, or constrained by different sorts of ideals, often projects a lower profile. Cities are pedestals for monuments to the past — the Acropolis in Athens, Palatine Hill and St. Peter's in Rome, the Sacré Coeur and the Louvre in Paris; or furnish settings for symbols of cultural imperatives — the Holmenkollen ski jump in Oslo, Tivoli Park and City Hall in Copenhagen, St. Paul's Cathedral and Big Ben in London.

Whether one judges American society as better or worse than the others depends on individual tastes more than on any absolute standards. But understanding the past informs judgment of the present, and history can, to some degree at least, be understood. The history of any country results from the interaction of its physical environment and the people who live in it, some of whom play a more important role than others.

Among the Americans, none played a more dynamic part than the manufacturers, for the country's ability to make things in massive quantity and acceptable quality at low cost did more than any other factor to propel it from colonial dependency to world power.

Other elements facilitated the passage, of course. The country's original economic viability grew from the capacity of its land, the benevolence of its climate, and the industry of its farmers. (In the long run, ironically enough, the ability to cling to vestigial prosperity may depend primarily on the same factors.) Other men, men who grew nothing and produced nothing, contributed by assembling the capital needed by those who did. But, more than anything else, America rode to prosperity on a man-made river of goods.

The goods-makers, then, deserve attention, not just as builders of prosperity, but also as architects of the society as a whole. Conversely, these men were themselves products of their society. The culture provided much of their mental equipment, shaped their aspirations, inculcated some sense of moral propriety and political pragmatism. That the culture was American made all the difference. Every society confronts the problem of coming to terms with its physical environment, and presumably does so with a core of universal instincts among its members, but the responses vary from the furiously energetic to the fatalistically passive, a variety too great to be explained by differences in climate and natural resources. Sweden is cold, resource-poor, and rich. Indonesia is warm, resource-rich, but poor. Even among societies that embrace history's most widely accepted creed, industrialization, dissimilar answers emerge in response to such fundamental questions as who raises capital and how, who decides what to produce, in what quantity, and how to price it.

American manufacturers' behavior formed a vital component of their society's particular response to mankind's fundamental dilemma: in the pure state of nature, every human awakens every day cold, hungry, and uncertain of living to see another dawn. As the human race tightropes across the tenuous span between cradle and grave, its necessities are few and simply stated: something to eat, some way to keep warm, something to believe in. These requirements, so simply put, have proven achingly difficult for most societies to fulfill, but mass production, for those that have achieved it, holds the wolf, if not the demons, at bay. In the nineteenth century, American manufacturers made mass production the core of the business system, and it has been a national way of life ever since.

As a supplier of goods and services, necessary and otherwise, the American business system remains the best yet. That is not to say that it is perfect; two of its major flaws — environmental damage and the persistence of a poverty-ridden under class — fester stubbornly. But the fact that these and other failings of our pluralist society are traced to economic causes reveals how deeply the business strand interweaves the social fabric. Businessmen were never a race apart and did not operate in a vacuum. On the contrary, constraints obtruded at every turn — their conception of what was legitimate and possible for them personally, their education, their estimate of public reaction to their activities, their desire to perpetuate their families' control of the business they built, the limitations and possibilities presented by existing laws, the prospect of government help, the fear of government interference, the obligation to answer to stockholders, and above all, the vagaries of a fluctuating, unpredictable, uncontrollable market.

To a large degree, the complexities of the American market resulted from the very prosperity of the country itself. To an extent unprecedented in history, Americans found themselves able to afford things they wanted, not just things they needed. The luxury of indulging laziness, or aesthetic tastes, of satisfying a craving for convenience or dissipation, hitherto reserved to the planet's plutocrats, came within range of much of the American population. So much disposable current income, coupled to the American penchant for expecting even better times ahead, constituted an enormous potential market that businessmen found ways to stimulate into immediate demand. Through advertisements and credit sales, businessmen convinced the public that yesterday's luxuries could be today's necessities, that the many could live now as only the rich had lived in the past, and that they had a right to do just that.

In a country dedicated to progress and persuaded that improvement could be measured in material terms, the proliferation of goods seemed moral, and those who made it possible seemed great benefactors. In 1888 Charles Elliott Perkins, president of the Chicago, Burlington, and Quincy Railroad asked:

Have not great merchants, great manufacturers, great inventors, done more for the world than preachers and philanthropists? . . . Can there be any doubt that cheapening the cost of necessities and conveniences of life is the most powerful agent of civilization and progress? Does not the fact that well-fed and well-warmed men make better citizens . . . than those who are cold and hungry, answer the question?

As far as Perkins was concerned, it surely did:

Poverty is the cause of most of the crime in the world — cheapening the cost of the necessaries and conveniences . . . is lessening poverty, and there is no other way to lessen it, absolutely none. History and experience demonstrate that as wealth has accumulated and things have cheapened, men have improved . . . in their habits of thought, their sympathy for others, their ideas of justice as well as of mercy. . . . Material progress must come first and . . . upon it is founded all other progress.

To a remarkable degree Perkins's fellow citizens agreed with him and always had, contributing to the creation of a market where Adam Smith's well-informed buyers and sellers were joined by unscrupulous producers and uncritical customers. In the "Great Barbecue" that ensued, most people got what they needed, many what they wanted, and a few what they deserved. The wicked often prospered; virtue sometimes found scant reward; and the innocent frequently suffered. Through it all, prosperity remained the goal of Americans from the top of society to the bottom. When asked "What is it labor wants?" Samuel Gompers, first president of the American Federation of Labor, philosophical and organizational father of modern American organized labor, answered with a word no capitalist, however greedy, could have improved upon: "More," said Gompers, "more, more, more."

Businessmen's conduct, laudable or otherwise, thus reflected a complex interaction between themselves and their culture, not simply the results of their own will, exercised unrestrained in pursuit of power and profit. For example, industrialization American style involved a disregard of life and limb that killed and maimed thousands of workers. But that fact says something not only about the men who presided over the carnage, but also about a society that lionized them, financed them, and worked for them, while rationalizing casualties as "the price of progress" and smoke as "the smell of money." Industrialization drove some people to despair, some to rebellion, and some back to the old country, but most tolerated it bec͏ ͏͏them hope for a better life for their children if not f͏ brought results in the form of a ris͏ pain had its consequences as wel͏ lasted a short time compared to͏ constituted most human experienc͏ action strong enough to propel ͏ agencies, institutionalized eviden͏ nomic system to counterbalance͏

These days, critics of busines͏ vealing, tacks. Business, they sa͏ consumer sovereignty with an advertising blitzkrieg, enabling it to fob off on the mesmerized public a massive array of trashy, tasteless products that exhibit the short life expectancy and disgusting sameness of maggots on a corpse. Dinner at McDonald's, followed by an evening watching television while squirming around in polyester pants, can heighten anyone's receptivity to this critique. But coupling the success of these mediocrities to the failure of such things as Corfam and the Edsel, the popularity of small cars, the proliferation of auto service shops selling parts with long guarantees, and the widespread enthusiasm for theatre and opera groups, limns a more intricate picture. Business stands willing to make and sell pretty much anything that people will buy, and certainly spends lots of money trying to make sure they buy plenty, but the power to produce goods (even shoddy goods) and mold opinion (even by willful deceit) adds up to something less than the power to dictate to the market.

In fact, the market has done much of the dictating throughout American history. It acted as a commercial polling place where sellers campaigned and buyers voted. Just as in politics, the commercial hustings accommodated knaves as well as knights, the tawdry and the sublime, the garish and the comely; for free enterprise, like democracy, counted on the wisdom of the people to sort things out eventually. The Americans themselves have always cherished their rights at both polls, including the right to be lazy, ill informed, and to go for tinsel instead of substance if they so chose.

That imperfections have resulted, no one could deny, but Americans generally have judged the market mechanism as Winston Churchill judged democracy, "the worst alternative, except for all the others," and they often bristle at paternalistic tampering with it. Informing the public is one thing — no one wants to buy children's pajamas fireproofed with carcinogens — telling buyers what to do with the information is something else again. American consumers sometimes reject legislative intrusion in the market as an unwarranted restriction on individual as witness the widespread hostility to mandatory seat-motorcycle-helmet laws. As long as these attitudes persist, the market — the sum of individual consumer preferences, not some mystical "force of history" — will, for better or worse, prescribe what is produced, including, no doubt, massive doses of drivel, dross, and chicken-fat frankfurters.

The men who successfully created the American system of mass production did so by giving this idiosyncratic market whatever it demanded, or at any rate, whatever it would buy at a price that returned a profit. Those who explicitly criticize business behavior thus implicitly criticize mass taste (both critiques valuable and legitimate, to be sure), and in fact, what the public wants offends John Kenneth Galbraith, Ralph Nader, and others as much as business's eagerness to supply it. Their philippics reflect the continued intertwining of cultural and economic imperatives in the marketplace, a process that has outrun, in terms of material wealth, the palmiest expectations of its advance men, Adam Smith and Alexander Hamilton.

But the business system that has so copiously provided for most Americans' material needs has, alas, proven less successful at feeding their spiritual hungers. Happiness remains an elusive goal, even among those least threatened by hunger and cold. Business, as one of the two locomotives assigned to haul the American express (the political system being the other), gets blamed when a lot of unhappy passengers turn up on board.

The intensity of recent criticism along these lines says much about the nature of past expectations: the higher the hopes, the deeper the potential for despair. Widespread use of the idiom "money can't buy happiness" obscures the fact that mankind generally accepts the reverse proposition, namely that poverty and misery go hand in hand. Now and then a Gandhi or a Dick Gregory transcends the equation temporarily, but on the whole, history validates Bertolt Brecht's observation that "even saintly folk may act like sinners, unless they've had their customary dinners."

The American colonies were born into a seventeenth-century world that could not remember when masses of poor did not present a continuing social and economic problem, as well as a potential political menace. The mother country, England, grappled with the dilemma of too many people, too little land, and too few jobs. "The land grows weary of its people," Englishmen lamented, and "the beggars are coming to town," where, as in the countryside, "like Caterpillars, Waspes, and Droanes, they eate and devoure uppe the Fruites and sweet Commodities of the Commonwealth."

The idle had an equally pernicious effect on the sturdy fabric and character of English society. With nothing else to do, and "abounding in all kinds of filthinesse and prophanenesse," they tended to "seeke out disordered Alehouses, where they sweare and forsweare ... Curse, Blaspheme God, disdain good things, slander and backbite their neighbors," as well as to afflict honest folk with "the theefe, the Rogue, the Strumpet, the sturdy Beggar, the Filcher, the Couzener, the Cut-purse, and such like."

Small wonder that the idea of exporting these vagabonds to a new world appealed to the English mentality, convinced as it was of the relationship of poverty, misery, and wickedness. Colonization promised many benefits to its sponsors — a market for British woolens; a chance to find gold as the Spaniards had done; a sure, cheap source of ship timber, cordage, tar, olive oil, wine; an arena for performing God's work by bringing the heathen Indians into the Christian fold — but the prospect of striking a blow for the economic and moral integrity of the kingdom proved particularly alluring.

The colonists themselves, even the most spiritually idealistic, knew from the beginning that the New World must be a paying proposition. Whether their minds turned to the Puritan exclusionism of New England, the Quaker tolerance of Pennsylvania, the Catholic solace of Maryland, or the Anglican pomp of Virginia, their hands turned to making money. Meanwhile, the clergy busied itself with explaining and justifying the interdependence of faith and materialism. "As soon as ever a man begins to look toward God and the way of his Grace," said the Reverend John Cotton, a pillar of early New England Puritanism, "he will not rest 'til he finds out some warrantable calling and employment." His grandson, Cotton Mather, declared, "Would a man *Rise* by his Business? I say, then let Him Rise to his Business. ... Let your *Business* ingross the most of your time." The Quaker William Penn urged diligence as "the Way to Wealth." *"The diligent Hand makes Rich,"* he declared; moreover, diligence coupled to frugality was the "better way to be rich," for it led to a more peaceful life, with "less Toil and Temptation."

By the time the colonies declared their independence, testimonials abounded to the energy with which Americans pursued wealth and property, and their widespread success in attaining it. "The only principle of Life propagated among the Young People," Cadwallader Colden observed in 1748, "is to get Money. . . . The hopes of having land of their own . . . is what chiefly induces people into America." Once there, they bought land as soon as they could, for such was "the desire of being independent and leaving [an] estate to their children that it [overcame] all other considerations."

Most men who wanted land got it. In 1751, Benjamin Franklin wrote that any "laboring man that understands husbandry can in a short time save enough money to purchase a piece of land sufficient for a plantation." In 1764, Thomas Hutchinson, royal governor of Massachusetts, observed that throughout the colonies, less than 2 percent of all farmers were tenants, and the research of modern historians confirms Hutchinson's general impression, if not his exact estimate. The cities exhibited similar evidence of the rewards of hard work. In 1776, a Philadelphia newspaper asked, "Is not one half the property in the city . . . owned by men who wear *Leather Aprons?* Does not the other half belong to men whose fathers or grandfathers wore Leather Aprons?" In New York and Boston, two-thirds of the Revolutionary era merchants had begun as poor men. Altogether, less than a third of the population held no property, and that third included slaves and indentured servants.

In colonial America, as elsewhere, the very rich owned a disproportionate share of the wealth and, in retrospect, the common folk's holdings seem pitifully small to have generated such excitement. But the rich had always prospered; what made

America different was the fact that most men could aspire to owning something and their children something more, a rousing prospect to settlers from England, where landless poverty had always been the lot of most men and their posterity.

Steeped in the ageless hunger for land as the foundation of wealth and fired by the seemingly limitless expanse of their continent, the Americans embraced a creed that intertwined property and liberty, wealth and happiness. These goals, so long unattainable to most of mankind, became a "self-evident" truth, one of the "unalienable rights" of the Declaration of Independence, "Life, Liberty and the pursuit of Happiness." The Constitution affirmed the relationship, protecting the people against loss of "life, liberty, or property, without due process of law . . . or just compensation," thus enshrining what Sinclair Lewis later called, in *Main Street,* "this treasure of American ideals. Sturdiness and democracy and opportunity," preserved for succeeding generations by "one of our favorite American myths that broad fields make broad minds and high mountains make high purposes."

However self-evident it may now seem to critics of the American economic system that wealth does not necessarily bring happiness, American businessmen through most of the country's history operated in a culture where the opposite assumption prevailed. Many Americans welcomed industrialization because it lessened their dependence on the mischievous, unpredictable Europeans, boosted farm productivity, exploited natural resources other than land, and generated wealth even faster than agriculture. Machines, moreover, had a quality that promised to provide jobs and goods in mind-boggling quantities: machines can reproduce themselves; the land cannot.

As masters of the new mechanized systems of production, manufacturers found themselves appointed chief caretakers of the American dream of universal prosperity and happiness. In this position they were admired, excused, encouraged, given free rein as long as times were good or hopes were high. When times were bad and despair prevailed, they were reviled, accused, restricted, and regulated. As long as "all was well, because all got better" (in the smug words of Andrew Carnegie), their most casually uttered absurdities carried the weight of divine writs; when things fell to pieces, their best-informed opinions were derided as self-serving chicanery, or as the rankest nonsense. And, since the very system they commanded further subdivided an already complex society into groups that perceived their self-interests as conflicting, manufacturers past and present have often found themselves damned on one side and praised on the other.

As men whose power shaped the past and molds the present, manufacturers are subject to the judgments of history. But in measuring their culpability for the stubborn spiritual malaise that has resisted the medications of prosperity, it is well to keep in mind the dialogue between one of Antoine de St. Exupéry's kings and the Little Prince:

" 'If I ordered a general to fly from one flower to another like a butterfly, or to write a tragic drama, or to change himself into a sea bird, and if the general did not [obey], which one of us would be in the wrong, the general or myself?'

" 'You,' said the Little Prince firmly.

" 'Exactly. One must require from each one the duty which each one can perform. . . . Accepted authority rests first of all on reason.' "

This latter proposition Americans have embraced throughout their history as an independent nation. Themselves children of what history has called the "Enlightenment," or the "Age of Reason," the writers of the Declaration of Independence and of the Constitution cited reason, not divine inspiration nor hereditary privilege, as the authority for dissolving the "political bands" that connected them to an old government in 1776, and for endorsing a new one in 1789. Newspapermen and song writers packaged for popular consumption the idea that scientific logic justified liberty, as in a 1789 song entitled "Ode on Science":

So Science spreads her lighted ray
O'er lands which long in darkness lay;

> *Fair Freedom, her attendant waits,*
> *To crown the young and rising States*
> *With laurels of immortal day.*

Reason itself, however, is a livery stable horse, ridable by anyone who can clamber aboard. Loyalists and anti-Federalists resorted to logic themselves, but denounced the Revolution and damned the Constitution. Ever since, Americans have relied on "reason," "logic," "common sense," and "rationality" to demonstrate the justice of this or that position. The Pope may have set crusading battalions on the road by crying "God wills it!" but "It makes sense!" has kept the Americans hustling.

Businessmen, like the rest of the citizenry, have endorsed logic as the justification for their behavior; indeed, they have often heralded themselves as embattled islands of reason in a sea of irrationality. Now and again one of them, besotted with his own magnificence, or puffed up by some tame clergyman, proclaimed himself, as the president of the Reading Coal and Iron Company did in 1902, the holder of a divine appointment as one of the "Christian men to whom God in his infinite wisdom has given control of the property interests of this country." But few capitalists have canonized themselves, at least not publicly. Most businessmen explained their success in terms of the reason that condoned private property, the natural laws that ruled the marketplace, the common sense that connected prosperity to the national welfare, or the science of social Darwinism, which rationalized competition as a natural process that elevated society by eliminating the unfit. In these arguments, and in the public's reaction to them, lies a key to understanding the American past because businessmen played such a central role in American history that their interpretation of themselves, and of the world around them, resonated with the pulse of American life.

All the men I've included here played just such a central role. Each made lasting contributions to the American manufacturing system, helping to shape it into the most potent economy in history, an economy that could, at full stretch, feed and equip half the world or more. I considered other manufacturers (Francis Cabot Lowell and Clarence Birdseye, to name two) but discarded them on the grounds of lesser historical importance, a judgment based on my reading of history and informed by my own experiences in business. I also excluded other possible categories, such as financiers (J. P. Morgan and John D. Rockefeller the most tempting) and leaders of organized labor (John L. Lewis and Walter Reuther are worthy of any economic historian's attention), because while I can conceive of the Carnegies without the Morgans and the Fords without the Reuthers, the reverse seems to me inconceivable.

In addition, I've made only passing references to the role of organized labor and of government in the development of American economic society, not because I think their roles unimportant — they deserve equal time — but because big labor and big government as we know them emerged as a response to big business far more than the other way around, and I want to deal first with first causes.

Making such choices, and standing or falling by them, is the essence of the historian's craft, but the fact that I wound up with an all-white, all-male cast (and would have even if I had expanded the book's scope to include the most influential figures in realms of finance, labor, and government) is symptomatic of the reality of American history itself. No black man, no red man, and no woman of any color has yet reached the first rank in American business, and this may be the most damning indictment of the system that can be made. To have included a George Washington Carver or an Elizabeth Arden in this book would have been to twist past and present realities to fit future hopes. My cast of characters, then, reflects both my own judgment and the historical reality that when one speaks of the builders of American business, one perforce speaks of businessmen, and white businessmen at that.

All the men in the chapters that follow wielded great power, but their power stemmed from their understanding of the market and their mastery of the machine, not from the traditional preindustrial sources: land, politics, the military, mercantile trade, or hereditary privilege. None of these manufacturers ever held a political office of consequence, and the few who tried cut ridiculous figures in the attempt. Most of them, however, knew Presidents (and sometimes kings) intimately, often advised or controlled politicians, and some of them ruled companies with incomes and output greater than most countries' of their times. None distinguished himself in military service, but several owed their fortunes at least partially to armed forces patronage; all produced goods that had significant military applications, and most of them commanded echelons of managers and armies of workers of greater size and sophistication than their military contemporaries.

None of these men could claim to be a successful merchant, and, in fact, their activities displaced the merchant's dominant role in the economy, often destroying it altogether. Many of them, however, survived and prospered through access to mercantile capital and reliance on mercantile expertise to supply raw materials and distribute products.

In background and training, these men shared no membership in an elitist caste. Indeed, their very diversity reflected the complexity and fluidity of American society. Some were born poor, some rich, most neither. Some were immigrants, or the children of immigrants; some came from families long established in America. Some grew up on farms, others in cities. Some had no education worthy of the name; others graduated from distinguished universities. Some were inventors or master craftsmen; some scarcely knew one end of a wrench from the other. Some built systems to manage their enterprise; others ruled personally, autocratically, and belligerently resisted bureaucratization that might dampen their authority. Some worked all their lives and died in harness; some retired to opulence or philanthropy. Many traveled abroad and became internationalists; some never left the American shore; a few evinced unsavory traits of nativism, parochialism, and bigotry. Some mastered the art of being family men; some made a mess of the whole thing. A few embraced religion; most did not. Some gloried in the public's attention; others found it frightening or despicable and retreated into reclusiveness. Some had personalities as unremarkable as dirt; others carried idiosyncrasies to the point of lunacy and used their wealth to trumpet their eccentricities across the land. Living in America, they existed in a culture that not only tolerated such diversity but propagated it. Inculcated with the sense that what mattered to their society was not who or what they were, but what they could do, they perceived opportunities and seized them. They, and others like them, left an indelible mark on America and cast an image that the rest of the world, whether friendly, envious, or hostile, could not ignore. "If they could," wrote one observer recently, "half the people in the world would start walking to America tomorrow." For some of these pilgrims, the lure might be American democracy and its tradition of individual liberties, but for most the magnet would be what it always was: America, the land of opportunity, toward which a good part of the world *did* start walking at one time or another. These men — "the Vital Few," "the Potentates," "the Robber Barons," "the Entrepreneurs," or whatever collective title one gives them — built and ran the dynamos that energized the American magnet. This is the land that made them, and this is the land they made.

Eli Whitney in 1821, weary and prosperous

2

The Artist of His Country
Eli Whitney

IN a previous incarnation, I made my living as a yardmaster
for the Pennsylvania Railroad. From time to time my domain included yards that delivered parts to automobile assembly plants of the "Big Three," General Motors, Ford, and
Chrysler. This experience introduced me to the practicalities
(and occasional absurdities) of the concept of interchangeable
parts, a notion that, before then, had existed for me largely as an
abstraction. Like most Americans, I had accepted as an obvious
truth the statement that our prosperity rested on mass production, and that mass production meant assembly of interchangeable parts.

Behind this tautology there lurks a complex and frantic world,
as I soon learned from the bedlamites who inhabited a crucial
part of it, my opposite numbers in the transportation offices of
the car companies. I discovered that the assembly line itself, "a
system designed," as Herman Wouk said of the U.S. Navy, "by
geniuses, to be operated by idiots," is child's play next to the web
of transportation and communications that keeps it supplied.
The jungle of apparatus that carries the parts to the line, props
them in place, welds, glues, or bolts them together, and drags the
whole contraption through the plant pales in cost and complexity
compared to the machines spawning streams of identical parts in
dozens of plants far removed from the assembly process itself.

The corporations that built and run these empires of supply, manufacture, and assembly wield enormous power, creating incomes through jobs and investments and supplying the market with swarms of products. The "economy" that is General Motors alone outsells and outspends all but a handful of the countries of the world. Power so great radiates invulnerability, and indeed, an installation such as Ford's River Rouge, where boatloads of iron ore, coal, limestone, and sand come in one end and trainloads of cars come out the other, seems a juggernaut with an unstoppable momentum of its own. In fact, the powerful engine created by mass assembly of interchangeable parts is finely tuned, delicate, and easily bogged down by anything that interrupts the flow of information or material.

Parts for today's assembly schedule may be in the plant, but tomorrow's ride the rails somewhere between manufacturing and assembly point, while next week's may not yet be fabricated. It won't do, moreover, for *most* of the bits and pieces to arrive on schedule; they *all* have to get there or everything stops. Consequently, a huge assembly plant's multimillion-dollar machinery and thousands of workers can be idled for the lack of a sack of hardware worth a few dollars.

I first encountered this reality on a July afternoon in a Delaware railroad yard. Squinting through the glare and the fog, I was amazed to see a motorized combat team from the nearby Chrysler plant assault a boxcar with a cutting torch, dragging the oxygen and acetylene hoses across the tracks to get at their quarry. By the time I got to the scene, they had fired up and begun slicing a hole in the side of a boxcar. "We need some bolts," said the foreman, by way of what he thought sufficient explanation. "If we don't get them, the line will stop in an hour."

"What about using the door?" I asked him.

"We think they're in this end and we don't have time to unload the whole car."

"What if they aren't in this end?"

"We've got a lot of gas. We'll cut 'til we find 'em."

"What about the car?"

"The hell with the car. The Company'll pay for it."

"I'll call the cops. You guys can't come on railroad property unless you sign a damages release, and you sure as hell can't cut cars open regardless."

"Call the cops. Call anybody you want. By the time they get here we'll be long gone, and even if we aren't, the Company'll pay the fine. It costs forty thousand dollars an hour to stop that line. You think the Company gives a damn about a two-bit fine from a hick-town judge? We're gonna get them bolts, whatever you do about it."

What I did about it was get the railroad crew to kick a boxcar full of fenders down the track, trifurcating the hoses, suffocating the torch, and sure enough stopping the line, about eighty thousand dollars' worth. I hadn't thought it possible, but they really did need those bolts.

Over the years I witnessed similar scenes many times, when a shortage of tires, batteries, nuts, bolts, washers, or cotter pins loomed. On paper such crises were impossible. The system translated dealers' orders into parts requisitions, shipping manifests, and assembly schedules that crisscrossed the communications network in precise columns of computer and Telex printouts. On paper, everything arrived on time. On the ground, however, things sometimes went haywire. Strikes, snowstorms, train wrecks, loading mistakes, sabotage, locomotive breakdowns, misdirected shipments, and a plethora of other mishaps betrayed the corporations' inability, for all their power, to make steel, rubber, and plastic march with the precision of their printed surrogates.

Knowing its fragilities, I was more impressed by the system, not less. Most of the time things went exactly as planned. And one thing never failed; when the parts got there, they fitted. Getting them there absorbed most of my energies, but the precision and symmetry of them excited my imagination, for it was that that made all the rest possible and necessary. For the first time, the schoolboy textbook phrase "Eli Whitney invented interchangeable parts" transmitted a fascination commensurate with the achievement. I felt pretty close to old Eli sometimes.

Later on, when I got to college, I found out I had been even closer than I knew — just about four engineering generations away, in fact. The assembly plants I strolled through were up-dated variations of Henry Ford's original; Ford was the "most distinguished disciple" of Henry M. Leland, who applied the concept of interchangeable parts to the manufacture of automobiles. Leland learned the concept and the precision machine work that effected it while working in the Springfield Armory and the Colt Arms works. At Springfield and Colt, Leland apprenticed with men who had known Eli Whitney: Simeon North, Roswell Lee, John H. Hall, and other pioneers who had struggled to transform interchangeability from engineering theory into manufacturing practice.

Among these pathfinders, Whitney ranks first, but not because he originated interchangeability, perfected it, or applied it successfully to mass production; he did none of these. What he did do was to perceive identical parts as a precondition to volume production, particularly in the circumstances of the early United States. He applied his energy and genius to the problem and influenced his contemporaries and successors who addressed the same challenge. Whitney built the first arch in the engineering bridge that spanned the gulf between the ancient world's handicraft methods of production and the modern world's mass manufacturing, a bridge across which his countrymen and the rest of the so-called developed world marched to prosperity.

Whitney was a practical man, a prototype of the pragmatic American. Like many of his contemporaries, he lived by and for his ambitions, aspiring to wealth and social position. These goals and the possibility of fulfilling them drove him forward in his work, not the kind of intellectual curiosity that led Ben Franklin to fly kites among the lightning bolts. A manufacturer before he became an inventor, Whitney yoked the two roles firmly together throughout his life, inventing things to make and sell in markets that existed right then, not squandering this creativity on gadgets that might be useful someday. These qualities, the hallmarks of the entrepreneurial personality, Whitney demonstrated while still a boy, growing up in rural New England.

Whitney was born on December 8, 1765, on his father's farm in Westborough, Massachusetts, about forty miles west of Boston. The town, now spelled Westboro, lies near Route 128, the belt highway that encircles Boston, but in Whitney's day, the lack of waterways connecting it to any urban center kept Westborough, like other landlocked American towns, a provincial outback, culturally and economically.

The Whitney farm generated little cash but provided a comfortable living for the family. But, like so many children growing up in long-settled New England, Eli knew that the home place was too small to be redivided among the children without reducing them and their parents from comfort to subsistence. Even before Whitney was born, New England farmers had encountered this bedeviling phenomenon of rural life. Successful farming required big families but, as the population expanded, land got scarce. Had there been no alternatives, Americans would have adapted their aspirations to the realities of scarcity, delaying marriage as the Irish did, or controlling the birth rate as the French peasantry did. But in America, of course, the open lands of the frontier offered an alternative, and one that a nation of farmers could exploit. For the young people of New England, as elsewhere in America, it came down to a choice: move, or abandon the ideals of independence and prosperity that had been part of the American cultural milieu from the outset. Land shortage thus drove people from New England as surely as from Olde England. As much pushed by the harsh realities behind them as pulled by roseate visions of what lay ahead, they spilled through the mountain gaps and filled up the land along the rivers and lakes of New York.

Preserving American materialistic ideals thus meant that, in many areas, American children were raised to be sent away. This environment reinforced the attitude of independence and individualism, even among the young, and was remarked upon by European visitors like Alexis de Tocqueville. It also injected a dynamic concept into the emerging American culture, the idea that freedom to move inherently preserved individual liberty. This notion pops up again and again in American history: as part of the enthusiasm that greeted the coming of canals, steamboats, and railroads; in the American obsession with everyman's freedom machine, the automobile; in the spirit that ennobled hoboes as "knights of the road"; and in a folklore that enshrines the train whistle as an anthem of free spirits:

> *I can settle down and be doin' just fine,*
> *'Til I hear an old freight blowin' down the line . . .*

Or as a canticle of escape:

> *Far from Folsom prison, that's where I long to stay;*
> *So I let that lonesome whistle blow my blues away.*

Whitney himself, ambitious and restless in the dead end that was Westborough, ultimately joined the ranks of his peregrinating countrymen; indeed, he spent much of his life hustling from one place to another. But his disposition closed the most obvious avenue of escape, because he detested farming, with its drudgery, isolation, and uncertainties. Whatever joy, nobility, and hope his peers found in tilling the soil and coaxing things to grow from it eluded young Eli. Like many another American who turned to the worlds of commerce and machinery, Whitney derived part of his impetus from the barbarities of bucolic life.

Fortunately for young Whitney, his father's farm included a workshop among its paraphernalia. There, where his father made wheels and implements for the farm, Whitney discovered a fascination with tools, particularly those that themselves shaped other tools. He also exhibited a gift, not only for the manual arts required by home manufacture (then, literally, a business of "making by hand") but also for grasping the logic through which machines can be devised to replace human energy and physical movements. In addition, he saw how to harness these skills to produce a marketable product, and he knew a market when he saw one.

The American Revolution broke out when Whitney was ten years old. Boston, Concord, and Lexington lay not far off; neighbors and, before the war ended, boys Eli's age marched away to join the ranks, but neither the political nor the military excitement enveloped him. What did stir him was the market opportunity presented by the wartime interruption to commerce. With

British trade stopped for the duration, hardware soon became scarce. Eli, aged fourteen, talked his father into installing a forge in the workshop. There he made nails and knife blades that sold well enough to justify hiring an additional worker. After the war, the British dumped shiploads of nails into American ports at prices no farm forge could equal. Undaunted, Eli shifted to the manufacture of hatpins and walking sticks, a move that sounds simple in the telling, but that demonstrated a combination of initiative, confidence, and flexibility rare at any time among people of any age, but extraordinary in an eighteen-year-old boy in the bushes of Massachusetts.

As a young man, Whitney thus met and mastered one of the harshest realities of the American marketplace: under the continuous pummeling of world events, internal migration, population growth, and technological change, the market often shifted unexpectedly. Entrepreneurs who developed a skill and equipped a shop to turn out a specific product often found, as Whitney did, that the market disappeared or became too competitive. The ability to assess such a change as temporary or permanent, and to react by shutting down, replacing obsolete equipment, or shifting to a new product, often determined success or failure, and determines it still. Whitney, shifting his tiny shop from nails to hatpins, exhibited the same supple survival instincts that Andrew Carnegie showed a century later, turning his giant Homestead steel works from railroad rails to structural iron beams as railroad construction dwindled and urban building boomed.

Despite gloomy predictions to the contrary, people like Whitney and Carnegie have continued to appear, constantly retooling industry to meet the fickle market, supplying much of the drive that has powered American economic growth. America has had no monopoly on such flexible minds, but its society has produced a disproportionate number of them, a fact that reveals something distinctive about the society itself. Here, as elsewhere, the dominant human tendency is inertial, a craving for stability and continuity. But American society, born free of traditional European class rigidity, kept kinetic by social mobility up and down, held in flux by immigration from without and migration within, its religious traditions undermined by secular faith in materialism, and dedicated to progress, nationally and individually, has remained incessantly in motion.

Americans have soothed the anxieties inherent in constant movement by convincing themselves that the special circumstances here made change the keystone of stability. Dedicated to progress, they equated movement with change, and change with progress. Clinging to the political ideals on which the country was founded, they justified alterations in law and society as necessary to preserve unchanged the original ideals themselves. In such an atmosphere, adaptability became a virtue, and the man with a flexible mind was a man to admire.

Movement thus encouraged movers, and the ambitious found that the rough, shifting surface of American society offered hand- and footholds not found on the smooth, unmoving class barriers of Europe. The climb was treacherous, but it could be made. Aspirants were spurred on by the knowledge that at the top awaited not only wealth and power, but also admiration and acclaim from the public and acceptance into the circles of the elite. This last was a plum withheld by the oligarchs of Prussia, France, and England, who despised businessmen and their posterity as vulgar unless they repudiated their professions and laundered their money through propitious marriage or several generations of country living.

In addition to offering great rewards for success, American society encouraged ambition by attaching little stigma to failure, even to bankruptcy. Failing once or a dozen times was no bar to starting over from the bottom if one had the grit to keep trying, another notion embedded in generations of American consciousness through Hickson's "If at first you don't succeed, /Try, try again," in *McGuffey's Reader,* through the "I think I can; I think I can" of *The Little Engine That Could,* to Tony Baretta's televised exhortation, "Keep Strokin'!"

Eli Whitney had plenty of ambition. By the time he was eighteen, he had considered alternative outlets for it, dismissed the farm and shop as too limiting, and decided to go off to college. The fact that college *was* an option for a young man like Whitney in the 1780s starkly differentiated American society from its counterparts in Europe. He had no money, a rudimentary education, and had never been out of his home district. He was, in fact, a rube, a clever, ambitious rube, but a rube nonetheless. In America he could surmount all these obstacles and matriculate at Yale. In England, a young man of Whitney's situation in life might as well have aspired to the archbishopric at Canterbury as to the baccalaureate at Oxford or Cambridge.

Whitney was a systematic man. He tackled the obstacles between Westborough and Yale one by one, but it took him six years, from 1783 to 1789, to surmount them all. By teaching school in nearby towns (his father, aware of Eli's meager qualifications, expected the worst, but Eli told him that with three weeks' head start he could keep ahead of his pupils all year) he financed summer study at Leicester Academy. There Whitney polished his mathematics and English grammar, and grappled with the intricacies of Latin and Greek. There also he became a beneficiary for the first time (many more were to come) of the Yale old-boy network, for the master at Leicester, Ebenezer Crafts, was a Yale alumnus and booster. Crafts persuaded Whitney to go to Yale rather than Harvard, and helped him get in when the time came.

Whitney's diligence, together with failing health brought on by his Möbian life as teacher-scholar, finally overcame his father's skepticism and won a promise of $1,000 support. In March, 1789, Eli set out for New Haven, stopping for a month in Durham, Connecticut, to study mathematics with the Reverend Elizur Goodrich, professor of divinity and professor of mathematics at Yale and a close friend of the college's president, Ezra Stiles. When Whitney presented himself to Stiles for his entrance examination in April, 1789, he came well prepared and highly recommended. The examination itself was a five-hour oral ordeal that few of today's university faculty, let alone students, would approach with much confidence, involving as it did parsing and translating Latin and Greek, in addition to demonstrating a knowledge of the fine points of English grammar and of mathematics.

Once admitted, Whitney flung himself into his studies. Poor, and old for a freshman, Whitney had no time to waste. Certainly the curriculum was arduous in schedule, if not in content. The school day began at five in the morning and proceeded through alternating study and class periods, with the first recitation at seven o'clock. Somehow Whitney found time to earn a little pocket money and to socialize. He fraternized successfully with his classmates, most of them from families far wealthier and more prominent than his own. His popularity was confirmed in 1791, when he was elected to Phi Beta Kappa, then a tribute to social, rather than scholastic, agility.

Acceptance by his peers meant a lot to Whitney, for he viewed Yale more as charm school than vocational school. He went there determined to acquire the genteel manners in dress, speech, correspondence, and general knowledge that would gain him entry to polite society. In short, he went to college to become a gentleman, accepted by other gentlemen. That Whitney could aspire to such a goal reflected another unique facet of his society. Only in America could a man not born a gentleman become one. Years later, his letters to a nephew at Yale, urging the merits of gentility, revealed the lifelong satisfaction he derived from his collegiate accomplishments, and the efforts put forth to achieve them.

He reached graduation in 1792, however, without any specific vocational objective in mind despite his father's urgings that he look to the future, and carefully. "As to your profession," the elder Whitney wrote, "my advice is to look forward and count the Cost before you plan ... and Consider your Surcomstances for I shall not be able to help you much after you are through college."

From time to time Eli, like many an undergraduate down to the present day, pondered a career at law, then as now one of America's great growth industries. Ultimately, he decided against it. (He was to get an education in law, nevertheless, but later, and the hard way, as a litigant.) The other professions for which Yale prepared its sons — the ministry, politics, mercantile trade, and teaching — didn't interest him either. As an undergraduate he evidenced a disillusionment with religion by writing home that he found "a great many Hypocrites" among the clergy. This comment alarmed his father who, steeped in orthodox New England religiosity, urged his son to "avoid infidelity and atheism.... We must not ... excuse ourselves and have no religion at all because others make a bad Use of it." The advice went unheeded; throughout his life, and after his death, the more pious among Whitney's friends and relatives feared for his salvation. ·

Politics he found distasteful as well, avoiding it always and keeping his opinions on the subject — whatever they might have been — to himself. He had neither the capital nor the connections to secure a partnership in a mercantile house, and he certainly hadn't gone to Yale to become a counting-house clerk. Schoolteaching he had had a bellyful of already. The profession for which, as a mechanic with a college education, he would have been most qualified a generation later, engineering, did not yet exist.

In the end Whitney, poor, urbane, polished, a bit cynical ("You know I always considered this a dam'd kind of world," he wrote a friend), and, at twenty-eight, approaching middle age, had to accept a post as tutor to the children of a South Carolina planter. A tutor, Whitney lamented, was just a jumped-up version of a schoolteacher; worse, he feared for his life in the unhealthy climate of the South. His first tutor and one of his classmates had died in Georgia. "Perhaps I shall lose my health and perhaps my life," he wrote his brother Josiah. On the other hand, the job paid well, eighty guineas a year, of which, he told his father, "I hope to save fifty Guineas pr. Year." President Stiles, who found a job for him, "thought it a good offer on the whole." Swallowing his fears and disappointments, Whitney presented himself to Phineas Miller, a Yale alumnus, "a Gentleman from Connecticut, a man of reputation and abilities," and the representative of Whitney's prospective employer.

Miller himself had originally gone south in similar fashion. In 1785, General Nathanael Greene, hero of the Revolution, had asked Stiles to recommend a tutor for the Greene children. Stiles proposed Miller. A year later Greene died and Miller became estate manager — and a whole lot more, as we shall see presently — to Greene's widow. The similarity of Miller's background to his own, and the fact that Miller "really treated [him] like a Gentleman," reassured Whitney. He accepted Miller's invitation to accompany him and Mrs. Greene on the voyage from New York to Savannah, whence he could easily reach his destination. The voyage, and his new friends, carried him to latitudes, both human and geographic, beyond anything he had experienced or anticipated.

In Catherine Greene, Whitney discovered a woman like none he had ever known. Born and raised in the merry and cultured society of Rhode Island, Catherine moved easily in the world of silk and brocade, among men and women who sat for Gilbert Stuart portraits and talked of the latest fashions in literature, dance, and science. Catherine saw no sin in pleasure. She wrung the utmost from life, and chided the sober Whitney, offering to teach him "how to enjoy the few fleeting years which any can calculate upon."

There was more to this woman than fluff and hedonism, however. Married to Nathanael Greene, Washington's most trusted lieutenant and commander of the southern armies in the Revolution, she had accompanied her husband throughout the Revolutionary War. Among her experiences was one that qualified her for membership in an exclusive and cherished circle: she had wintered with Washington at Valley Forge. Catherine's admirers included virtually everyone worth knowing in the Revolutionary generation: Washington, Jefferson, Lafayette, von Steuben, Kosciuszko, Hamilton, Burr. Though recently widowed when Whitney met her, Catherine had rebounded quickly. She exuded charm, joie de vivre, and sexuality. Whitney at once was smitten, and remained so until Catherine's death in 1812. An inconvenient circumstance, however, obtruded, preventing his affection from progressing beyond friendship. Catherine, as Whitney soon discovered, had promoted his friend Miller from estate manager to consort. Whitney's background had ill prepared him for association with a gentleman who cohabited with a lady not his wife, but Catherine's charm, Miller's friendship, and the couple's eventual marriage (in 1796) overcame his instinctive reactions. The South itself, when Whitney arrived in late 1792, was a revelation. Still reeling from the neglect and devastation of the Revolutionary years, the South was mired in economic stagnation, groping for a crop that could restore prosperity. Tobacco had exhausted much of the soil; the market for rice and indigo had collapsed. The land that later billowed with white oceans of cotton remained yet an inland thicket, patrolled by bears and wildcats. Most of the inhabitants squatted along the coast and the shallow rivers and inlets, swatting mosquitoes, hacking at underbrush, and scratching out provisions to feed themselves. The slave population, once looked upon as a valuable resource, hung ever more heavily on the feeble neck of the economy. Violence, so rarely seen in Whitney's New England past, was a way of life. Casual tavern conversations erupted at the drop of an ill-chosen word into eye-gouging, ear-ripping brawls. Surveying all this, Whitney wrote, "I find myself in a new natural world and as for the moral world I believe it does not exist so far south."

Paradoxically, this feral environment supported many devotees of manners, grace, and good living. Along the Savannah River, where Catherine's plantation, Mulberry Grove, was located, the climate was so gentle and the soil so rich that no man's best efforts could ruin it entirely. "Oranges, Pomegranates, Figgs, Olives all grow within ten rods of the place where I now sit," Whitney wrote home. Like the Garden of Eden, Georgia boasted "several fruits which grow spontaneously in the fields . . . the figg tree putteth forth its figgs, the pomegranate its blossoms, the Indian corn its tassel and we have peas and Salad all winter."

Mulberry Grove, when Whitney arrived, was a shambles. Once the residence of the royal lieutenant governor, it had been confiscated by the state of Georgia, which had given it, a prize of war, to General Greene. Greene needed all the help he could get because he had passed out personal notes to the contractors who fed his army. After the war, the Confederation government, less grateful than Georgia's, had repudiated these obligations, stranding Greene in a morass of debt from which he was never able to extricate himself.

The plantation itself and the trees from which it took its name were monuments to the long romance with the silkworm carried on by North Americans. Mulberry trees lined the streets of Whitney's New Haven, and Ezra Stiles's diary recorded "The Spirit for *raising Silk worms* [which] is great in this town ... & other places in Connecticut." Stiles himself spread the silk fever, distributing "Mulberry Seeds ... in this State, some up Mohawk R[iver], & Vermont Towns on L[ake] Champlain." Mulberry Streets in a hundred east coast towns attest to the pervasiveness of America's durable flirtation with the silkworm and its gossamer product. (In retrospect, the obsession with this will-o'-the-wisp seems silly, unless one realizes that the silkworm, contentedly munching mulberry leaves on one end and extruding a ready-to-weave filament on the other, accomplishes, within its little body, a task that man requires flocks of sheep, fields of cotton, and stacks of machinery to duplicate. Unfortunately, the silkworm, like seaweed, is an oriental delicacy that never did well in America.)

Greene had labored to get Mulberry Grove on its feet as a rice plantation by repairing dikes and fields ravaged by wartime floods. This Herculean chore ("The cultivation of rice requires much more labor than I had imagined," Whitney observed) Miller had assumed on Greene's death. What the end result might have been can't be known, but given the state of the rice market, the omens were unpropitious. Fate, and Whitney's genius, intervened to rescue Miller from the paddies.

After a brief stay at Mulberry Grove, Whitney duly crossed the river to assume his tutor's duties. He soon returned, however, claiming the actual salary offered was less than half that promised. Now at loose ends, he succumbed readily to Catherine's invitation to stay on at Mulberry Grove. His mechanical skills made him an asset around the plantation, and his social graces made him an ornament to Catherine's parlor. "He can do anything," she boasted to her friends. Catherine's salon drew the local gentry like moths to a candle. There, Whitney "heard much said of extreme difficulty of ginning Cotton, that is, separating it from its seed.... A number of very respectable Gentlemen at Mrs. Greene's ... agreed that if a machine could be invented [to] clean the Cotton with expedition, it would be a great thing both to the country and to the inventor."

A great thing indeed. If ever in history a chain of potentially explosive economic power awaited only the insertion of a single missing link, the time was 1792, and Whitney stood squarely at the gap. A world sweltering and chafing in woolen and linen offered a global market of incomprehensible dimensions. English craftsmen had successfully mechanized every step of cotton manufacture. The fields, climate, and slave-labor force of southern America could grow the scarce raw material in vast quantities. Only the problem of removing the seeds, which clung to the fibers like burrs to a woolen sock, remained. Picking the seeds out by hand required so much labor that the expense was prohibitive. So alluring, however, were the prospects of the cotton market that some planters put in a crop in 1792, hoping that by the time it matured, some genius would have figured out a way to remove the seeds.

This optimism proved premature, but not by much. Whitney put his mind to the problem, conceived a solution in early 1793, and soon produced a working model, for which he declined an offer of a hundred guineas. The machine was simple, so simple that Georgia schoolboys described its essentials in a phrase, "wire teeth which worked thro' slats, and a brush." The promise, on the other hand, was enormous. Whitney, who had earlier described "the world" as "a Lottery in which many draw Blanks, one of which may fall to [me]," could now boast to his father, " 'Tis generally said by those who know anything about it that I shall make a Fortune out of it." "I am now so sure of success," he added, "that ten thousand dollars, if I saw the money counted out to me, would not tempt me to give up my right and relinquish the object."

Encouraged by the enthusiasm of those who saw his first

model, Whitney built a larger one and tested it, with dynamic
results.

> With [this machine] one man will clean ten times as much cotton as
> ... any other way before known and ... clean it much better. ... This
> machine can be turned by water ... or a horse, with the greatest ease,
> and one man and a horse will do more than fifty men with the old
> [method].

The machine, he added, "makes the labor fifty times less, *without
throwing any class of People out of business*" (italics mine). Whitney thus articulated one of the principles that led people to seize
upon industrialization as the remedy to misery and poverty. If
the machine could put more people to work, lighten their labor,
and generate wealth for everybody without injuring anyone, who
could resist its appeal?

Thus was Prometheus unbound. This little machine — inspired, according to legend, by Whitney's observing a cat reach
through a fence, snatch at a chicken, and come away with only a
pawful of feathers, and by Catherine Greene's handing Whitney
a hearth brush, saying, "La, Mr. Whitney, here's what you
need," to remove the clean cotton from the gin's teeth — this
machine unleashed a cataclysmic force. The southern cotton
crop, insignificant when Whitney invented the gin, exceeded 200
million pounds annually by the time he died in 1825.

The total effects, however, defy the power of numbers to con-
vey. A southern judge remarked, in 1806, that before Whitney's
machine, "The whole interior of the Southern states was lan-
guishing," and people were leaving the South. Thanks to the gin,
"Individuals who were depressed with poverty, and sunk with
idleness, have suddenly risen to wealth and *respectability* [italics
mine]. Our debts have been paid off, our capitals increased; and
our lands are treble in value." Cotton cleared the southern wilderness, enriched northern merchants and shipowners, financed
industrialization, and built the factories that soaked up much of
the surplus population of England and Ireland. But there was a
dark side as well. Cotton reinvigorated slavery, hitherto expiring
from its own weakness, and laid its curse on Americans white

and black. Cotton built the mill towns, squalid and stinking, that horrified Karl Marx and galvanized his speculations into a creed that shakes the world even now.

But all that, good and bad, lay far beyond Whitney's ken in 1793. He had his invention and that was new, but nothing else had changed. Even the most dramatic movements in history begin with a small step in a world that remains, for the moment, unchanged. Whitney, rejoicing in his little model there on the banks of the Savannah, had visions of wealth and glory dancing in his head. But the exact route from inspiration to riches was obscure, and strewn with obstacles. He had no capital, no business organization, no factory, no plan to sell or distribute the machines, and no precedents he could follow.

Meanwhile, Catherine's pride in her protégé's skill had led her to show off the machine to her friends; any of them might copy it, and Whitney had no patent to stop them. A patent he must have, and soon; furthermore, he must build lots of machines, and quickly; otherwise, the whole chance must go on a-glimmering. None of this could be accomplished down there in the "chigger and pellagra latitudes," as Henry Mencken derided them. Not only was the South the "Sahara" of the beaux arts, but it was barren of the industrial arts as well. As Whitney realized, the southern swamps and thickets abounded with men clever enough to make individual copies of so simple a machine, but every-thing — labor, raw materials, machinery — was lacking for a factory to produce in volume.

Whitney concluded he must go north to get a patent and set up manufacture. In New England he knew where to find everything he needed. Forming a partnership with Miller, who advanced the necessary capital, Whitney sailed back to New York on June 1, 1793. Detouring to the national capital, Philadelphia, where he filed his patent application, he moved on to New Haven to set up shop. The way he equipped his establishment demonstrated an embryonic grasp of modern manufacturing arrangements. He might simply have hired enough skilled workers to build gins one at a time by hand, but skilled workers were scarce and com-manded high wages, an omnipresent incentive that encouraged generations of American manufacturers to mechanize. Moreover, hand production would have been a slow business, far too slow to keep up with demand.

In order to accelerate the process he needed tools, machine tools that could produce components in volume. Such devices could not be bought in the United States; he had to make them himself. Drawing on his experience in his father's workshop and as a manufacturer of nails and hatpins, Whitney built a lathe, a wire drawing block, and a machine to cut the wire teeth for the gin. A forerunner of later tools, the tooth-cutting machine produced parts of uniform size, but "equally on both sides." "It feeds itself," Whitney added, "and goes remarkably easy."

Making the machines to make the parts to make the gins took time — so much time that not until May, 1794, could Whitney set out for Georgia with six gins. Before sailing, he returned to Philadelphia to complete the patent formalities. (This included depositing a model of his invention, as the patent law then required. The model collection burned in a Patent Office fire in 1836, a loss as grievous to historians of technology as Henry VIII's confiscation of the monasteries was to medievalists. Heaven only knows what marvelous contraptions went up in smoke.) Whitney carried a letter of introduction from his old tutor Elizur Goodrich to Oliver Wolcott, comptroller of the treasury, citizen of Connecticut, and Yale graduate, 1778. This connection with Goodrich ultimately proved more valuable than the cotton gin patent that he secured on March 14, 1784. Whitney, wrote Goodrich,

sustained a very fair reputation in the academic studies and is perhaps inferior to none in accordance with the mechanic powers, and those of the branches of natural philosophy which are applicable to the manufacturers and commerce of our country. He happily unites talents to reduce it to practice; a circumstance which is rarely found in our young men of collegiate education.

Buoyed by this praise (which few could merit today) and by the enthusiasm shown by Secretary of State Thomas Jefferson, who wanted a small gin for use on his plantation at Monticello,

Whitney sailed south with high hopes. He wrote his father that he had

accomplished everything agreeable to my wishes. I had the satisfaction to hear . . . a number of the first men in America [say] that my machine is the most perfect & most valuable invention that has ever appeared in this country . . . and I shall probably gain some honor as well as profit by the Invention. . . . One of the most Respectable Gentlemen in N. Haven [said] that he would rather be the author of the Invention than the prime minister of England.

When Whitney arrived in Georgia he discovered that Miller had already worked out a marketing scheme and begun ballyhooing the gin to the countryside. Miller planned to sell not the gin itself but its services. He offered to clean any quantity of cotton that planters might bring and to return one pound of clean cotton for every five pounds presented. This plan meant that Miller and Whitney would acquire two fifths of a pound of clean cotton for every one pound returned to the planter and demonstrated the timeless principle that men attack new problems with old ideas since these are the only ideas that they have. Miller's plan resembled the traditional arrangement between the owners of gristmills and their farmer customers. In theory at least, it solved two perplexing problems that confronted businessmen all over America. Few planters had the ready cash to purchase a gin outright, and Miller, grappling with the debts that beset the Greene estate, had no mind to sell on credit. In addition, the United States at this time had no currency worthy of the name, or rather labored under a blizzard of currencies scarcely worthy of the name. Business was transacted with a bewildering array of state banknotes, personal notes, commercial paper, and foreign currencies. Most of these "monies" were of uncertain value, particularly in places as far removed from their origins as New Haven was from Georgia. Even small change was hard to come by. In port cities merchants accepted exotic coins such as Russian kopeks and Portuguese escudos brought back by sailors, much as postage stamps, telephone tokens, and pizza parlor scrip circulate in Italy today.

Under the conditions that prevailed, then, selling for cash could be even riskier than selling on credit. Cotton was another matter: cotton was as good as gold; white gold, they called it. Throughout the period before the Civil War, businessmen readily accepted cotton in payment and often preferred it to cash or promissory notes. Cotton could be sold in England in exchange for English merchants' drafts, which, if issued by a reputable house, had a more certain value than any of the money or near money available in the United States. Cotton could also be held as a speculation, waiting for a rise in the market.

If Miller's scheme had worked, he and Whitney would have become wealthy men indeed, for they would have acquired title to one third of the South's cotton crop. Miller apparently intended to gin the entire cotton output of the South. Unfortunately, cotton agriculture expanded far more swiftly than Whitney's production of gins. The planters would not, or could not, wait and found many reasons not to. Once Catherine Greene let the secret out of the bag, it ran free. Within a year, three hundred unauthorized copies or "improvements" of Whitney's gin churned merrily away in southern towns and in plantation sheds. Even the news that Whitney had secured a patent on his machine failed to act as a deterrent. A patent supposedly converted an idea into a property, and vested it with the same rights as any other kind of property, including protection against trespass and thievery. Most Americans — squatters on the frontier were an exception — accepted such restrictions when applied to real, tangible property. After all, most of them had property of their own to protect. But restricting the use of an idea to its originator smacked of "monopoly," a battle cry that has always got the American blood up, whether raised against the British East India Company, the English king, Eli Whitney, the Second Bank of the United States, or Standard Oil. This howl the planters soon raised, adding to it a charge that would be repeated with increasing frequency as the friction between North and South intensified: northern capitalists, in this case Whitney and Miller, had fastened themselves parasitically on the body of the South, sucking its blood and growing wealthy upon the sweat and capital of southerners.

Behind this bluster, some of it no doubt rooted in genuine resentment, lay cold calculation. The federal government was in its infancy. Whether it could, or would, enforce its patent law remained to be seen. Even if it did, it might take a long time to bring offenders to heel. In the meantime, so much money might be made that the penalties, whatever they turned out to be, might be tiny compared to the profits accumulated.

Whitney returned north to speed up production, the first line of defense against interlopers. "Do not let a deficiency of money, do not let anything hinder the speedy construction of the gins," Miller wrote to Whitney; "the people of the country are almost running mad for them." Meanwhile, Miller initiated a series of lawsuits designed to hold the imitators at bay. He soon discovered that a lawsuit, as Ambrose Bierce later remarked, was "a machine that you go into as a pig and come out as a sausage." Throughout the rest of Miller's life (he died in 1802) and most of the rest of Whitney's, the partners found themselves embroiled in an endless series of lawsuits that consumed time, money, and energy, and for a long time brought scant reward.

Some defendants argued that they didn't use the gin, in one case shouting to make their disclaimers heard above the roar of gins thundering away next door to the courtroom. Others claimed that they did not use Whitney's gin at all, but rather an improved model of their own making, or one purchased legitimately from some other manufacturer. A few squeezed through a loophole in the wording of the patent law. Even after Congress filled this cavity in 1800, the two Yankee capitalists found it difficult to convince southern juries to bring judgments against their neighbors. Eventually the tide turned, and, state by state, Whitney managed to win vindication and some recompense. He always claimed, however, that the sums received fell short of the money he expended in production, legal fees, and traveling back and forth to attend court.

It is hard not to sympathize, as most of Whitney's biographers did, with his predicament. Having created a machine that un-locked the enormous potential for wealth that lay in unused southern fields and idle southern slaves, Whitney himself re-ceived very little in return.

From the point of view of the growth of the national economy, however, it may have been just as well. Enforced patents did cre-ate monopolies; monopolies slowed the diffusion of technology and delayed economic benefits of inventions. The fact that pa-tent laws functioned poorly in the early years of the United States meant that technology spread very quickly. Theoretically, patent laws encouraged creativity by protecting the inventors' prospects, but whether they worked that way in practice seems doubtful. Inventors could, as Whitney himself later proved, pros-per mightily without the benefits of patent protection. On the whole, the feebleness of the laws probably served the country's best interests, at least in its early years, just as the destruction of the Second National Bank probably facilitated development of the frontier, whether Andrew Jackson intended it that way or not.

Long before the final resolution of the cotton gin lawsuits, however, Whitney had diverted much of his energy to another area. Watching the southern markets slip away, despairing of legal redress, mired in a debt deepened by a fire in his factory, Whitney sought another outlet for his talent as a manufacturer. In the late 1790s, however, the market for manufactured goods in the United States offered scant prospects for men of Whitney's abilities. British manufacturers controlled much of it, and at prices that no American manufacturers could match.

Whitney's unhappy experience with the cotton gin had taught him several valuable lessons. First, the mere fact that one owned a patent guaranteed nothing. The only safeguard lay in produc-ing in such quantity and at such a price that no competitor could succeed, even if he ignored the patent laws. Second, a manufac-turer faced an uphill struggle finding the capital he needed. The most obvious sources, banks and wealthy merchants (the latter invariably controlled the former), underwrote agriculture and mercantile trade, with which they had been familiar for centuries. They proved reluctant, however, to finance manufacturing, which they regarded as an unfamiliar risk. Attuned to the seasons and to the timing of transatlantic voyages, they rarely granted credit for longer than sixty days to anyone. "But that," remarked Whitney, "is not a credit which, in the present state of the business, can be of much service to me." A manufacturer, as Whitney had learned the hard way, required considerable time to tool up for production. His creditors had to have patience; banks and merchants did not. Not until the War of 1812 blocked the usual outlets for their capital, and a Boston merchant, Francis Cabot Lowell, convinced his colleagues that the potential profits justified the wait and the risk, did merchants in significant numbers make their resources available to manufacturers. Thereafter, much of American industrialization resulted from partnerships between merchant capitalists and mechanics. But in 1797, when Whitney decided to look for a new venture, that happy partnership lay in the future.

Whitney understood Adam Smith's maxim that the size of the market determined the division of labor. Given a large enough market, he thought he knew both theoretically and practically how to achieve the necessary division of labor by substituting machines for skilled hands. Such a method of production would, coincidentally, bypass what Alexander Hamilton had called in 1791 "the greatest obstacle to success," the shortage of skilled labor in the United States and would bear out Hamilton's prediction that the solution lay "in the genius of people of this country, a peculiar aptitude for mechanical improvements." Despite Hamilton's optimism, few of Whitney's contemporaries could boast of his qualifications to set up a mechanized factory. But before Whitney and his country could profit from his unusual talents, Whitney had to find an appropriate market and adequate capital. He found both in the same spot, the federal government.

In the early 1790s, the deteriorating political situation in Europe increasingly alarmed the American Congress. One way and another the United States might find itself embroiled in a war with England, France, or both. The country had no armaments with which to fight such a war and no way to make them. In an effort to achieve a self-sufficiency in weapons, Congress set up the Springfield Armory in 1794, and later added an establishment at Harper's Ferry. Congress soon realized, however, that the two government armories together could not do the job, or at any rate could not do it soon enough. In 1797, after three years of effort, the Springfield Armory had turned out a thousand muskets; Harper's Ferry had as yet produced none. Congress began debating the advisability of buying arms from private contractors.

Whitney at once perceived this as the opportunity he needed. He wrote to his old friend and fellow Yale alumnus Oliver Wolcott, now Secretary of the Treasury, "By the Debates of Congress I observe that they [may make] some appropriations for procuring Arms etc for the U.S. . . . I have a number of workmen & apprentices whom I have instructed in working Wood & Metals and whom I wish to keep employed. These circumstances induced me to address you. . . . I should like to undertake to Manufacture ten or Fifteen Thousand Stand of Arms."

By any standards then known — Springfield Armory's output, for example — such a quantity of weapons constituted an enormous order for a single contractor to fill. Whitney made it plain that he intended to mechanize the process: "I am persuaded that Machinery moved by water adapted to this Business would greatly diminish the labor and facilitate the Manufacture of this Article. Machines for forging, rolling, floating, boreing, Grinding, Polishing etc may all be made use of to advantage." He added, "There is a good fall of Water in the Vicinity of this Town which I can procure and could have works erected in a short time. It would not answer however to go to the expense of erecting works for this purpose unless I could contract to make a considerable number."

There, in his last sentence, Whitney expressed the manufacturer's dilemma in early American capitalism. Machinery was expensive and the cost had to be recaptured with something to spare, or no investor would put up the money. The best bet was a product for which a volume market existed, thus enabling the manufacturer to spread his capital costs over many units of production. If the product was one in which machine production offered significant savings over hand labor, so much the better. Best of all was a combination of the two, such as the pin factory that inspired Adam Smith to rhapsodize on the wealth potential of mechanization and division of labor.

Unfortunately, in 1798 America, few such markets beckoned. Most of those that did — hardware and textiles, for instance — were dominated by British producers, who had something Americans lacked: cheap labor and plenty of it. Eventually the combination of population growth, protective tariffs, transportation costs across the Atlantic, and technological progress created markets for American-made goods and lured American capital. But as Whitney surveyed his shop, his "workmen & apprentices," and his own talents, all idled by the collapse of his cotton gin expectations, he faced bleak prospects until the federal government's determination to create an American arms industry came to the rescue.

The government presented Whitney with a volume market and a noncompetitive one at that. British manufacturers were excluded by definition and no American ones existed. The government would accept a price that assured a profit and would advance the necessary capital. If he could secure such a contract, Whitney thought, his compound miseries would be alleviated at a stroke. He had in mind a more ambitious and detailed plan of manufacture than he vouchsafed to Wolcott (having learned the hard way with the cotton gin, he kept his best ideas to himself). With this scheme he expected (mistakenly, as it turned out) to expedite production, cut costs, and get rich quickly. What inspired him were not Hamiltonian visions of American industrial glory, nor interest and skill in arms-making (he knew nothing about it, in fact), but the opportunity to use his skill and assets to fulfill his personal ambitions.

Wolcott may have had his doubts about Whitney's grandiose proposal, but his letter arrived just as Congress appropriated $800,000 for the purchase of arms, without having any clear idea of where to get them. Contractors had to be found, and Wolcott's general faith in Whitney as a fellow Yale alumnus, a fellow gentleman, and a craftsman of some reputation led him to endorse Whitney's proposal. "Knowing your skill in Mechanick," Wolcott wrote to Whitney, "I had before spoken of you to the Secretary of War as a person whose services might possibly be rendered highly useful."

On June 14, 1798, Whitney signed a contract with the United States government to supply 10,000 muskets and their accouterments within twenty-eight months, the first 4,000 to be delivered before September 30, 1799. The government advanced Whitney $5,000 to begin setting up his works, and promised another $5,000 when needed. The federal Purveyor of Supplies thought Whitney's offer too good to be true. He wrote Wolcott, "I have my doubts about this matter and suspect that Mr. Whitney cannot perform as to time." But war with France seemed an imminent possibility, and Whitney seemed the best bet, so Wolcott brushed these objections aside.

With a contract for $134,000 and an advance of $5,000 in his pocket, Whitney returned to New Haven rescued from the brink of disaster. "Bankruptcy & ruin," he wrote a friend, "were . . . staring me in the face & disappointment Trip'd me up every step I attempted to take. I was miserable . . . Loaded with a Debt of 3 or 4000 Dollars, without resources and without any business that would ever furnish me a support."

The longed-for security remained elusive, despite the government's largesse. Difficulties beset Whitney at every turn. He had to find workers ("I have not only the arms, but the armorers to make," he wrote Wolcott); floods, a severe winter, and a shortage of materials plagued him. By the spring of 1799 he had run out of money and was running out of time. To these concerns was added the exhaustion brought on by the need to be everything and to be everywhere at once. Purchasing agent, construction supervisor, employment officer, machine designer and fabricator: all these and other roles Whitney fulfilled himself. He concluded he must ask Wolcott for further help. "Cannot some arrangement be made by which I may obtain such indulgences as will enable me to pursue the business . . . and relieve me from the extreme anxiety which now . . . overpowers my ardor and dampens my resolution?" he wrote in June, 1799. He reiterated his faith in his plan of manufacture, again without elaborating on the details.

Fortunately for Whitney, the government inspector on the site, Captain Decius Wadsworth, a classmate of Phineas Miller at Yale, expressed similar views in the report he submitted to Wolcott. Encouraged by Wadsworth's report, and determined to carry through the "wish of the Government to diffuse such a degree of skill in the manufacture of Musquets as will exempt this country from arranging further importations," Wolcott took Whitney off the hook:

If you feel entire confidence in your project and will furnish me with additional security for a further advance, money shall be granted to enable you to make a fair trial. I should consider a *real improvement* in machinery for manufacturing arms as a great acquisition to the United States. For present purposes & to give you time to look out for good security, I enclose you a [letter] of credit . . . for 1500 Dols.

Wolcott did not entirely suppress his doubts, however. Pointing out that the government could have acquired muskets in the old way, he added, "My mind is inclined to scepticism with respect to all theories which have not been sanctioned by experience."

Alarmed by this shot across his bows, Whitney abandoned secrecy and for the first time gave the Secretary a detailed account of the method he had in mind:

My general plan does not consist in one great complicated machine, wherever one small part being out of order or not answering to the purpose expected, the whole must stop & be considered useless. . . . *One of my primary objects is to form the tools so that the tools themselves shall fashion the work and give to every part its just proportion — which when once accomplished will give expedition, uniformity, and exactness to the whole.*

If each . . . workman must form . . . every part according to his own fancy & regulate the size & proportion by his own Eye or even by a measure, I should have as many varieties as I have . . . part[s]. . . . By long practice . . . mere Mechanics who have no correct taste acquire the art of giving a particular uniformity . . . to particular substances. But very few really good experienced workmen in this branch of business are to be had in this country. In order to supply ourselves in the course of the next few years with any considerable number of really good muskets, such means must be devised as will preclude the necessity of every workman's being bred to the business. An accurate Eye, close attention and much time are necessary to form things rightly.

In short, the tools which I contemplate are similar to an engraving on copper plate from which may be taken a great number of impressions perceptibly alike.

There, in this brief statement made in 1799, Whitney summarized the prerequisites to mass production: the subdivision of the final product into component parts, shaped by machine to a standard size and thus interchangeable, with the work to be done by unskilled or semiskilled labor. (In fact, Whitney, like Henry Ford a century later, preferred unskilled workers as machine operators because, having nothing to unlearn, they could absorb his teachings more readily.) In practice he never succeeded completely in mechanizing production or in making all parts of the weapon interchangeable. The fault lay not with Whitney's perception of what had to be done, but rather with the lack of proper tools to do it. In Whitney's lifetime, his mechanized production theory ran ahead of machine tool practice. How quickly the gap closed, however, was shown by the fact that his son, executing a contract for one thousand of Samuel Colt's six-shooters in 1847, tooled up and finished production in six months.

Whitney himself surmounted the prevailing state of the art and fulfilled his contracts by resorting to hand labor, achieving uniformity, or something close to it, in the firing mechanisms by having the workers measure their product against standard patterns and gauges. He did, however, mechanize many steps of the process, inventing some of the necessary machines, and borrowing others. He achieved a greater degree of interchangeability than any manufacturer before him. He showed what could be done and kept neither the results nor the method a secret. He never bothered to patent any of his machines, and he communicated freely with other arms manufacturers, such as Colonel Roswell Lee, a former employee of Whitney and Miller, and longtime superintendent of the Springfield Armories. From the Whitney works, from the Springfield Armory, from the factory of Simeon North, and from other New England armories came a whole generation of craftsmen like Henry Leland, whose skill at designing machine tools and production methods made interchangeable parts a widespread reality in America.

By the 1850s the engineering generation that followed Whitney's had a large enough market, created by the growth of population and transportation, to justify this new "American system of production" (as British observers titled it) in many fields of manufacture. Interchangeability had diffused from the arms industry into consumer products such as locks, clocks and watches, sewing machines, farm machinery, and pianos, and was spreading fast. A British industrial commission, making an American tour of inspection in 1851, found that U.S. manufacturers "call in the aid of machinery in almost every department of industry. Wherever it can . . . substitute for manual labor, it is universally and willingly resorted to."

The British visitors, accustomed to the hostility between English industrialists and their workers, remarked a startling commonality of purpose between American employers and employees. No outbreaks of Luddite machine-wrecking impeded mechanization in the United States. To the contrary, they discovered an "extreme desire, manifested by masters and workmen to adopt all labour-saving devices" because all parties thought mechanization to be in "their mutual interest." American workmen, on whom "traditional methods had little hold . . . as compared with the English artisan," not only accepted improvements introduced by the boss, but also were themselves "continually devising some new thing to assist . . . in [the] work" and demanding to be "posted up" on new developments.

In such a propitious atmosphere machine tools had become amazingly sophisticated. At Springfield Armory, the Englishmen found machines "in which a succession of tools were brought to bear on the work one after another (with the 'most rigid accuracy')" and "edging machines" that traced "irregular figures and impart[ed] an exact outline" from a model to the part. The process virtually eliminated handwork (two and a half minutes, as opposed to twenty-nine minutes' machine work on each musket) and produced "parts . . . so exactly alike that any . . . part will . . . fit any musket."

American factories also produced high volume at low cost. In Whitney's hometown of New Haven, English engineer Joseph Whitworth inspected a padlock factory that turned out two thousand a day, "of a superior quality to those of the same class ordinarily imported from England and not more expensive. . . . Special machines were applied to every part, and the parts . . . can be interchanged." Whitworth also visited a New Haven clock factory that produced six hundred a day with similar methods and successfully exported to England and the European continent.

The Englishmen reported their findings with foreboding. By making manufacturing the province of "large factories with machinery applied to almost every process, the extreme subdivision of labor, and all reduced to an almost perfect system of manufacture," the Americans demonstrated an "ingenuity, combined with undaunted energy, which we would do well to imitate if we meant to hold our present position in the Great Markets of the world." Even by 1851, some harbingers of future American potency had appeared in Britain itself. From 1847 on, some British manufacturers imported American machine tools and, in a move that particularly shocked Britons, the famous Enfield Arsenal reequipped itself with machine tools imported from Windsor "in the wilds of Vermont."

Oliver Wolcott, by answering Whitney's supplications for money to keep going, proved a crucial catalyst for the evolution of American manufacturing supremacy and made the federal government a partner in forging what proved to be free enterprise's most potent tool. But Whitney's tribulations did not end with Wolcott's gesture in July, 1799. In fact, it took him ten years to fulfill the original contract, what with delays caused by trips to southern courts, fires at the factory, and harassment from government officials. But things improved steadily thereafter, and Whitney gradually achieved the recognition and wealth he had so long sought. In September, 1799, ten of the leading citizens of New Haven, most of them Yale graduates, signed a bond that secured a further $10,000 advance from the government. In January, 1801, Whitney went to the new capital, Washington, D.C., and put on a triumphant demonstration of interchangeability. Disassembling several firing mechanisms into their constituent parts, and mixing the parts, Whitney invited the dignitaries present to pick the parts at random and reassemble them. The reassembled mechanisms all fitted on the musket that Whitney had brought along. Among the impressed spectators was the President-elect, Thomas Jefferson, who had granted Whitney his original patent on the cotton gin. Jefferson's interest in and support for interchangeability had been aroused in the 1780s when, on a visit to France, he had witnessed a similar demonstration by a French locksmith. At the time, Jefferson had tried to persuade the Frenchman to immigrate to the United States, but had failed.

After this demonstration, the government indulged Whitney with all the patience and money he required. The public acclaimed him as "The Artist of His Country." With his methods perfected, the muskets rolled out and the money rolled in through a succession of contracts with federal and state governments. With the advice of his old friend Oliver Wolcott, retired from government service into a private banking and brokerage firm, Whitney invested his profits wisely and achieved financial security.

In 1817 he married, subsequently fathering three children, including a son, Eli Whitney, Jr., who eventually succeeded to the business. In 1825 Eli Whitney, Sr., died, leaving a large estate to his family but an even more magnificent legacy to his country. His life spanned a period that saw the people of the United States rise from discontented colonialists to armed revolutionists to a place secure among the nations of the world. In the political and military adventures of his lifetime, he played no direct part. But he figured largely in the economic transformation of this country from a colonial dependency, where the few manufactured goods were the product of handicraft, to a rising industrial power, well on its way to manufacturing self-sufficiency, using a system that would become the most powerful on earth.

His career clearly revealed the impact of his society upon him. His ambition, his education, and the opportunities it provided him were as much products of America as the cotton gin was. His life's work produced cataclysmic results, including the Civil War, where the forces of southern plantation agriculture and northern industrialism, both of which he did so much to unleash, collided. But perhaps more important, his life revealed patterns of behavior characteristic of subsequent generations of American manufacturing entrepreneurs. Driven by his ambition, seeing in it a pole star on which he could set the course of his life, Whitney perceived a market, assembled the assets necessary to meet it, kept those assets employed by shifting into a new product when the old failed. Striving for mechanization and standardization, Whitney blazed a trail that became a path and ultimately an expressway to prosperity.

Cyrus Hall McCormick: the Grim Reaper as millionaire

3

The Grim Reaper
Cyrus Hall McCormick

I KNOW that Anthony Burgess is a smart man. I know this because in a *New York Times* article he expressed two opinions
that I endorse — that Los Caracoles restaurant in Barcelona
is a diner's delight, and that it is better to travel by train than by
plane. Like Burgess, I fear that every time I board a plane I run
the risk of not surviving, and I suspect that I have worsened the
odds by running the risk so often. I know that mathematically
this is nonsense: each trip is a lottery in which the odds of drawing one of the "blanks" that Eli Whitney feared are the same
every time, regardless of past experience, just as the odds of toss-
ing heads or tails are always fifty-fifty, even if heads has come up
a hundred times in a row. I have, nevertheless, returned to the
trains and use them whenever I can.

I find trains a more civilized way to travel for many reasons,
not least of which is the fact that one meets interesting people
and talks to them in a civilized way across a dining car table-
cloth, rather than in the elbows-in, half-shouted, side-of-the-
mouth manner necessitated by airplanes. Among the interesting
denizens of the dining car, I have found many Europeans, who
ride trains here because they are accustomed to the excellence of
rail travel at home and because they come to this country to see
it, not to fly over it.

On one trip from Seattle to Chicago I enjoyed the company of
two elderly German couples who practiced their tourists' English

on me while I inflicted my pidgin German on them. As the train ambled across North Dakota, our seats in the dome car gave us a close-up view of one of North America's most intriguing annual spectacles, the wheat harvest on the Great Plains. As we watched, the giant combines moved in echelon, like scarlet locusts cutting a half-mile swath through wheatfields that stretched in every direction as far as the eye could see. The combines' reels, rising above the waves of grain, then plunging forward and down to stroke the stalks into the cutting knives, looked for all the world like paddlewheels on the Ohio River towboats that I had watched as a boy. In the towns, the lines of trucks and strings of railroad cars at the grain elevators formed another link in the mechanized conveyer that moved the crop from field to market without the touch of a human hand.

The next day, as the train rolled through Milwaukee, one of my companions said to me: "And now the factories begin, yes?"

"Yes," I replied, "I'm afraid so."

"That is not so much to see," he said. "In Germany you can see that also. In Essen, in Mannheim, in Frankfurt, you can see all the factories you want. But three thousand kilometers of forests and wheatfields, that you cannot see. I think you Americans have not as much to fear as you think you have."

That's true, of course, and a fact that we often forget. Any people that can feed itself has less to fear than one that cannot. In the fields and towns of the Great Plains we had witnessed the confluence of industrial technology, fertile land, and a benevolent climate with the river of agricultural productivity that makes Americans fat and well fed in a world that is lean and hungry. However valuable crude oil may seem, it cannot be eaten, and, once harvested, it cannot be replanted. This harsh reality, which eludes so many Americans, has haunted the Shah of Iran, Sheikh Yamani of Saudia Arabia, and other potentates of the petroleum-producing states. As a guarantee of survival for oneself and one's posterity, a wheatfield in North Dakota is a better bet than an oil well in the Persian Gulf.

As we have seen in the case of Whitney's cotton gin, the potential agricultural productivity of the American expanses presented manufacturers with a great opportunity. The generation of innovators that followed Whitney busied itself seizing the market for labor-saving machines inherent in a land so vast and a people so few. Dozens, then hundreds, of mechanics rushed to patent devices designed to perform the tasks traditionally handled by peasant hands in Europe. The northern states, which would not countenance slavery, suffered perpetually from a shortage of farm labor. Few people would work another man's land when they could farm their own, and those who would demanded high wages. Farmers themselves and the editors of newspapers and magazines directed to the farm audience recognized the necessity for mechanization, a need that intensified as settlement moved westward, creating larger farms that specialized in grain as a market crop.

In 1823, Jonathan Roberts, president of the Pennsylvania Agricultural Society, wrote in the *American Farmer* magazine:

In practical husbandry the expense of labor is a cardinal consideration. Since the year 1818, farmers have . . . felt that labor has been much dearer than produce. . . . A mitigation of this effect may be sought . . . by improved implements. . . . Nothing is more wanted than the application of animal labor [to machines] in the cutting of grain. It is the business on the farm which requires the most [speed], and it is always the most expensive labor. Such an invention can be no easy task, or the ingenuity of our fellow citizens would, ere this, have effected it.

In England, as the whirling machinery of Lancashire cotton mills sucked manpower from the countryside, as emigration to the United States further depleted it, and as political agitation fractured the tractability of those workers who remained on the land, the English press took up the cry. In 1834 the *Farmer's Magazine* of London wrote, "It is certainly a remarkable circumstance in the history of mechanical science in this country, that the art of cutting down the cultivated crops should be so inadequately supplied with instruments."

In fact, farmers of the 1830s still assaulted their foremost problem, harvesting the ripe grain, with weapons thousands of years old, the sickle and the scythe. From the Book of Ruth through American primitive painters, observers romanticized the harvest in story, song, and picture. But a brief sojourn in a wheatfield on an August afternoon, laying about with a scythe, was a demythologizing experience. Certainly neither farmers nor their laborers had any illusions about the brutal nature of the work. Furthermore, it had to be done quickly, for about ten days after ripening, the husks opened, the grains of wheat fell to the ground, and the crop was lost.

In such circumstances, workers could demand high wages and an expensive fringe benefit in the form of a wagon, laden with refreshment to slake their thirsts. The preferred beverage was Monongahela whiskey, but the cost and the temperance scruples of many farmer-employers often dictated a substitute. The *Southern Planter* advised its readers, "The next best thing to the 'ra-al Monongaly' to string up the nerves of those who wield the scythe, is a drink composed of five gallons of iced water well mixed with half a gallon of molasses, one quart of vinegar, and two ounces of ginger." The *American Farmer* suggested that a recipe of five gallons of water, one half gallon of molasses, and one quarter pound of ginger, mixed and served hourly, was "invigorating, refreshing, and safe, no matter how cold the water may be. The cooler the water, the more grateful will it be to the pallet, — the more refreshing to the system, the surer of giving tone and strength to the harvester."

Even when toned, strengthened, and well strung up in the nerves, the scythemen and their helpers who bound and stacked the cut grain cost the farmer a lot of money. In 1830 it required six laborers to harvest two acres of wheat a day. Any machine that reduced this cost would find a ready market among farmers with large acreage, provided it could be sold at a reasonable price.

In the open spaces of the American Midwest, old Northwest, and Great Plains lay a potential wealth equal to that of the cotton fields in the South. Three keys were needed to unlock this bonanza: people, transportation, and machines. Immigration supplied the first, railroads and canals the second, American manufacturing the last. The mechanical harvester, the machine that most facilitated the transformation of these open spaces into a cornucopia, emerged from a farm workshop in the Shenandoah valley, the "Valley of Virginia," as it was styled in the nineteenth century. Cyrus Hall McCormick, the harvester's inventor, contributed the first of a series of technological innovations that culminated in the combine that mechanized the entire harvesting process, but it was his skill in manufacturing and marketing that carried his firm to the top of the farm machinery industry and kept it there. In addition, McCormick's distribution methods were emulated by all successful competitors, and subsequently adapted to other products, most particularly the automobile. The methods by which modern automobile firms manufacture and sell their product, itself the apotheosis of urban, industrialized America, thus have pedigrees that run directly back to Eli Whitney and Cyrus McCormick, farm boys who sought their fortunes in serving an agricultural, rural economy.

Cyrus McCormick was born in 1809, the year that Eli Whitney finally completed his first musket contract for the United States government. McCormick's immediate ancestors traced a common pattern of American immigration, migration, and settlement. His great-grandfather, a Scotch-Irishman, immigrated in 1734, and eventually settled in Cumberland County, Pennsylvania, on the west bank of the Susquehanna River near Harrisburg. Cyrus's grandfather, Robert McCormick, settled first in Juniata County, Pennsylvania, on the Juniata River, a Susquehanna tributary. In 1779 he removed himself and his family to Rockbridge County, Virginia, in the Shenandoah valley, midway between Lexington and Staunton, where Cyrus's father, Robert, was born and died.

The McCormicks illustrated how topography determined patterns of settlement before the advent of railroads and automobiles. The east coast of the United States was blessed with a large number of river systems that penetrated the coastal plain into the foothills of the mountains. Settlers clung to these waterways, floating their goods upstream until they reached open land. Whenever they could, they set up their farms along a stream because only by water could they profitably send produce to market. Carting crops to town over primitive roads was a bone- and wagon-shattering affair. Worse, it was prohibitively expensive: the cost of hauling grain to market often exceeded its selling price. The same transportation requirements dictated the location of factories. A Senate report in 1816 declared, "A coal mine may exist in the United States not more than ten miles from valuable ores of iron and other materials, and both of them be useless unless a canal is established between them, as the price of land carriage is too great to be borne by either."

In addition to water routes, the location of the mountains shaped the direction of migration. In Juniata County, the first Robert McCormick had gone about as far west as a man could go without encountering the parallel spines of the Alleghenies, which run from southwest to northeast across the state. Transmontane migration with heavily laden wagons was a ticklish operation, not so much because of the difficulty of hauling wagons up the mountain (a slow but sure process), but rather because of the nightmarish tendency of wagons to hurtle themselves down the far side. The steep ridges of central Pennsylvania were a teamster's horror in the days of wagons, and even now truckers dread them more in the winter than the gentle escarpments of the Rockies. When Robert McCormick decided he needed and could afford more space, he took the path of least resistance, moving southwestward across the Potomac River at Harper's Ferry, and then up its tributary, the Shenandoah, into the broad valley that bears its name. The northern half of the valley filled with German and Scotch-Irish settlers, as the Pennsylvania mountains deflected the stream of migrants into the Valley of Virginia.

They were a tough bunch, these Scotch-Irishmen. Like the Cromwellites a century before, they marched with the Bible in one hand and a musket in the other, ready to smite their enemies with either weapon. Hating the British, and ever fearful lest some American version of British privileged oligarchy establish itself in the United States, they rallied to the colonial banner in the Revolution and to the standard of Jeffersonian democracy afterward. Cyrus's grandfather fought with the colonial forces at

Yorktown. Cyrus himself remained a staunch Democrat all his life, in marked contrast to most of his fellow industrialists, who hewed to the Whig, and then the Republican, line.

Deeply Calvinistic, these Scotch-Irish farmers saw in them-selves the personification of Thomas Jefferson's declaration that "Those who labor in the earth are the chosen people of God, if ever He had a chosen people, whose breasts He has made His peculiar deposit for substantial and genuine virtue." Glorying in their religious faith, their political creed, and their virtuous oc-cupation, the McCormicks and their neighbors went about their business "in an armor of militant self-righteousness." They also exhibited a nice talent for selectivity, fastening upon those texts that justified their behavior and ignoring others less convenient.

As farmers, the McCormicks could rejoice in Jefferson's cele-bration of them as a chosen people; as slaveholders they ignored his warning that slavery made him "tremble for [his] country when [he] reflect[ed] that God is just." Robert McCormick could refuse, on religious grounds, to supply his harvest hands with their cherished alcoholic refreshment; the same scruples did not prevent him from converting his surplus corn to whiskey and selling it for 25 cents a gallon in distant bastions of sin such as Lynchburg and Richmond. Cyrus McCormick once gave $10,-000 to found a Presbyterian church in Chicago; in the same year he collected $110 rent on two aged slaves he still owned in Virginia.

Throughout his life, Cyrus expected the Lord to bless his en-deavors and thought his faith vindicated when he thrived in the ferocious American marketplace. Crushing competitors, ha-rassing railroads for rebates, besieging potential customers with advertising, he did battle confident of the continued assistance of his mighty ally. "Business is not inconsistent with Christianity," he said in 1845, as he set out to carry his reaper into markets be-yond his native state's. In meeting past obstacles, he reflected, "Providence . . . seemed to assist me in our business." In avoid-ing future pitfalls, "I believe the Lord will help us out." And so it came to pass, or seemed to anyway. In 1857, a millionaire and the dominant figure in the American farm machinery industry,

McCormick rejoiced, "Providence is with us and will defend us as heretofor."

Before industrialization, generations of successful businessmen and farmers like Cyrus McCormick's ancestors had sought and found religious justification for private property, for borrowing and lending money at interest, for buying and selling labor and commodities at prices set by the market, for slavery, for saving, investing, and speculating, for the whole panoply of activities that built the mercantile, agricultural economy of preindustrial America. Most prosperous men found sanction, not stricture, in religion; some, like Eli Whitney, discarded formal religion altogether.

Unsurprisingly, the generations that presided over industrialization followed a similar course, sometimes adapting, with the help of cooperative clerics, the old creeds to the new needs; sometimes, as we shall see with Andrew Carnegie, finding an adequate faith in the new process itself.

Thus Cyrus McCormick, sallying forth to do savage battle with his competitors, confident that "Providence . . . will defend us," could proclaim "the feeling that should be cherished [is] unconditional submission and resignation to the will and hand of Providence . . . rejoicing that unworthy as we are, the law has been satisfied, and we may be saved by *faith.*"

Whatever absolute rules the Protestant deity might enforce at the heavenly bar, his earthly adherents propounded a pliable secular code, readily shaped to cover capitalism in its industrial as well as in its agricultural permutations. In religion then, as in politics, Americans defended specific changes as the logical outgrowth of the impact of absolute values on a progressively evolving society. Cyrus McCormick, whose lifetime spanned the American age of industrialization, personified the extension of militant Protestant values from farm to shop, factory, and global business enterprise.

By 1830, when Cyrus McCormick was twenty-one years old, his father had expanded the original four hundred acres, bought by Cyrus's grandfather in 1779 with the proceeds from the sale of his Pennsylvania farm and named Walnut Grove, to a twelve-hundred-acre estate. Walnut Grove produced grain, fruit, timber, and limestone, and had gristmills, a distillery, a sawmill, and limekilns to process its products. These installations furnished the farm with much of its needs. The elder Robert McCormick's move to Rockbridge County had carried him beyond the navigable headwaters of the Shenandoah, so transportation costs gave the McCormicks an incentive to process raw materials into more valuable and compact commodities, before shipping. The same incentive later induced Gustavus Swift in the late nineteenth century to ship dressed beef to the east coast, leaving hooves, hides, and horns in Chicago, and now makes oil refineries a tempting investment for petroleum-producing countries. To help him work his extensive holdings, the younger Robert McCormick had acquired by 1830 five children, nine slaves, and eighteen horses. These assets made him a prominent man, influential in his community and his church, with extensive credit available to him when he needed it. And sometimes he did need it, for like most successful farmers past and present, he was land-rich but cash-poor.

The McCormick farm, like the Whitney farm, had a workshop, including a blacksmith's forge. As he grew old and prosperous, the second Robert McCormick spent more and more of his time there, indulging a penchant for invention, particularly inventions that might lessen farm labor.

Like many another farm tinkerer in England and America, Cyrus McCormick's father invented a reaper, a horse-drawn device to cut the wheat in the fields. No grain farmer needed agricultural journalists to tell him what a boon such a machine could be. Unfortunately, it proved devilishly difficult to make one that worked. A number of variables had to be accommodated, and a machine that cut wondrously in a flat field of dry wheat often bogged down in rough ground or in wheat that was heavy, wet, or tangled. The machines also had a tendency to shatter their cutting teeth on the rocks that in the Shenandoah valley often seemed to sprout as thickly as the wheat itself. In addition, the cutting action, which had to be powerful enough to sever a swath of tough wheat stalks, often proved so violent that it shook the kernels out of the husks, whereupon they fell uselessly to the ground.

Cyrus, who often helped his father in the shop and early demonstrated an inventive knack of his own, took up the task. He fashioned a reaper that operated successfully on a neighboring farm during the harvest of 1831. Later, Cyrus McCormick claimed to have realized at once that that machine was worth a million dollars to him. If so, he had a more sanguine imagination than Eli Whitney's, or perhaps he simply reflected the increased scale on which Americans could dream after the forty years of expansion that took place between Whitney's invention and McCormick's. More likely, he simply indulged in the omniscience of hindsight, since he set aside the new gadget for several years while he pursued other and, as it turned out, worthless, schemes to make his fortune. First he crossed the mountains into Kentucky, where he passed a fruitless year trying to sell a hemp-breaking machine that his father had invented. These days hemp cultivation takes place largely in remote areas of the world like Bangladesh, but in the early nineteenth century many Kentuckians, including their most distinguished statesman, Henry Clay, thought hemp might do for Kentucky what cotton had done for states farther south.

After the failure of this venture, Cyrus McCormick returned to the workshop to improve his reaper. In 1834, satisfied that he had perfected it to a point of marketability, McCormick received a patent for his machine. With patent in hand, and standing on the very threshold of success, McCormick once again deflected his efforts. Manifesting a weakness that reappeared throughout his life, McCormick went haring off in pursuit of quick riches in a nearby iron mine and furnace. McCormick knew nothing about the iron business, but plunged in with his energies and his resources, piling up lots of debt but not much iron. In 1840 McCormick abandoned this unrewarding venture and returned to work on the reaper, but he never lost his penchant for get-rich-quick schemes.

Fighting his way to the top of the farm machinery business, McCormick displayed a knowledge of manufacturing, a subtle understanding of the market for his products, and a farsighted perception of the shape and direction of American agricultural development. But these instincts often deserted him when he confronted an opportunity to engage in speculation. The glittering prospect of wealth waiting to be dug out of the earth particularly addled him. Even late in life, when his business had made him a very wealthy man, he poured $200,000 into a hole in the ground, investing in a gold mine that he never saw, complaining afterward that he had been victimized by "the most *outrageous swindle* that could be perpetrated." Like many another businessman, McCormick demonstrated that beyond the qualities that made him wealthy and successful, his personality included a large dose of childlike naïveté, which money and power only magnified.

In contrast with his leap into the iron business, McCormick crept forward cautiously with his reaper. In December, 1839, he advertised in the Richmond *Enquirer,* declaring that the reaper was ready for general sale, and promised to fill any orders in time for the next harvest. Certainly he had incentives to get going. The machine worked, at least sometimes, and when it did, it halved the labor cost of harvesting. Many farmers had already seen it in action, and their testimonials, together with a number of articles in the press, aroused a significant interest. In addition, a competitor, the first of many that McCormick faced in his career, had been in the field since 1833. This worthy, who sported the picturesque name of Obed Hussey, had invaded McCormick's territory with a reaper of his own invention. Goaded to action, McCormick sold two machines in 1840, but his claims of perfection proved premature when both failed. Consequently, he withdrew from the market in 1841 to spend a year in the Walnut Grove workshop, getting the bugs out of the mechanism. In 1842 he reentered the market and sold six; in 1843, twenty-nine.

By 1844 McCormick felt that at last he had a machine good enough to capture a large share of the market. The market itself, however, was on the move. The Erie and other canals, the Great Lakes, and the rivers of the Midwest had opened the grain markets of the east coast and Europe to western farmers. Furthermore, the railroad, as everyone knew, was coming to open up those areas not reached by waterways. By 1840, a single county in western New York grew more wheat than all the New England states, and two New York counties outstripped Virginia and Maryland combined. The future lay even farther westward, in the great flat open spaces that stretched to the Rockies. In 1845, when New York led the United States by producing 16 million bushels of wheat, Ohio ran a close second with 13 million bushels. A steady stream of settlers, including immigrants from Europe and native New Englanders, poured west. "I sing New England," lyricized William Ellery Channing, "as she lights her fires in every Prairie's midst." In New England itself, some fires went out. In the 1880s Matthew Arnold saw long-derelict farms in the Connecticut River valley, depopulated in favor of the broad prairie expanses where "hundreds, nay thousands, of acres ... enclosed by one fence [form] a campania of waving grain the like of which one may search the rest of the world in vain to find."

As the settlers spread west, they pushed the frontier of commercial agriculture ahead of them. Between 1840 and 1850 the population of Ohio expanded from one-and-a-half million to two million, of Indiana from 700,000 to one million, of Illinois from 500,000 to 900,000. During the same period, wheat production rose from 84 million to 100 million bushels. Because of a fortunate combination of factors, the demand for wheat expanded as rapidly as did production. Population increase in the United States and in Europe, together with bad European harvests and a reduction of import duties on American grain, created a market that absorbed all the wheat American farmers could grow and then some.

"Western Farmer!" exhorted one American observer from his post overseas, "what are you going to do for the Old World next year? Are you going to feed them, or let them die of hunger? If you cannot ... grow *one thousand millions* of bushels ... for them the coming season, and send it over ... they will come after it themselves, and your prairies will swarm with them, as with an ocean of bull frogs. So be up now and at it. There will be no potatoes raised [in Great Britain] this season, and you must plant . . . for half the world."

Planting, however, was not the problem; harvesting was. With so much land available for settlement, farm labor grew more scarce despite immigration. One western New York farmer commented in 1845, "Many a farmer with an excited woebegone face have I seen this season, riding about in search of [workers] . . . but experienced [men] were few indeed." Not only the shortage of labor, but also the large acreage of western farms made them ideal for mechanization. Westerners needed machinery and urged their eastern brethren to supply it. In 1842 the *Union Agriculturalist and Western Prairie Farmer* of Chicago wrote, "Inventors — here is a field for you to operate in; anything that you wish to have introduced into extensive use, which you know to be really valuable, you can bring here with a good prospect of success. Bring along your machines."

In June, 1844, Cyrus McCormick went west and took along his machine. Jolting and swaying in crowded stagecoaches, wading through spittle and tobacco juice on the decks of canal boats, surviving the rancid food of travelers' hostelries, McCormick journeyed to western New York, Ohio, Michigan, Indiana, Illinois, Wisconsin, Missouri, and Kentucky, demonstrating the reaper as he went. In the Ohio valley McCormick saw, as Whitney had seen in Georgia forty years before, crops rotting in the fields for want of a machine to process them.

McCormick returned home and announced triumphantly that his machines had performed "without a failure and with the most perfect success." The western agricultural press echoed his enthusiasm. The Chicago *Daily Journal* declared that the reapers "are just the thing for our prairies, where more grain is sown than can possibly be gathered in the ordinary way, and their comparative cheapness puts them within reach of every tiller of the soil. So indispensable will be their use that hereafter the sickle [and] the scythe . . . may as well hang themselves 'upon the willow.' " The Chicago *Daily Democrat* reported "the . . . universal opinion of the farmers of the prairies [is] that the quantity of

wheat grown [will be] greatly increased by the facilities for harvesting afforded by the Reaper . . . and if they can get enough of
McCormick's Reapers, they can beat the world . . . growing
wheat."

McCormick himself, as well as his machine, came in for lavish
praise, a delicacy for which he developed an insatiable appetite.
Even in the 1840s he seemed destined for a place in the pantheon
of greats, which the pragmatic Americans reserved not for think-
ers who idled away their hours pondering recondite abstractions
but for men who could bring dreams into practical realization.
The same American attitudes, which had anointed an inventor as
"The Artist of His Country," were expressed forty years later by
an Iowan who lauded McCormick as one of the men bringing
America into "the *'golden age'* of agriculture," as significant to
mankind as the golden philosophical ages of Greece and Rome.
"The introduction of machinery for harvesting forms a new era
in farming on the prairies," he declared, "and had the inventor
chanced to live in old Greece or Rome they would have held a
high place in mythology. . . . One such practical man as McCormick, does more for his kind than a thousand theorizers on
Guano." William H. Seward, one of McCormick's patent attor-
neys (and later Lincoln's Secretary of State) also invoked the
classical comparisons favored by educated Americans to find
suitable praise for the reaper's inventor: "No General or Consul
drawn in a chariot through the streets of Rome by order of the
Senate ever conferred upon mankind benefits so great as he."

It is one thing to have one's invention and one's talents ap-
plauded. It is quite another, however, to convert these assets into
a successful business organization. Between the machine and its
market lay a welter of obstacles in manufacturing, transportation, and sales. Moreover, by the time McCormick returned to
Virginia in the fall of 1844, confident of a western market, his
original patent had only four years left to run, and renewal was
by no means a certainty. Farmers' hostility to monopoly in the
form of patents had abated not a whit since Whitney's day. Their
sentiments found powerful expression in Congress, as did the

opposition of competitors like Hussey, each of whom had his champion in the nation's capital.

McCormick needed to produce a lot of machines in a hurry, and his small workshop at Walnut Grove could not turn out more than forty or fifty a year. It was, moreover, poorly located to supply the western markets. In order to get his demonstration machines to the western states in 1844, McCormick had had to cart them up the valley to Scottsville, Virginia, ship them by canal boat to Richmond, by freighter to New Orleans, and then up the Mississippi by steamboat. The expense of this circuitous route, added to the costs of manufacture and an allowance for profit, would price the machines beyond the reach of most prospective customers and present a golden opportunity to western manufacturers, of which a dozen had appeared in Illinois alone by 1847.

To step up production swiftly in locations central to western markets, McCormick took a step that Whitney and Miller had considered and rejected: he temporarily licensed manufacturers in other cities to produce his machine. Such arrangements between patentees and manufacturers were not uncommon by the 1840s. The manufacturer paid a stipulated fee for each machine produced (if the inventor had his way) or sold (if the manufacturer had his). McCormick made such arrangements in Brockport, New York, Cincinnati, Chicago, St. Louis, and elsewhere. At the same time he enlisted his brothers William and Leander to push the Walnut Grove shop to its utmost. Together these installations produced and sold some 1,200 machines between 1844 and 1848, when McCormick closed the Walnut Grove shop and opened a factory in Chicago.

Submanufacturing, however, worked poorly; the licensees tended to be slow in production and sloppy in manufacture. Since harvesting was a seasonal business and had to be done quickly, ten days' tardiness in delivery was as bad as a year; moreover, delivering a poorly made machine that broke down at the crucial moment or damaged the crop generated almost as much customer fury as delivering no machine at all. Consequently, when submanufacturing agreements expired, McCormick did not renew them. After 1851 his entire output came from his own factory.

Manufacturing involved only the application of known methods to achieve mass production. By the time McCormick moved to Chicago in 1848, Whitney's legacy of machine-made interchangeable parts was understood and available. McCormick could bring the required tools and a steam engine to drive them, and hire experts to install and run them. Nor, as we have seen, was mass production any novelty either. This, too, could be imported to Chicago.

But selling the harvester presented unprecedented problems. Rarely had American business had to sell complex machines to nonexpert buyers. In the East, the better railroads relied more and more on designated purchasing officers who kept up with the increasingly complex railroad equipment. As time passed, the railroads' agents dealt directly with manufacturers, eliminating the commission merchants, who had served as middlemen in the railroads' early years. But these transactions took place in a market populated by a relatively small number of expert buyers and sellers.

McCormick faced a market made up of thousands of independent farmers. Tough customers in every sense of the term, they refused to buy reapers the way McCormick bought gold mines, sight unseen. They demanded demonstrations, especially ones where manufacturers pitted their products against one another. Success at such competitions demanded the presence of an expert at the reap-off to adjust the machines to local conditions and to make running repairs. In the early days, McCormick himself attended many exhibitions. As the search for markets and submanufacturers took up more of his time, he dragooned his brothers into service. Relying on family members or on old, trusted acquaintances was traditional in preindustrial America, as it had been for centuries before in Europe. But mass markets made such nepotistic methods obsolete. No one had a family that large. For manufacturers who, like McCormick, produced volume goods for diffuse markets, mass distribution presented greater problems than mass production and forced the manufacturers to create organizations to handle sales as well as manufacturing.

Marketing the reaper involved more than competitions and displays at county fairs. After the move to Chicago in 1848, McCormick participated in fewer such events because the outcome was often uncertain. Sometimes his machine lost; sometimes the local judges turned out to be biased in favor of a competitor's product. The McCormick reaper did win its share of medals, prizes, and certificates of merit, which the company proudly displayed. But competitors did the same, and farmers, facing conflicting claims, often believed none. In addition, farmers found that results of hard daily usage fell suspiciously short of those of the staged competitions. The result, as the editor of the *Farmers' Register* observed, was

grave injury inflicted on deserving inventors themselves, as well as on the public by the *puffing system*. Every new invention . . . whatever may be its . . . merit or demerit, is ushered forth with puffs upon puffs. Dupes are made, and knaves who puff, and sell, profit at the expense of the fools who believe and buy. . . . The more discreet . . . who know the working of the puffing system, stand aloof, and trust [neither] true statements [nor] false.

Since reaper marketing demanded extensive personal contact, McCormick gradually relied more on a far-flung network of salesmen, on his company's reputation, and on his factory's ability to outproduce any competitor's, than on showboating before increasingly skeptical audiences at bucolic gatherings.

The reaper was for its time a delicate and complicated machine. In fact, nothing so complex had ever been widely marketed before. Few customers, moreover, could claim much mechanical expertise; unlike the manufacturers of railway equipment, McCormick sold to a nonexpert clientele. From the outset McCormick salesmen had to instruct farmers in the use and care of the machine. Even the mules and horses that pulled it had to be broken to the task; otherwise they had a tendency to bolt across the fields, trying to escape the rattling contraption that pursued them.

In the 1840s, when sales were numbered in the dozens, McCormick often urged his brothers to handle deliveries personally: "William or Leander could attend to . . . putting together, explaining, and having printed direction [for the machine]." Later, printed instructions accompanied every machine, explaining its operation, adjustment, the need for lubrication, the best technique for sharpening the cutting knives, and the replacement of broken parts.

Printed instructions or not, the machines often broke down, requiring repairs or adjustments that the farmers would not or could not perform. The early reapers acquired a reputation for fragility that constituted one of the major sales obstacles to be overcome. This reputation survived long after the reaper passed from the experimental stage. In the 1850s, for example, one farm journalist wrote that all reapers, even McCormick's, were of little value unless there was "a Blacksmith shop at each corner of the field."

Breakdowns often resulted from farmers' attitude toward maintenance, an attitude similar to one once encountered by an automobile service manager friend of mine. A furious customer confronted him with a car that rattled, shook, and belched smoke. A quick check showed that the car had sixty-four thousand miles on the odometer and no oil in the crankcase. "Did you ever change the oil?" my friend asked. "Change the oil! Why the hell should I change the oil?" the customer demanded heatedly. "I paid eight thousand dollars for this car. What the hell was wrong with the oil they put in it? I'll never buy this make again." Like this frustrated motorist, many farmers felt that a machine that cost so much should run by itself and forever. One frustrated reaper repairman commented, "I am sorry I enlisted [for this job] but there is no use I shall go through with the Job if I live . . . the Machiens are in the worst plight imaginable. I have found them outdoors and frozen down Just where they used them last." But even the most bullheaded characters had to be accommodated, as McCormick knew, lest they become enemies. In the early years the factory supplied the farmers with the name of a nearby mechanic, in addition to the printed instructions. "I think it would be well to refer persons in the vicinity of Richmond to Mr. Parker for repairs," one of McCormick's agents wrote in 1845. "It is desirable to give satisfaction to all if possible, for now in the infancy of the reaper's existence a few dissatisfied persons might do you serious injury." But such casual arrangements with people who owed no particular allegiance to the company proved as unsatisfactory as agreements with submanufacturers. The need to provide reliable service over a widespread area contributed to the development of a network of company agents.

The company also had to supply spare parts. After the first few years the parts were interchangeable, but the fact that the reaper was frequently redesigned meant that parts for one year's model often would not fit another's. The company tried to meet this difficulty by furnishing a set of spares with each machine. When this proved unsatisfactory, a parts department was established at the Chicago factory. Farmers could send a defective part to the plant, where it was matched against a collection of all the machines the company had ever built. Once identified, the drawings could be pulled from the files and the part duplicated in the company shop. This method proved slow, expensive, and unsatisfactory. The machines broke down during the harvest, when they were most needed, and few farmers could wait for the factory to duplicate the defective component and return it. Parts stockpiles had to be established so that they could be got quickly when needed.

Finally, the reaper cost a lot of money — an average of $130 before the Civil War. Few farmers had that kind of cash, and banks, which had no interest in consumer finance, would rarely lend it to them. The company, therefore, had to interpose itself as a credit intermediary, selling machines on the installment plan and using its own superior credit to borrow operating funds until farmers paid up. Obviously the company couldn't restrict credit sales to members of the McCormick family, its friends, and their acquaintances; in effect, McCormick had to pawn his firm's resources and lend the proceeds to thousands of strangers scattered across the prairie outback. No small sum was involved: by 1858 farmers owed McCormick half a million dollars; two years later this had grown to a million dollars.

To survive in this kind of risky business, the firm needed reliable credit information before the sale and aggressive debt collection after it. In the East, formal credit rating services, the forerunners of Dun & Bradstreet, appeared in the 1840s and 1850s, but these agencies supplied no information on the probity of midwestern farmers.

Some structure thus had to be devised to demonstrate the machines, sell and repair them, supply spare parts, evaluate credit, and make collections. During the Virginia years, McCormick had relied on a motley troop consisting of himself, other family members, newspaper editors (thought useful because of their potential value as publicists), and blacksmiths. These catch-as-catch-can arrangements worked badly enough in Virginia, but broke down entirely after the company moved to Chicago and began mass production. Searching for a solution to this combination of marketing problems, McCormick found himself in unexplored territory, for no manufacturer had yet encountered similar vexations. What McCormick had to have was a widespread network of dependable agents, loyal to the Chicago factory and its products but familiar with local business conditions, farming practices, and, above all, the creditworthiness of prospective customers. No prototype of such a network existed; however, distribution of general merchandise, much of it sold on credit, had long since been perfected in small-town, rural America. It was the province of merchants and storekeepers in the towns and peddlers in the countryside.

On this existing foundation, McCormick found he could build. Successful merchants, though he could know but few of them personally, at least belonged to a trustworthy category and had long experience with credit sales. Beginning with an adaptation of the merchant-peddler system of the 1850s, the company developed a sales and service system that evolved from a loose-knit assortment of agents and subagents (whose functions corresponded roughly to those of merchants and peddlers respectively) into a highly structured, closely regulated network of franchised dealerships. These marketing problems, ultimately encountered by all mass producers of goods with similar inherent problems of sales, service, and finance, thus contributed to the shift from personalized to bureaucratic business methods that invariably accompanied industrialization.

McCormick's new sales methods roused the ire of his farmer customers, who regarded dealers as unwelcome intruders that disrupted the farmers' direct relationship with the company and had the gall to charge for the depersonalization. Responding to these attacks, denying that its agents were "parasitic middlemen," the firm used examples it thought its rustic critics could comprehend. His agents, McCormick argued, were as necessary to him "as clerks were to the owner of a store." After all, the company asked, "Would you, a farmer, sell a horse on credit to the first stranger who came along?" In the 1870s and '80s this plan evolved into a network of franchised dealerships. Copied and expanded to national scale by wagon and carriage manufacturers, it became the prototype for modern dealerships that sell automobiles and other consumer durables requiring demonstrations, service, and financing.

The success of this system of sales and service, the first of its kind, and not simply the productivity of his factory carried McCormick to the top of the farm machinery industry and kept him there despite fierce competition and the expiration of his patents.

In the beginning the company's agents and subagents restricted themselves largely to sales and credit functions, leaving mechanical problems to the factory's parts and repairs departments, or to company mechanics sent out from Chicago after the season's production was finished. As the years passed, the agents assumed these responsibilities as well. The company expected its agents not only to provide showrooms to display the machines, "travel thoroughly . . . through the wheat growing portions" of a specific district, sell to "responsible and trustworthy farmers only," hire "efficient assistant agents," deliver machines, "devote themselves actively to putting up, starting and setting to work the . . . reapers," and make collections, but also to stock spare parts and make repairs. Eventually the company got out of the repair business altogether, telling its agents that the factory "should not be made a graveyard for broken down or imperfect machines. . . . Our rule . . . is that every general shall take care of his own wounded and bury his own dead." This ukase meant that dealers also had to repair and resell trade-ins, although in practice the overhauls were often limited to whatever a paintbrush could accomplish.

Dealers also had to perform auxiliary services, such as stocking twine for the binders (machines that tied the wheat in bundles as it was cut) that came on the market after the Civil War, and negotiating with railroads for rebates on shipments to their territories.

Originally, the company made year-to-year arrangements with their representatives. Soon, however, the principal agents became permanent company employees, working on a salary rather than a commission basis, restricted to the sale of McCormick products, and held responsible for hiring and supervising subagents. The agent's lot was not always a happy one. When the factory overproduced, he came under great pressure to push the machines into the market. This often led to sales to farmers who could ill afford further debts. McCormick thus engaged in a forerunner of the modern technique of restoring the market's vital signs by injections of consumer-credit adrenalin, a method that reflected traditional American confidence in the better days to come.

When factory output fell short of demand, angry customers swarmed about the agent like hornets. Most burdensome of all, the company hounded its dealers to collect from the farmers, many of whom could not pay, and some of whom felt that old man McCormick with all his money could, like the dentist, wait.

Obviously a successful agent had to be an aggressive character indeed. The company exhorted its representatives to have "spunk," "grit," and "sand," to "spit on your fists," "make it hot for them," and "to keep on top of the heap." When the competition got hot, apparently something more was required. One home office representative, commenting on the failure of a Minnesota agent, wrote, "Edgar [has] trouble all over his dist[rict]. . . . The only reason I can assign is that he has too many *churchmen* for [sub-] agts. I believe in religion & temperance but it ain't worth a 'cuss' to run the Reaper trade on in Minnesota: it requires cheek & muscle and I am sorry to say some 'evasions' from the truth to successfully sell McCormick harvesters with the opposition we have. . . . You have got to fight the Devil with fire and it is no use trying to fool him on sweetened water."

As the field organizations expanded, the company offices in Chicago underwent an evolution of their own. A subdivision of labor soon separated the manufacturing function from the others. By 1859, the company's office had specialists who dealt exclusively with one particular aspect of business outside the factory, including agent supervision, collections, purchasing, shipping, repairs and spare parts, and accounting. In time each of these individuals metamorphosed into a department with an office and field staff. A printing department published a company newspaper called *The Farmers' Advance* that reached a circulation of 350,000 in the early 1880s. The company also published 800,000 thirty-page pamphlets annually, printed in five or six different languages, some 8,000 colored show cards, and repair catalogs listing spare parts and their prices.

From his first days in business, McCormick had pioneered in widespread advertising. As sales expanded, the policy continued with unabated vigor and soon boasted a specialized staff of its own. "Trying to do business without advertising," the company declared in *The Farmers' Advance,* "is like winking at a pretty girl through a pair of green goggles. You may know what you are doing, but no one else does." Advertising not only reached the market, but, as the company found, expanded it as well, persuading many a farmer to buy machines he neither needed nor could afford.

Development of the field sales force and the office staff began under Orloff M. Dorman, a Chicago merchant and quondam partner of Cyrus McCormick, who joined the firm in 1848. Orloff worked in tandem with William McCormick, who soon took sole charge. When William died in 1865, control of the field and office forces passed to professional managers, another milestone on the road from family to bureaucratic management.

By fair means or foul, the whirlwind activities of the sales staff created a forced draft that kept the factory boilers at full steam. Production rose from 1,500 in 1849 to 4,500 in 1858 to 8,000 in 1868. In 1871 the original factory burned in the great Chicago fire. A new and larger one was built and then expanded as production rose to ten, twelve, and fifteen thousand machines per year. All this made Cyrus McCormick a rich man. In 1849 profits totaled $65,000; in 1856, $300,000; in 1878, $600,000; in 1880, $1,200,000. Floods, droughts, Hessian flies, weevils, army worms, wheat blight, chinch bugs, and grasshoppers beset the farmers, but the McCormick machine churned on.

By 1858 Cyrus McCormick was a millionaire; when he died in 1882 he was a millionaire ten times over. After 1858, millionaire McCormick devoted increasingly less time to the immediate supervision of his business. In fact, between 1858 and 1871, when he returned to supervise the rebuilding after the Chicago fire, McCormick spent little time in Chicago. Most of the day-to-day responsibility fell to his brothers: William ran the office, Leander the factory. Crying family unity, Cyrus had induced his brothers to come to Chicago in 1840, though both they and their wives were loath to leave the soil of Virginia. Like an Oriental satrap, McCormick arrayed his family about him, harrying his sisters and brothers-in-law to join the clan in Chicago.

But McCormick's zest for family unity stopped at the factory gate. During their first ten years in Chicago his brothers received only a salary while Cyrus grew wealthy on the profits. Eventually they protested big brother's meanness. William demanded "something considerable more than a salary out of the business." Leander added, "I have done *not a little* for the machine and I am resolved not to be satisfied without a pretty strong interest if I remain in the business." These demands first came in 1857, but the brothers did not become partners until 1859, when they threatened to quit. By that time they had become nearly indispensable to Cyrus McCormick, particularly since he had in mind spending less, not more, time on the reaper business.

Partnership, however, did little to heal the wounds of long exploitation. The brothers grew increasingly resentful at doing the lion's share of the work while Cyrus indulged his hobbies and perambulated the world collecting trophies and applause. "C.[yrus] H. is the picture of health," complained William's wife; "he takes it easy and thinks ... he does the hardest of work." Exhausted by his responsibilities, William had a nervous breakdown and died in 1865. Leander toiled on, but grew increasingly embittered, particularly when Cyrus dragged his feet about admitting Leander's son to partnership.

In 1858, C. H. McCormick married Nancy Fowler, a Presbyterian choir-singer twenty-five years his junior. The union further divided the brothers when Cyrus's wife proved a tough-minded woman with a strong business sense. She became his most, and often his only, trusted business confidant, to the anger and frustration of his brothers. McCormick legend has it that she, not they, persuaded him to rebuild after the Chicago fire of 1871. Unquestionably her social pretensions and religious fervor encouraged him in the activities that diverted his attention from the business after their marriage. Leaving his brothers to "fight the Devil with fire," and supply the necessary "cheek," "muscle," and "evasions," McCormick reveled in the company of "churchmen" and lapped at the "sweetened water" of health spas. He developed a taste for musical soirees and enjoyed hobnobbing with moguls like August Belmont and Cyrus Field and playing power broker with political luminaries like Samuel J. Tilden. In Chicago and New York, where he bought a house after his marriage, he dabbled in politics. In 1860 he maneuvered to get the Democratic nomination for mayor of Chicago, but failed. He served as chairman of the county central committeee of the Democratic party in Chicago. In 1864 he ran for Congress as a Democratic peace candidate and was trounced three to one. For years he bid for a role as political kingmaker, but the party bosses took his money, drank his wine, shook his hand, and ignored him.

He fared better in the religious world. Always a conservative, he financed churches and a seminary staffed by divines who shared, or at least professed to share, his negative views on abolition of slavery and revision of church dogma. In these matters he showed plenty of cheek and muscle of his own. On one occasion he cut off the salary, credit, and coal supply of a minister who transgressed the doctrine according to McCormick.

Urged on by his brother William, he invested in real estate, becoming the largest landlord in Chicago. To his goldmining speculations, he added a series of ventures in railroads. For a man with such rigid criteria in selecting worshippers, McCormick joined some tacky predators on the hunt for the railroad dollar. In association with the gentlemen of the Crédit Mobilier, who plundered the stockholders of the Union Pacific Railroad, McCormick profited nicely; however, he got fleeced by the Southern Railway Association. In the Southern Association, McCormick, a diehard southern sympathizer and postwar contributor to southern causes, allied himself with Henry S. McComb, a rogue and a carpetbagger, though, like McCormick, a loudly proclaimed Christian.

The Civil War brought a further separation of McCormick from his business. A Virginian, a slaveholder, and an outspoken supporter of the southern cause, McCormick opposed, avowedly on constitutional grounds, forceful preservation of the union. But his legalese did little to deter the wrath of the public, or of the Chicago *Tribune,* which denounced him as a "rebel" and a "slave-driver." As a man with a lot of property that might be torched by patriotic mobs, McCormick issued a public statement in April, 1861, declaring that his "utmost efforts were directed toward the maintenance of peace, believing . . . that the best interests of the country would be thereby promoted." Now that the war had come, however, he proclaimed his allegiance:

Born and reared in the South, I would disgrace my manhood did I not say that my heart sickens at the prospect of the conflict which must ensue. Yet while I regard the war as a great calamity, I am fully aware that there are greater calamities even in war, and the loss of national honor is one of them. Though a native of the south, I am a citizen of Illinois and of the United States, and as such shall bear true allegiance to the Government. That allegiance I shall never violate. . . . I am and ever shall be on the side of my country in war — without considering whether my country is right or wrong.

So much for his public position. Private behavior suggested quite a different point of view. Early in 1862, he sailed to Europe, ostensibly on business, but with the ulterior motive of soliciting intervention on behalf of the Confederacy.

His company meanwhile trimmed its sails to the winds of war and sailed a prosperous tack. In the months before fighting broke out, the company reminded its southern agents to emphasize McCormick's southern birth, and the southern heritage of the reaper itself. Copies of Chicago newspaper articles denouncing McCormick were sent south to show that he was "right" on slavery. Virginia agents were reminded that "our heart still yields allegiance to the 'Old Dominion.' " At the same time, the company told its northern representatives that it opposed secession and would rally to the "Stars and Stripes first, last, and always."

Like many northern manufacturers, the McCormicks had a relatively small southern market, but one that they were reluctant to abandon. Weeks after Fort Sumter, the company stood willing to sell machines in the South, provided customers would pay cash. But this attitude was not unique to the McCormicks; manufacturers on both sides of the Mason-Dixon Line shared it. For example, as hostilities approached, Samuel Colt, an arms manufacturer born and raised in New England, offered to build gun factories for southern states and rushed his agents south to take orders. "Make hay while the sun shines," Colt urged his factory superintendents, ordering a step-up in production. Nor was such behavior limited to northern industrialists. Weeks after Fort Sumter had fallen, Joseph Anderson, proprietor of the Tredegar Iron Works in Richmond, Virginia, submitted a bid for an artillery ammunition contract being let by the federal government. His company had had such contracts in the past, Anderson argued, had always filled them on time, and would do so now. The McCormicks, like other manufacturers, subjugated patriotism to business until the troops drew impassable lines. Luckily for them, patriotism (or protestations of it) proved compatible with profits.

After a brief downturn in 1861 and 1862, the war proved a bonanza for the McCormick firm. Farm labor marched off to war; crop failures in Europe produced a soaring export market; government spending flooded the land with greenbacks. Finding themselves with a booming market, a greater shortage of hands than ever, and cash a-plenty, farmers rushed to buy machinery. Many paid cash for the first time in their lives, and long-overdue notes were paid with inflated wartime currency. For years the McCormicks, like other businessmen, had badgered their creditors for payment. Now the tables were turned, bringing a situation, where, as William McCormick wrote his brother, "creditors were running away from debtors who pursued them in triumph and paid them without mercy." "I . . . told you long ago," he added, that "[the law that made greenbacks] legal tender would in the end be a good bankrupt law. 'Money' *may* be brought by the bushel to pay . . . us. This legal tender law is . . . a great *leveler*. It will enable the creditor to pay his honest debts with scraps of paper."

Cyrus McCormick was no more a great leveler than the greenback dollar turned out to be, despite his lifelong adherence to the people's party of Jefferson and Jackson. His career put a great distance between him and hoi polloi, and he liked it that way. Suspicious of all reform movements, he also had no sympathy for the Granger organizations, through which grainbelt farmers voiced their protests in the 1870s and '80s. As a politician and a farm machinery manufacturer, McCormick tempered his public criticisms of the Grangers, who were, after all, potential voters and customers. On issues he thought irrelevant to his own self-interest, such as opposition to monopoly, McCormick publicly expressed sympathy with the Grangers' aims. Privately he instructed the company's staff to stand fast against any demands that affected the McCormick harvester company directly. Rubbing elbows in Grange halls full of sweaty farmers had no charms for Cyrus. His wealth had opened the doors of society's inner sanctums, and he much preferred hobnobbing with the elite at watering holes like the Manhattan Club and Saratoga Springs. Like many another citizen of the republic, McCormick relished the approval of the Europeans, the more aristocratic the better. In 1851 he exhibited the reaper at the Crystal Palace exhibition in London, winning a Grand Council Medal. In 1855 the French International Exposition awarded him the Grand Medal of Honor. Delighting in these baubles and others collected from lesser European states, he decided in 1866 that selection for the French Legion of Honor would make a crowning touch to his achievements, so he campaigned for the award. "I might," he wrote to a friend in France, "get the 'Cross of Honor' for the Invention & improvement of the Reaping Machine." His friend replied that the award was possible "with proper management." McCormick's influential friends in France lobbied hard on his behalf, and on January 5, 1868, the Emperor Napoleon III made McCormick a Chevalier of the Legion of Honor. Thereafter, McCormick proudly wore the Legion's red rosette in his lapel. (What McCormick's fiercely independent Scotch-Irish forebears would have thought of his preening before a petty, third-rate French dictator can only be imagined, but it probably would have been mild compared to their reaction when he tried to have his daughter presented to Victoria, queen of hated England.)

The citation that accompanied the award of the Legion of Honor acclaimed McCormick as the "inventor of the reaper." When he received it he had invented nothing significant for twenty years. The original Virginia Reaper underwent more or less continual improvement and was finally replaced in 1870 by a lighter, more efficient model called "the Advance." But these changes were merely refinements of the original design. Over the years the company expanded its line by adding a mower, a combination reaper-mower, a harvester that not only cut grain but also raked it automatically into piles, and finally a binder that cut the grain and bound it into bundles ready for threshing. All these machines incorporated new and patented ideas, but none of them was McCormick's. When he sought to renew his original patent in 1848, his application was rejected. In 1855 he sued a major competitor for infringement of his own patents, but lost.

These setbacks, however, made little difference. As his brother William remarked, "I have often said your money has been made *not* out of your patents but by making and selling the machines." As the most powerful competitor in the field, McCormick could simply buy whatever patents he needed to keep pace with competition. His factory and sales force did the rest. As he himself remarked on the subject of twine binders, "The self binding part of these machines [was] invented by others, while they have been brought to the present state of practical utility, economy & adaptation to public wants in my works & by their operation in the field by men engaged with me in my business."

With such a powerful rival already in the field, few inventors could find the capital necessary to commence manufacture on their own. It made more sense for them to license an established firm to use their patent in return for royalty on each machine built. Although his opponents might denounce him as "monied monopolist" who siphoned money from the farmers' pockets into his own, and denounce his patent suits as attempts to "protect [himself] from the improvements of anybody else and so to stop the whole inventive genius of the country," it can be argued that the presence of wealthy potential customers like McCormick encouraged inventors rather than discouraged them and thus accelerated rather than retarded the diffusion of technology. If so, then this was one of the ways that big business preserved individual initiative while destroying competition in their bailiwicks of the economy. In any case, McCormick's patent-buying typified a pattern that appeared with increasing frequency in the nineteenth century.

Cyrus McCormick was born into a world where farmers harvested their grain crops as they had since time immemorial; when he died in 1882 the mechanical reaper was in use around the world. As on the British Empire, the sun never set on the McCormick reaper. He and his competitors had converted the American prairies from open space to the breadbasket that fed the United States and much of Europe. In some ways his firm, which did so much to modernize the American agricultural economy, remained an anachronism at his death, stranded half-way between traditional family management and modern bureaucratic control. McCormick would neither relinquish control of his business nor exercise it consistently after 1858. Together with his brothers' disaffection, this led to diminishing efficiency and loss of direction.

By the time McCormick died, his firm had become something of a rudderless ship, its lack of direction masked by the fact that American farmers had entered a period of unparalleled prosperity that kept demand for farm machinery high. When McCormick's son was ready to enter the business in 1879, W. J. Hanna, who had succeeded William McCormick as head of the company's office, wrote that the firm "practically has no head — every man in the office seems to do what is right in his own eyes — makes his own hours, and goes home when he pleases without leave. . . . A general laxity prevails, and that laxity extends to the agents likewise. They are allowed far too much freedom, and feel quite independent of the *apparent* government of the office." A similar laxity prevailed in the factory itself, as evidenced by the fact that despite significant increases in annual production, the cost of constructing each machine remained constant.

Despite these failings, McCormick, in reaching the diffuse market for farm equipment, and expanding it through advertising and credit, had created a system of sales and service that became one component of the modern industrial firm. A complex man, McCormick was shrewd enough to foresee Chicago's future role as the hub of American agricultural commerce and naïve enough to be swindled by gold-mine and railroad promoters. Sometimes generous and forgiving, he contributed hundreds of thousands of dollars to his church and to Washington and Lee University; he became friends with generals Grant, Sherman, and Sheridan, who had scourged his beloved South during the war. But he could be mean and petty as well, particularly to his inferiors: he upbraided subordinates for wasting the company's money on unnecessary postage stamps or superfluous words in telegrams. Secretaries and servants never lasted long. When offended, he became a venomous, indefatigable enemy. He once declined to pay the Pennsylvania Railroad an excess baggage charge of $8.70 that he considered unjust, although he was a millionaire at the time and his obstinance meant that his wife and two small children had to cancel their trip and return to their hotel. When the railroad subsequently lost the baggage, he instituted a suit for damages and pursued it for eighteen years.

His character thus exhibited paradoxes common among his countrymen. Generous and stingy, ambitious and lazy, clever and naïve, energetic and narrowminded, unscrupulous and self-righteous, he pursued self-aggrandizement, flattening obstacles human and otherwise that stood in his way. In the process he multiplied mankind's ability to feed itself and made an enduring contribution to the American business system. Ultimately his name disappeared into the corporate anonymity of International Harvester (formed in 1902), but his work lives on. The giant combines that move through wheatfields all over the world are the direct descendants of the clumsy little reaper born in the Shenandoah valley of Virginia.

Andrew Carnegie: the Steel King as philanthropist

4

The Star-Spangled Scotchman Andrew Carnegie

WE go back a long way, Andy and I. Even before I could read, I heard the story of this Scottish immigrant boy whose rise to wealth and power became part of the American "rags to riches" legend. When I went to school the teacher directed me to the nearby Carnegie Library, where I discovered Zane Grey and Richard Halliburton, who convinced me that I might some day play shortstop in the major leagues, or swim in the Panama Canal. (I'm batting 50 percent so far.)

In my salad days as an academic, Carnegie's life provided the material for one book, and one of his foundations supported the research for another. Some day I expect I'll retire (though why any academic wants to retire is something I haven't discovered yet) on a pension fund for which Carnegie furnished the seed money. In a hiatus between the railroad and college, however, I discovered another aspect of Carnegie's handiwork, the steel industry.

Somebody told me there was gold in that thar steel; all you had to do was buy a truck and go haul it. I should have known better, but my mother never heard Waylon Jennings's advice about babies:

> *Don't let 'em pick guitars and drive them ol' trucks;*
> *Let em be doctors and lawyers and such.*

It took a while to learn that lesson on my own, and an expensive session it was. A friend once asked my partner, "Is there any money in the trucking business?" "Damn right," he replied, "there's seven thousand dollars of my money in it somewhere."

Although at the time I couldn't see the benefits that lay obscured by a stack of unpaid fuel bills, I realize now that I got a bargain. As an "independent owner-operator," I joined a fraternity for which the traditional tie of movement and individual liberty survives as a living creed. Though much truckers' conversation tends to be, as one cynic remarked, "lies about them waitresses and how fast them trucks will go," I nevertheless learned a good bit about independence, self-reliance, and the pros and cons of Brother James Hoffa, as well as the diabolical nature of government interference with individual initiative and how to avoid it. I learned how to fake the Interstate Commerce Commission logbook so as to drive as many hours a day as I could stay awake, regardless of what the law mandated; I mastered the art of running the rig's outside wheels over the curb instead of over the scales at a turnpike tollbooth, thereby holding down the weight and the toll; I memorized the locations of treacherous downhill grades, as well as the names of small towns where cops carrying flashlights and wearing white socks lurked to trap the unwary, conveying them first to the scales and then to all-night justices of the peace; I ate lots of bad food and saw lots of beautiful country; I explored mills where steel poured out in a continuous ribbon at thirty miles an hour and factories that made bathtubs and fenceposts on assembly lines.

During long layovers between loads, spent in dozens of cinder-block modern motels, the desk clerks, chambermaids, and waitresses told me their life stories. Around the pools and bars of these hostelries, the natives — airline crews and working girls — regaled me with stories of trips around the world, while we all waited for our next haul. In fact, for a business that attracted the independent-minded who craved freedom of movement, trucking turned out to involve a lot of truckling: to the tyranny of the telephone, the vanity of the commission agent who arranged loads, and the cupidity of loading crews, who often had to be bribed lest death take care of you before they did.

Steel hauling particularly involved protracted waits, both inside the mill and out. Twelve-hour delays were too commonplace to deserve comment; twenty-four hours was not unusual; forty-eight hours not unheard-of. Some mills were notorious. It was widely reported and believed that a driver had frozen to death in his truck while waiting to be loaded at one plant noted for its leisurely pace. Drivers especially dreaded assignments to United States Steel (the direct descendant of Carnegie Steel), where confusion and indifference dominated everything. After being beached for twenty-four hours, along with a school of other trucks, at Carnegie's original mill in Pittsburgh, I met a colleague who had become a history buff in his plentiful spare time. "I've been reading about old Carnegie," he said, "and if Andy could see this, he'd clean house in a hurry."

Confusion and idleness, however, were not the only inefficiencies besetting Carnegie's once-streamlined industry. Plying the turnpikes of Ohio, Pennsylvania, and New Jersey, endless lines of trucks shuttled back and forth, carrying steel from the mills of the Delaware valley to the factories of Ohio, and from the steel mills of Ohio to the factories of the Delaware valley. Many of the loads at opposite ends were identical except for slight variations in weight. Since steel products and their prices were standardized, and since the manufacturers absorbed the shipping charges, which are standardized by law, price competition played little part in the selling and shipping of steel. Assuming a dependable delivery schedule, a manufacturer in Philadelphia didn't care whether he bought his steel from a mill nearby or from one in Cleveland. Once the steel was sold, it made no financial difference to buyer or seller which trucking company hauled it. Competing for sales and loads, salesmen therefore showered purchasing agents and shipping clerks with emoluments such as Playboy calendars, dinners, and baseball tickets (Cleveland-based salesmen had a handicap: you couldn't give Indians' tickets away).

The resulting inefficiency kept a lot of truckers busy burning a lot of fuel, but also created a market opportunity perceived by one of my more acute brethren. Under his auspices, drivers gathered nightly at a truck stop outside of Philadelphia, made a list of their loads and destinations, then telephoned a similar group in Ohio. When a driver could match his load to a similar one on the other end of the line, he saved himself a long trip. Representatives from each end drove their cars to Somerset, Pennsylvania, exchanged paperwork for the matching loads, and returned home. Next morning, each lucky driver delivered the wrong load, but the right paperwork. The system worked because all the steel looked alike and because the trucks were weighed on dispatch, but not on delivery. Eventually, of course, logorrhea overthrew discretion; the story got out, and established inefficiency deposed extemporaneous efficiency. Years later, after I had rummaged through Carnegie's life, I concluded that if Andy had been around, he would first have laughed, then fired the man in charge of shipping and replaced him with the truck driver who found a better way.

Andy wanted things moving around his place, so he promoted hustlers and fired slackers. Sluggishness wasted time as well as money, and time *was money,* that he knew. Waste offended him because he had the Scot's fetish for thrift combined with the American's fascination with efficiency. These and other personal qualities he translated into management methods that created America's first manufacturing "Big Business," carried him from poor Scottish immigrant boy to richest man in the world, and made him a hero to his countrymen. Like Cyrus McCormick's, his firm's identity eventually disappeared into the anonymity of a corporate merger, but Carnegie himself left an indelible mark on American business and society. His career became a legend, inspiring to some, notorious to others. His wealth became a legacy to the people of both his native and adopted homelands. His system became, like Whitney's theory of production and McCormick's distribution methods, a component of the modern American industrial machine.

Carnegie was born in November, 1835, in Dunfermline, County Fife, Scotland. Andrew Jackson was then President of the United States, which comprised 24 states and some 15 million people, 90 percent of whom were rural residents. The American economy was overwhelmingly one of farming and trading. Industrialization had begun and household manufacturing was declining, but aside from the New England textile mills and a handful of other exceptions, manufacturing remained the province of small shops. Only the first thousand miles of what grew to be a railroad network of a quarter of a million miles had been constructed. Cyrus McCormick was embarking on his ill-fated excursion into the iron business. Karl Marx was a seventeen-year-old middle-class student in Germany.

In Britain, the Industrial Revolution, powered by steam, was sweeping across the land, eliminating the remaining pockets of traditional handicraft production. Dunfermline, a town of hand-loom weavers, lay squarely in its path. In its wake arose the Chartist ferment, demanding political reform and legislative protection against rampaging capitalists. During Carnegie's boy-hood, both the Industrial Revolution and the Chartist agitation engulfed Dunfermline. Industrialization succeeded, inflicting the ills of dislocation on the Carnegies and thousands of other Scottish families. Chartism failed.

In the bleak decade that became known as "the hungry forties," a quarter of a million British citizens gave up the unequal struggle against the machine and sailed to America. In 1848, the year that Karl Marx published the *Communist Manifesto*, calling on the "workers of the world [to] unite," the Carnegies joined the diaspora.

In the thirteen years between Andy's birth in Scotland and his family's departure for America, Scotland made a vivid impression on him, inculcating attitudes that affected his behavior the rest of his life. Measuring American realities against Scottish ideals, he found scope and outlet for his driving ambitions and developed a paradoxical character that reflected the contrasting worlds of his boyhood in preindustrial Scotland and his man-hood in the mechanized United States. Carnegie, whose work made Pittsburgh the nineteenth-century American industrial city par excellence, replete with bleak factories, grimy air, and an unskilled labor force regulated by factory discipline and wages, grew up in a town as unlike Pittsburgh as any that can be imagined.

Dunfermline's prosperity and stability rested upon an ancient and honorable craft, the handloom weaving of linen. More than half the town's eleven thousand inhabitants practiced this craft, handed down from father to son essentially unchanged for centuries. Self-employed, working hours of their own choosing in their own home workshops, earning good wages, the weavers were men of substance and self-respect, indebted to no one and subject to no man's beck and call. As one of Dunfermline's more skillful practitioners, Andrew's father, Will Carnegie, enjoyed the respect of his fellow townsmen and the security of a home and family. In 1836 he had such a prosperous year that he moved his family to a larger house, bought three additional looms, and took on apprentices to work them.

Father's
business
declined

But the very factors that made linen weaving such a special art — the large amount of skilled labor and time required to produce each piece — rendered the trade particularly susceptible to mechanization. By 1838 steam mills elsewhere were producing goods in such volume that Dunfermline's handloom weavers found prices and demand sinking. This decline, discounted at first as one of the temporary slumps that occurred from time to time, soon proved to be an irreversible trend. In 1843 the decline became an avalanche when a steam mill opened in Dunfermline. The mill's whistle, sounding the beginning and end of the working day, was the death knell for Will Carnegie and his fellow artisans. Since he was unable to work for himself and unwilling to work for others, Will Carnegie's world collapsed around him.

✗ For young Andy, Dunfermline had been a magical place, filled with the romance of Scotland's past and ferment of its present. Although it was the largest town in County Fife and the center of handicraft production, Dunfermline had a rural setting among hills and glens, overlooking the Firth of Forth. Relics and ruins of Scottish history dotted the landscape. As a boy, Andy explored Dunfermline Abbey, Malcolm's Tower, monuments to

Mary Queen of Scots, and the palace and tomb of King Robert the Bruce.

Carnegie's uncle George Lauder cast a troubadour's spell over the boy, peopling the ruins with the paladins of Scotland's past — William Wallace, Robert the Bruce, and Shakespearean heroes. To this heady brew the uncle added liberal doses of Scottish ballads and, above all, the poetry of Robert Burns. A self-respecting people must be a free people, Andy learned, but peace could be achieved only through peaceful means. The Scots had been warriors for centuries, the uncle argued, but heroic tales were a poor return for all the valor and bloodshed. Scotland's cherished independence had been swallowed up by the United Kingdom; Scottish boys, whose grandfathers had marched proudly under the cross of St. Andrew, now tramped under the English flag along the highways and byways of the British Empire. Democracy, not war, could fashion the key with which a people could unlock the greatness that lay within them. The United States, Uncle Lauder told Andy, showed what a free people could do. Under his uncle's tutelage, Andy added Franklin, Washington, and Jefferson to his stock of heroic figures.

To the enchantments found in days wandering sun-dappled glens and among rain-streaked monuments, young Carnegie added the nocturnal excitements of Dunfermline's political agitation. Dunfermline was "reknowned as perhaps the most radical town in the kingdom," according to Carnegie. Convinced that the People's Charter, with its provision for universal manhood suffrage, could bring to Scotland what the Constitution had provided the people of the United States, Carnegie's father and uncles joined the Chartist movement. In torchlit squares and lamplit parlors, Andy absorbed the guiding principle of the radical reformers: "political equality, that is all we ask, and then everything else will follow: the prosperous yeoman, the respected artisan, the happy child. Give us the Charter and we can take care of ourselves." By 1847, when Will Carnegie told his son, "Andra, I can get nae mair work," Carnegie's boyhood had instilled attitudes that endured throughout his life: a reverence for the heroic figure; a faith in nationalism; a belief in political equality as a remedy for mankind's woes. This mental equipment, fashioned in old, decaying Scotland, proved ideally suited to the challenge of young, booming America.

By 1848 the Carnegie family had fallen on desperate times. The father, recognizing that he would never practice his craft again, had sold his idle looms. The responsibility for the family's support had passed to the mother, who squeezed a meager living out of cobbling and storekeeping. Although Samuel Johnson once remarked that "the noblest prospect which a Scotchman e'er perceives is the high-road that leads him to England," the Carnegies looked not toward England, whence came Scotland's misery, but toward the United States, where many a Scot had already found hope. Margaret Carnegie, Andy's mother, had two sisters who had emigrated to the United States in 1840. The sisters had written home often, the tone of their letters reflecting the fluctuating economic climate of their new home:

I wish I had . . . not come to America this soon — the banking system has made sad havoc . . . business is at a stand. . . . I would not advise any person to come who can get livelihood at home, as trade is very dull here, indeed many who are both willing & able to work find it impossible to find employment. [1842]

Later, the outlook brightened and America proved "far better for the working man. . . . You seem to breath a freer atmosphere here." In the face of such conflicting advice, the Carnegies clung to their home as long as they could. Only when Dunfermline seemed to offer no hope for the future did the family abandon it. The mother borrowed the passage money, and on May 17, 1848, the Carnegies left Dunfermline on the trek:

> *To the west, to the west, to the land of the free*
> *Where mighty Missouri rolls down to the sea;*
> *Where a man is a man if he's willing to toil,*
> *And the humblest may gather the fruits of the soil. . . .*
> *Where the young may exult and the aged may rest,*
> *Away far away, to the land of the west.*

Many millions before the Carnegies had followed this siren song, and many millions more were to come. For some, the new land delivered all the song promised and more. For others, the new world proved not a fertile field, but a graveyard of their hopes.

Emigration was traumatic for all but the very young. In some individuals, the decision to emigrate signaled not a courageous determination to carry on, but rather the ultimate admission of defeat, the inability to cope with circumstances that some — those who stayed behind — found ways to surmount. Like Joseph Conrad's Lord Jim, or Herman Wouk's Tom Kiefer, who abandoned what they thought were sinking ships only to find that sturdier souls remained aboard and kept the vessel afloat, some immigrants blighted the rest of their lives with the self-damnation of shame. To this category belonged Will Carnegie, aged forty-three at the time of sailing: reduced from proud, self-employed craftsman, family head, and prominent figure in his ancestral home to penniless nonentity, dependent upon his wife's labor and courage to keep the family together. Emasculated by his shattering experience in Scotland, Will Carnegie found neither manhood, exultation, nor rest in "the land of the west." America needed handloom weavers even less than Scotland did; politics offered no foothold, for the Americans already had the Charter; religion provided no solace, for Will had long ago repudiated the Calvinist faith of his ancestors. In the last seven years of his life, as his will to live dwindled, Will became a vagabond peddler and died a beaten man.

Many immigrants, however, responded energetically to their new surroundings. Like oysters converting the irritation of a grain of sand into the beauty of a pearl, they vindicated their flight in letters home that bristled with pride in the virtues of their new homeland and their own achievements there. Andrew Carnegie and his mother belonged to this group. Margaret, aged thirty-three, burned with shame at her husband's failure and despair, at leaving poor and defeated, and at having to beg, borrow, and sell out to get the passage money. Margaret was determined that her sons would succeed where her husband had failed, and that she herself would someday return to Dunfermline in triumph. Andrew, aged thirteen, aware of his father's failure and his mother's contempt for it, looked to the future for redemption of the past. Only the younger son, Tom, aged five, boarded ship unburdened with the baggage of failure.

For the Carnegies, as for millions of other immigrant families, the presence in America of relatives, friends, and fellow countrymen cushioned the shock of landing in their new home. A strong sense of community pervaded the Scots in America, regardless of their position in the old country. From the day of their arrival the Carnegie family benefited from the aid of informal Scottish brotherhood. Time and again throughout Andy's career, some Scot appeared at a crucial moment to lend a hand, just as the Yale "old-boy network" had so often rescued Whitney.

In New York the Carnegies were met by the James Sloane family. Sloane himself had been a Dunfermline weaver; Mrs. Sloane was a girlhood friend of Margaret Carnegie. In Pittsburgh, Mrs. Carnegie's sisters welcomed them, and other Scots provided employment. Henry Phipps gave Margaret a job cobbling; Andy found work in the textile mill of a Mr. Blackstock, who gave preferential treatment to his countrymen. The job paid $1.20 a week. "I have made millions since," Andy later remarked, "but none of these gave me so much happiness as my first week's earnings. I was now a helper of the family, a bread winner." He soon found a better job in the bobbin factory of John Jay, another Dunfermline expatriate.

At the bobbin factory, young Carnegie demonstrated many of the qualities that would carry him to the top: reliability, a willingness to work hard, an ability to perceive opportunities and to make the most of them. He attacked his pedestrian duties — dipping bobbins into oil and firing the factory boiler — energetically, although the oil smell nauseated him and the boiler frightened him (ironic reactions in a lad who later became an oil speculator and a railroad superintendent). Andy's employer rewarded his ardor with occasional stints in the office. There, Carnegie learned the rudiments of accounting, acquiring the first in a set of management tools he assembled while still a young man. He polished this skill by enrolling in a night school course in double-entry bookkeeping, trudging back and forth through snow and to class at the end of fourteen-hour days at the bobbin factory.

Young Andy thus showed that he had plenty of pluck, but as all dutiful readers of Horatio Alger know, pluck alone will not suffice; you have to have a little luck as well. Sure enough, luck ("Fortunatus," as Carnegie called it) arrived, and after only a year of waiting. "My Good Fairy found me in a cellar," Andy rejoiced. As might be expected, the good fairy was a Scot, David Brooks, manager of O'Reilly's Telegraph office in Pittsburgh and a crony of Carnegie's Uncle Hogan. Brooks needed a messenger boy for the telegraph office, and whenever possible he hired Scottish immigrant boys. Uncle Hogan nominated Andy, who rushed home for parental consent. Margaret, who thought Andy's subterranean chores at the oil vat and coal bin beneath her son, rejoiced at the new opportunity. She and Andy quickly put down the father's objections, and Andy presented himself at the telegraph office the next day. It was a momentous step. Not only did Andy escape to "paradise . . . heaven, as it seemed to me, with newspapers, pins, pencils, and sunshine," but more important, as he later recalled, "I felt that my foot was on the ladder and that I was bound to climb."

Opportunity had knocked and Andy, as he so often did, recognized the chance and flung open the door. In leaving the bobbin factory for the telegraph office, however, Carnegie did much more than exchange a tedious job for a more pleasant one; he moved from a business backwater to a mainstream, one that was revolutionizing American commerce and industry. The railroad and telegraph together brought the first significant increase in the speed of commerce and communication in centuries. Passengers and goods, hitherto restricted by the snail's pace of wagons, coaches, canal and steamboats, now rushed through weather and across mountains that often brought more primitive methods to a standstill. Communications, agonizingly slow and frustratingly uncertain in the past, now took place virtually instantaneously.

The rails and the wires battered down ancient barriers of space and time, opening land for settlement and markets for exploitation.

Thanks to its ideal location, Pittsburgh thrived on America's economy of agriculture and industry. Transportation routes radiated from Pittsburgh like the spokes of a wheel. The Ohio River, together with the Pennsylvania and Ohio canal systems, tied the city to the emerging granary of the Ohio valley and Great Lakes region and to the established cotton economy of the Mississippi valley. The Conemaugh River reached eastward to the iron mines and furnaces on the slopes of the Alleghenies; the Monongahela and Youghiogheny rivers penetrated the coal deposits of Connellsville and West Virginia; the Allegheny and Clarion rivers flowed from the iron and oil fields to the north. As these natural resources were discovered and developed, the rivers funneled them to Pittsburgh, making the city an industrial center just as it had become a commercial center earlier. By 1849, when Carnegie moved to the telegraph office, the city's iron smelters and mills clouded its sky with smoke and its rivers with slime.

From the clicking keys at the telegraph company, Carnegie learned firsthand of the rise and fall of agricultural markets as well as the negotiations through which merchants and manufacturers joined hands to finance industrial enterprises. He got to know many of the city's prime movers personally by delivering messages to them. The telegraph office thus served as an informal but effective school of commerce and business methods. Bright and eager, Andy soon knew as much about Pittsburgh's business as anyone in town. He knew who sold what to whom, at what price, and on what terms. He learned who succeeded and who failed as the credit standing of individuals and firms passed through his hands every day.

Distinguishing himself by coming early, staying late, and sweeping out the office when he had no messages to deliver, Andy soon garnered the rewards of virtue. His salary rose from $2.50 to $3.00 a week. The company promoted him, first to part-time telegrapher, then in 1851 to full-time telegraph operator.

(The superintendent who approved his promotion was James D. Reid, born in Dunfermline.)

As a qualified telegraph operator at the age of sixteen, Carnegie had achieved a position in the world that might have satisfied a less ambitious man for life. It was a job that rewarded responsibility with respect, a salary large enough to support a family, and a prospect of future promotion. But for Carnegie, as for many another ambitious American — Thomas Edison among them — the telegraph office served as a stepping stone to better things. It did justify, however, writing home to Scotland to boast of his success and the virtues of his new country. "I am past delivering messages now," he wrote to his cousin "Dod" Lauder in Scotland, "and have got to operating. I am to have $4 a week and a good prospect of getting more." In Scotland, he added, "I would have been a poor weaver all my days, but here, I can surely do something better . . . if I don't it will be my own fault, for anyone can get along in this country."

His success, he declared in an argument he would advance throughout his life, reflected the merits of the American political system. "We now possess what the working classes of Your Country look forward to as constituting their political millennium. We have the charter which you have been fighting for for years as the panacea for all Britain's woes, the bulwark of the liberties of the people. . . . The best proof of the superiority of our system is . . . the general prosperity."

Under this benevolent government that existed by consent of the governed, the national treasury held a surplus; the public debt was paid as it matured; the western lands were opening up; 13 thousand miles of railroad and 21 thousand miles of telegraph had been built with thousands more on the way; pauperism rarely occurred. Only political equality, Carnegie thought, explained

the contrast between the United States and the Canadas. They were settled by the same people at the same time under the same government — and look at the difference! Where are her Railroads, Telegraphs and Canals? her commercial marine and her unrivaled steamships? her fast clippers or her potent Press? We have given to the world a Washington, a Franklin, a Fulton, a Morse — what has Canada ever produced?

While still a young man, then, Carnegie articulated the principle of interdependence between political equality and economic superiority that most of his countrymen, rich and poor alike, embraced. This equation served Carnegie as a two-edged sword: with one side he attacked other countries' systems as inferior; with the other he defended American institutions against criticism. In the United States most things were right; those which were not would improve or disappear because the system was self-correcting. That being the case, Americans could look forward to a brighter future for their children, and, as often as not, for themselves.

The credo not only excused economic abuses but also justified opposition to economic reforms either by government intervention or by labor agitation. Should reformist intervention eventually become necessary, then, Carnegie argued, the political system would make it easy. Such a view most nineteenth-century Americans shared with Carnegie. Even in the twentieth century, when reform seemed blocked or perilously delayed on every hand, Americans preferred working through the existing political system to overthrowing capitalism in favor of some alternative economic arrangement.

In America — its prosperity, democracy, its opportunities, its heroic figures, its rich men humble enough to be kind to the poor telegraph boy who conveyed their messages — Carnegie perceived Scottish radicalism incarnate, and it was good. Soon it got better.

In 1852, another good fairy appeared in the personage of Tom Scott, superintendent of the western division of the Pennsylvania Railroad. The Pennsylvania, which replaced a cumbersome system of canals and inclined plane railroads across the Alleghenies, linked Pittsburgh, with its transportation network west and south, to the markets of the eastern seaboard. Scott needed a personal telegrapher and secretary; he hired Carnegie, the office hotshot, at a salary of $35 a month. The opportunity, more than the salary, lured Carnegie away from the telegraph company. "In my old berth," he wrote to his cousin in Scotland, "I must always have been an employee. The highest station I could attain was Manager of an office." Even before Scott showed up, he had resolved to accept any offer "which would be better for the future," even if it paid less than telegraphy.

Carnegie spent twelve years on the Pennsylvania Railroad, resigning as superintendent of the Pittsburgh division in 1865. His railroad service shaped the rest of his business life: on the railroad he assimilated the managerial skills, grasped the economic principles, and cemented the personal relationships that enabled him to become successively manager, capitalist, and entrepreneur. If he had exercised a conscious choice of training grounds in up-to-date managerial methods, Carnegie could have chosen no better than the Pennsylvania Railroad, which he had joined by chance. In America, the railroads pioneered in the development of sophisticated management structures, and the Pennsylvania led the way. Ironic as it may seem to those familiar only with the declining years of the Pennsylvania, its misbegotten alliance with the New York Central, or its bankruptcy and collapse into the dilapidated contraption known as "Conrail," the Pennsylvania was in the nineteenth and early twentieth centuries justifiably called "the standard railroad of the world." Charles Francis Adams, a ferocious critic of railroads in general, called the Pennsylvania "that superb organization, every detail of whose wonderful system is a fit subject for study to all interested in the operation of railroads." And, in fact, other American railroads and many abroad copied its methods and organization.

Carnegie, joining the Pennsylvania during its formative years, absorbed the methods that carried it to excellence. Railroads like the Pennsylvania pioneered in management techniques because they had to. In size of physical plant, in cost of construction, in complexity of technology and operation, in number of employees, in revenues, and in expenses, they quickly dwarfed even the New England textile mills, the largest previous business enter-

prises. The railroads' voracious appetite for capital led to modern
investment banking and the stock exchange. Their equipment
needs created a market that called forth a whole industry to supply rails, locomotives, cars. On the railroad itself, systematic
methods had to be employed to run trains without running them
into one another, to hire and fire workers, to perform necessary
maintenance, to keep track of thousands of shipments and millions of dollars (much of it literally in nickels and dimes) that
passed through the hands of hundreds of employees. All this
Carnegie saw and learned. But above all, he absorbed the railroad's dual obsession as to costs: knowing what they were, and
reducing them.

Circumstances forced the railroads, more than any other business before them, to apply cost accounting to management. The
railroads were built with other people's money; whether the year
ended in a profit or a loss, investors had a right to know how
much money was taken in and where it was spent. The Pennsylvania did this so effectively that a stockholders' committee reported that "a charge or entry of a day's labor, of the purchase of
a keg of nails, or the largest order goes through such a system of
checks and audits as to make fraud almost an impossibility."

Detailed cost accounting also greatly aided management decision making. In an operation as complex as the Pennsylvania
Railroad's, it was often hard to tell which services made money
and which did not. Cost accounting pinpointed the sources of
profit and loss. It also helped measure employee performance. In
addition, it permitted cost-based pricing, enabling the railroads
to assess charges that assured a profit. And a profit there had to
be, to avoid bankruptcy by meeting interest charges and paying
dividends high enough to attract further investment. Costs also
determined investment decisions. New equipment that could pay
for itself by reducing cost or attracting business was worth buying, regardless of price; otherwise, it was a waste of money no
matter how cheaply it could be bought.

Scott, with Carnegie at his elbow, set about making the Pennsylvania a paying proposition by getting volume up and holding
costs down. The structure that Scott developed to effect this pol-

icy involved a labyrinthine, departmentalized bureaucracy, a blizzard of paperwork assaulting its desks. That maze, which Carnegie memorized, we need not wander into here, but the underlying principles, which Carnegie later applied to the steel business, were simple. From Scott, Carnegie learned these rules: install whatever arrangements are necessary to know all costs all the time; to customers who can opt for a competitor's services, keep the price barely above costs and rely on volume to make a profit; with shippers, charge the limit; promote cost-conscious subordinates and fire the others; if business volume strains capacity, drive your men and equipment as hard as you can before hiring or buying more; buy what pays for itself and nothing that doesn't. The last two guidelines Carnegie fastened upon in particular, loading cars to capacity, marshaling them into the heaviest trains that locomotives could haul, and then running them as fast as conditions would permit (or faster, when a Casey Jones had the throttle). Since an adequate return on capital depended on the fact that it cost very little more to run big trains fast than it did to run small trains slowly, while the revenues were much greater, investment was concentrated in more durable rails, more powerful locomotives, and cars with greater capacity, all contributing to reduced cost of hauling each ton of freight, each sack of mail, each passenger.

When Scott was promoted to vice-president of the Pennsylvania in 1859, he named Carnegie his successor as superintendent. The position was a taxing one, demanding twenty-four-hour-a-day attention. As Carnegie described it:

the superintendent of a division in those days was expected to run trains by telegraph at night, to go and remove all wrecks, and indeed to do everything. At one time for eight days I was constantly upon the line, day and night at one obstruction or the other.

Carnegie gloried in it.

When Scott offered the appointment, Carnegie said, "I was only 24 years old, but my model then was Lord John Russell of whom it was said he would take command of the Channel fleet tomorrow." As superintendent he demonstrated his expertise with Scott's cost-volume-velocity doctrines, the complex statistical analyses that had produced them, and the operating strategies that put them into practice. He would burn wrecked cars to clear the line, or lay new tracks around a wreck. He originated night train dispatchers to expedite twenty-four-hour service and kept all telegraph stations open around the clock. When he forwarded to headquarters proposals for improved service at lower costs, he supported them with statistical analyses. He advocated double-tracking the entire main line between Altoona and Pittsburgh to reduce train delays, and urged that train crews' shifts be lengthened from ten to thirteen hours to eliminate a change between the two cities. He kept trains full by cutting Pittsburgh commuter fares to meet competition, and by holding back the company's own coal and lumber shipments until traffic was light.

In 1865, Scott, following his own maxim of promoting cost-cutters, offered to make Carnegie general superintendent. Carnegie declined because he had bigger ideas; he had learned the lessons of crucial years. By 1865, when Carnegie left, the Pennsylvania Railroad had become the largest business firm in the world in revenues, employees, and value of physical assets. Carnegie had shown his mastery of the Pennsylvania's complex system by superintending its most important division in terms of revenues generated, and its most demanding in terms of operations. Carnegie came to the Pennsylvania a callow telegrapher; he left it a mature, polished manager trained to run a big business by the biggest business of them all. Nor was this the only change. He came there a poor boy and left a rich man. This, too, he owed to Tom Scott, who liked to let "my boy Andy" in on things, and to his own genius at making the most of his chances. Carnegie justified Scott's faith, while validating Samuel Johnson's observation that "much can be made of a Scot, if you catch him young enough."

Tom Scott introduced Carnegie to the magic of capital investment, and Carnegie proved as apt a pupil in this art as he had been in management. Scott showed Carnegie a trick better than the making of bricks without straw; he showed how a shrewd capitalist could make a lot of money without having any. Starting in 1856, literally without a nickel to spare, Carnegie built a fortune. By 1863 his investments were providing him with an income of $45,000; to a friend who asked how he was, Carnegie replied, "I'm rich; I'm rich." By 1868 he was even richer; he owned securities and partnership shares worth $400,000 that paid him $56,000 a year. Thus by the time he was twenty-eight Carnegie had followed two paths in the world of business, paths that had done much more than make him rich. By mastering the new art of large-scale management and by fathoming the mysteries of capitalism, Carnegie had prepared himself uniquely to benefit from the combination of big industry and big finance that drove America's economy to world prominence after the Civil War.

Ultimately Carnegie was to demonstrate his skills by vanquishing or stalemating a formidable array of business rivals, including the entire American iron and steel industry, Cornelius Vanderbilt, John Murray Forbes, Jay Gould, John D. Rockefeller, and J. P. Morgan. His career as capitalist and speculator, however, began modestly. In 1856, Tom Scott persuaded Carnegie to buy ten shares of Adams Express Company stock for $600, lending him the money. Carnegie, broke, a tyro at investment, shared his mother's Scottish distaste for debt. He took the plunge, nevertheless, because his hero told him to: "I had not $50 saved for investment, but I was not going to miss the chance of becoming financially connected with my leader and great man." His devotion paid Carnegie quick dividends in the form of a $10 check from Adams Express.

"I shall remember that check . . . as long as I live," Carnegie later recalled, "it gave me the first penny of revenue from capital — something that I had not worked for with the sweat of my brow. 'Eureka,' I cried, 'Here's the goose that lays the golden eggs.' " Here was a new world indeed, the world of the capitalist, where a man could make money without toiling for it. With Scott's guidance, Carnegie acquired a whole new perspective on money, scrapping the consumer's mentality in favor of the investor's. He learned to see money as a commodity, untrammeled by emotions; as something to use to make more money, not as something to spend; as something whose value depended on what it could earn, not on what it could buy.

Once gripped by the investor's mentality, no man can be a Silas Marner, basking in the glow from a pile of cash. Money idle becomes money wasted; it has to be invested for income and gain. Carnegie's Adams Express stock venture taught him an important corollary: it made no difference whose money was invested. If expected dividends exceeded the interest rate on a loan, it made good sense to invest borrowed money, and better sense yet if the value of the shares rose. The Adams Express investment paid dividends ten times the interest on the loan during the first year that Carnegie held it. Money from credit thus could be invested as readily as cash from savings, but in both cases only when one's estimate of the future was sound. Englishmen had invested in colonial America not out of some Rousseau-like admiration for the beauty of wilderness, but out of the expectation that the wilderness could be made to produce cash. The original optimism took root and flourished, becoming an inherent characteristic of American society. With its vast lands, enormous resources, and a people bent on proving themselves by making good, the United States was a magnet for investment, first in agriculture and then in manufacturing. The country's rapid growth, furthermore, served to keep American capital at home, while attracting massive investments from abroad.

What kept capital coming, Carnegie learned, was the prospect of income. Investors didn't want their principal back, for that only required finding another place to put the money. Indeed, shrewd capitalists lavished loans on reliable borrowers, rather than demanding payment. In the long run, of course, there had to be some relationship between the quantity of capital invested and the productivity of the assets — land, plant, equipment, patents — that it bought. As Scott's managerial protégé, Carnegie learned how to divert some of the flow of investment and dividends into his own pockets.

In particular, Carnegie mastered the art of minimizing risks. Investors, like insurance actuaries, know that some of their clients will die on their hands. Success depends on spreading individual risks in such a way that in the aggregate there is no risk at all.

Scott's financial wizardry may have fascinated Carnegie, but it never mesmerized him. "I am sure," Carnegie said, "that any competent judge would be surprised how little I ever risked. . . . When I did big things some large corporation was behind me and was the responsible party." Most often, the "corporation" behind him was in fact the Pennsylvania Railroad. The Pennsylvania bought a lot of goods and services. Carnegie, in association with Scott and J. Edgar Thomson, the Pennsylvania's president, invested in firms that supplied them. This mixture, now outlawed by "conflict of interest" and "inside information" statutes, was perfectly legal then and produced fireproof insulation against risk. Almost as useful was Carnegie's encyclopedic knowledge of the strong and the weak in the Pittsburgh business community; the former telegrapher kept his data bank current as a railroad official. Carnegie rarely ventured beyond the financial magnetic field generated by the Pennsylvania dynamo; when he did, he carefully allied himself with a local businessman or financier of amply demonstrated shrewdness.

In 1858 Carnegie joined Thomson and Scott in financing the T. T. Woodruff Sleeping Car Company. The partners arranged to pay for their shares in installments, a common practice in nineteenth-century finance. Investors committed themselves to pay a specific amount of capital in a fixed number of payments over a specified period — sometimes at designated intervals, sometimes on call. During the War of 1812, Francis Cabot Lowell had induced skeptical Boston merchants to invest in the first integrated textile mill by offering just such a deal.

There were advantages to all involved. If the stockholders' list contained the names of the prominent and well-to-do, the firm got credit and customers more easily. (In England it was customary to trot in an aristocrat or two.) Meanwhile, the firm in effect had the leverage of its total capital but paid dividends on only a part. Another common arrangement spared the managers from parting with any actual profits. Until initial capitalization was achieved, they had the right to apply all dividends to unpaid stock subscriptions. In return this let investors hold on to much of their own cash, while allowing managers to retain company earnings for business use.

Such relaxed mid-nineteenth-century practices made it relatively easy to establish businesses. Many operations returned quick profits so that investors might never be called on for full subscriptions, as dividends liquidated promised installments. A shrewd investor might thus acquire a large interest in many firms with little actual money. Indeed, if he were bold enough, or informed enough an insider, he didn't even need money. Carnegie grasped precisely such an opportunity with the T. T. Woodruff Co. Without cash, he subscribed for a one-eighth share, "trusting," as he said, "to be able to make payments somehow or other." There was little need for "trusting." Carnegie knew that Thomson and Scott would see to it that Woodruff cars went on Pennsylvania trains. Carnegie got a bank loan to meet the first installment of $217.50, but he never made another payment. In the first year, dividends paid off the entire share balance; from the second year on, he received $5,000 or more annually until he sold out in the early 1870s.

Under a similar arrangement, Carnegie joined William Coleman, a wealthy ironmaster and elder statesman among Pittsburgh businessmen, to form the Columbia Oil Company in 1861. The Columbia Company sailed briskly into the booming flood of the oil that had recently gushed on the banks of Pennsylvania's Oil Creek. Carnegie subscribed for $110,000 worth of stock, with $11,000 in cash, drawn from his Woodruff dividends. The $11,000 investment returned him $17,800 the first year, and eventually brought more than a million dollars altogether.

Carnegie also became a partner in the Keystone Bridge Company, which opened for business in 1862. Keystone Bridge manufactured and erected iron railway bridges of a type patented by John Piper, supervisor of bridge construction for the Pennsylvania Railroad. The cost-conscious Pennsylvania seemed certain to replace its wooden bridges with iron because the trend toward heavier locomotives and trains, for which the Pennsylvania set the pace for the industry, demanded spans of ever-greater capacity. That the Pennsylvania would buy its bridges from Keystone Bridge seemed even more certain since Keystone's partners included, in addition to Piper himself, the following Pennsylvania Railroad officers: J. Edgar Thomson, president; Thomas A. Scott, vice-president; W. H. Wilson, chief engineer; Enoch Lewis, superintendent of transportation; Aaron Shiffler, bridge supervisor; J. H. Linville, bridge engineer; and Carnegie, superintendent of the western division.

Unsurprisingly, the firm prospered immediately. Carnegie held a one-fifth share; the first and only assessment of $1,250 he borrowed from a bank. In 1863 Keystone paid him $7,500 in dividends and continued to do well throughout the Civil War. After the war it did even better, expanding its operations from coast to coast, including construction of the Eads Bridge over the Mississippi at St. Louis, a nineteenth-century marvel still in daily use.

In the seven years that followed Carnegie's decision to leave the railroad's employ for a full-time career as investor, he ascended into the stratosphere of high finance, winging it with the highest flyers in Europe and the United States. He sold 30 millions' worth of bridge and railroad bonds, some of them good, some of them not so good, some of them worthless; but all of them paid him a commission. He borrowed cheap and lent dear; he manipulated stock prices up and down, buying and selling to take advantage of the fluctuations; he was a party to clandestine stock deals in the Union Pacific Railroad, Western Union, and the Pullman Company. He became the confidant of the Morgans and other moguls of finance; he became a very wealthy man. Then, in 1872, he abruptly changed course, abandoning his career as a financier and speculator, liquidating his assets, and pouring the proceeds into a new steel mill.

Carnegie's decision to abandon finance for manufacturing had many roots, some in practical calculations, some in conscience. Greed played a part, but a minor one. By 1872 he had assembled more than enough wealth to last him a lifetime; moreover, while the following year, 1873, brought a panic that bankrupted many, Carnegie, like the Morgans, was in a position to survive easily and go on to greater riches.

By 1872, however, Carnegie had perceived a distinction between investment and speculation, and developed a distaste for the latter. Investment, to Carnegie and others of a similar conservative bent, meant providing the capital necessary for a firm to produce tangible goods or real services — wheat, steel, railroad transportation. Carefully managed, such firms could be expected to generate a profit sufficient to pay a satisfactory return on the original investment. Of course the point where investment ended and speculation began was a question on which men with conscience could differ, and those without could ignore.

In the 1860s and '70s, with the Civil War over and the threat of sectional division apparently put to rest once and for all, a fresh burst of optimism swept through America. Limitless expansion became the order of the day: immigration, the Pacific Railroad Act, the Homestead Act, all pointed to swift settlement of the land between the Missouri and the Pacific. The business world took on a carnival atmosphere, as barkers of every stripe and hue, crying the boundless promise of the future, lured investors into the capitalist big top. Promising to expand existing businesses, or to create new ones, promoters hawked stocks, bonds, and partnership shares in massive quantities. In this era the only law governing the investment marketplace was "let the buyer beware." Would-be investors had nothing but their own wits to protect them against the most extravagant claims. The rosy forecasts of future profits that invariably accompanied solicitations for capital frequently bore only remote relationship, if any at all, to a firm's current earning power. As to future prospects, even the most conservative prognostications depended upon variables so numerous and so imponderable that they had as little claim to prescience as had the work of astrologers and fortune-tellers, as many businessmen realized. The hard-headed Commodore Vanderbilt, for instance, consulted a Staten Island mystic and invoked the ghost of the dear departed Jim Fisk for guidance in the stock market.

Many of the stock-jobbers who swarmed into the capital markets on both sides of the Atlantic were honest enough. These worthies genuinely believed that the heat from the expanding national market would dry up virtually any quantity of stock, no matter how wet (overpriced) when issued. Sometimes they were right. The Union Pacific Railroad, built at great cost across empty spaces in anticipation of massive but unpredictable freight and passenger traffic, eventually paid dividends and today is one of the country's healthiest railroads. But many other ventures, particularly when they involved borrowed money that required fixed interest payments, failed as overcapitalization proved itself a virulent side effect of the speculative fever. Firms large and small foundered trying to keep their heads above their own water. (And have continued to do so; doubters are referred to the performance records of the conglomerates formed in the 1960s.)

In addition to falling prey to well-intentioned but ill-advised promoters, investors also ran afoul of charlatans and mountebanks. Jay Gould and his brethren created stock purely for the purpose of selling it, neither knowing nor caring whether dividends would ever be paid. Under their tender ministrations, once-healthy firms like the Erie Railroad became bloated carcasses that not even the buoyant American economy could keep afloat. All these scenarios, and multiple variations upon them, Carnegie saw played out. In a few cases he served, wittingly or unwittingly, as a contributor. Although he liked to describe himself as a "first-class, steady-going securities man," he often dealt in paper of dubious value and knew it. He foisted bonds of the Davenport and St. Paul, the Missouri, Iowa, and Nebraska Railroads, and the Keokuk Bridge on European investors; all went bankrupt. Other ventures staggered along on the verge of collapse.

Later in life Carnegie claimed, "I have never bought or sold a share of stock speculatively in my life," but he had, and often. At one time or another he lied, concealing information, and misrepresenting the facts, all in pursuit of speculative manipulation. In the end, however, the game palled. Speculative fever continued to sweep the country, but in Carnegie something — his radical past, memories of the abuses of Scottish landlords, thoughts of his father, perhaps — caused him to withdraw. When his mentor, Thomas Scott, plunged into the Texas and Pacific Railroad, the venture that ultimately led to his downfall, Carnegie declined to follow his "leader and great man" into the depths. When Jay Gould offered to buy the Pennsylvania Railroad and install him as president, Carnegie declined. Whether cured by shrewdness or conscience, Carnegie survived the speculative fever with an immunization that lasted him a lifetime.

Another factor that drove Carnegie out of finance and into manufacturing was his changing view of wealth. In his early years Carnegie pursued money as an antidote to poverty and the cold, hunger, and shabbiness that went with it. In 1863 he had rejoiced, "I'm rich; I'm rich." But by 1868 he no longer saw money as a guarantee of a rewarding life, and feared, in fact, that continued pursuit of it might be his undoing:

Man must have an idol — The amassing of wealth is one of the worst species of idolatry. No idol more debasing than the worship of money. Whatever I engage in I must push inordinately therefor should I be careful to choose that life which will be the most elevating in its character. To continue much longer overwhelmed by business cares and with most of my thoughts wholly upon the way to make more money in the shortest time, must degrade me beyond hope of permanent recovery.

This memorandum, which Carnegie wrote for himself, not for public consumption, contained a program for self-improvement. He planned to arrange all his

business as to make no effort to increase fortune, but spend the surplus each year for benevolent purposes. . . . Settle in Oxford & get a thorough education making the acquaintance of literary men. . . . Settle then in London & purchase a controlling interest in some newspaper or live review . . . taking a part in public matters especially those connected with education & improvement of the poorer classes.

These sentiments marked a transition in Carnegie's motivation. Once the personification of David Hume's maxim that avarice was the spur of industry, Carnegie now evinced more complex sentiments, similar to those expressed by John Ruskin in 1870, "Life without industry is guilt; [but] Industry without art is brutality." Other successful American businessmen testified to a similar change in motivation, one that reflected the shifting perspective of American society as a whole. James E. Caldwell, a utilities magnate, said, "As a younger man, I was urged on by the necessity for food and raiment." Later, he found commerce "a fascinating game," and creating a telephone system "highly entertained" him. Joseph E. Sheffield, a New England railroad builder and founder of the Sheffield Scientific School at Yale, related that originally " 'getting gain' was a leading purpose" as well as a desire to *"stand well* with my fellows and people." When he entered business he hoped "to make money. But I distinctly recollect that my *pride of opinion* and great desire to be found *correct* in my *estimates* and *statistics* was paramount to all other considerations." As a wealthy man *"unselfish* public spirited enterprise [became] far more intense than any hope of making money."

Most of Carnegie's plan for self-improvement was postponed; some of it never came to pass. He did, however, read extensively, attend plays and concerts, master the grammar of the English language, cultivate friendships with literati such as Matthew Arnold and John Morley, and undertake a program of philanthropy.

Entering the steel business in 1872 Carnegie showed that business still fascinated him, but he had had enough of paper and speculation. "I wish to make something tangible," he said. He "had lived long enough in Pittsburgh to acquire the manufacturing, as distinguished from the speculative, spirit." Opening his own steel mill not only gave him the chance to make something tangible, but also to be his own boss, something he had wanted for many years. Leaving the railroad in 1865, he had commented, "A man must necessarily occupy a narrow field who is at the beck and call of others." He had set out "determined to make a fortune," and he had certainly made one, but found that it had not freed him from the beck and call of others. As a stock-

and-bond salesman he had still been a minion, a wealthy minion, to be sure, but nevertheless an acolyte to their sacerdotal majesties, the Barings, the Morgans, and others.

Starting his own business would make him his own master and he meant to keep it that way. He sold no stock in Carnegie Steel, ever. To raise the initial capital he did take in partners, but he himself always retained the majority interest. In addition, he forced his partners to sign the "Iron-Clad Agreement," which in effect enabled Carnegie to expel anyone he didn't like, while no combination of the other partners could force him out. In addition, the "Iron-Clad" prevented any partner from willing or selling his interest to anyone outside the company. By retaining absolute control, Carnegie retained a free hand to adopt any strategies he pleased, whether his partners approved of them or not. One of his policies in particular — using the firm's profits to finance expansion rather than pay dividends — drove many partners to distraction, but Carnegie stuck to it because it kept him and his firm clear of the stock market and its pitfalls.

To Carnegie, as to so many of his contemporaries, his business was an extension of himself; its reputation and his own were inextricably intertwined. This fact contributed to his obsession with controlling his own affairs. He was determined that none of his associates should be in a position to besmirch Carnegie's own reputation by engaging in shady business dealings. It sometimes happened in spite of him: his first superintendent, W. P. Shinn, speculated in the pig iron market; his general manager, Henry Clay Frick, tried to trick him into selling his business to three notorious speculators, the Moore brothers ("those Chicago adventurers," Carnegie called them) and John W. ("Bet a Million") Gates, a man known to have wagered a thousand dollars on which raindrop would run down a Pullman car window first. Shinn, Frick, and other transgressors found themselves punished by expulsion.

Finally, steel itself had an intrinsic appeal to Carnegie's newly established sense of virtue. It was a tangible, solid product, the very foundation of progress, the web that bound the nation's vast expanse together in a commercial, political, and social entity.

Steel also offered Carnegie a unique opportunity to utilize his manifold talents and connections. Always in touch with developments in the railroad industry, Carnegie knew that railroads would soon replace iron rails with steel. In this development, as in so many others, the Pennsylvania Railroad would lead the way, for its president, J. Edgar Thomson, believed in "steel for everything." A huge market loomed — the Pennsylvania alone could keep several large mills going — and Carnegie not unreasonably expected to get his share of it. Metallurgy and machine technology had advanced to the point that mass production of durable steel rails seemed feasible.

Carnegie knew nothing of metallurgy and little about machinery, but he had learned on the railroad that he could hire any kind of expertise he lacked. He did know something about the iron business from his experiences with Keystone Bridge and Union Mills, a firm he had purchased to supply Keystone's materials. Much of what he found out about the iron business and the traditional way it operated, he didn't like.

Developing Keystone and Union, Carnegie had quickly learned that the iron industry was organized much the same as the British textile industry. Each stage of manufacture from raw material to finished product took place in a separate independent production unit, almost always a small proprietorship or partnership. Iron furnaces smelted the ore into pig iron; forges and rolling mills converted the iron into bars and slabs; other mills then rolled plates, rails, and sheets, and cut nails. Separate factories fabricated tools, hardware, pots, and pans; foundries made stoves.

The dominant figures in the industry were specialized merchants who controlled the flow of materials from one manufacturing stage to another and then into the market. This dispersion of control was expensive for two reasons. First, every middleman added to the cost; second, the movement of material proceeded slowly through many hands and over a wide geographic area. The large quantity of material in the pipeline at any time kept a good deal of money tied up in inventory. Invariably this was borrowed money, and the finance charges on it added significantly to the cost of the final product. Such cost would skyrocket if the complicated supply train were coupled to the kind of high volume manufacturing plant that Carnegie had in mind. In building his new steel mill, Carnegie planned to eliminate the cost and undependability of the traditional, dispersed operations by following the example of Francis Cabot Lowell, who had put all stages of textile manufacture under a single roof.

Carnegie also discovered to his dismay that most iron masters used bookkeeping systems unchanged since the Renaissance:

I was greatly surprised to find that the cost of each of the various processes was unknown. Inquiries made of the leading manufacturers of Pittsburgh proved this. It was a lump business, and until stock was taken and the books balanced at the end of the year, the manufacturers were in total ignorance of the results. I heard of men who thought their business at the end of the year would show a loss and had found a profit, and *vice versa.*

Such primitive cost accounting consisted merely in dividing the year's expenses by the year's total output.

Obviously none of this would do; Carnegie wanted to build the largest steel business in the world, in the face of formidable competition from established mills at home and abroad. Such a business couldn't be run like a corner grocery. "I felt as if we were moles, burrowing in the dark," Carnegie remarked, "and this to me was intolerable." He resolved to rectify and modernize these slipshod methods. The first step was to find out what all costs were, all the time. "I insisted upon such a system of weighing and accounting being introduced throughout our works as would enable us to know what our cost was for each process."

Once costs were known, Carnegie set about mercilessly beating them down while getting production up. He pursued this campaign on many fronts. To reduce production costs he hired Alexander Holley, the world's foremost expert on Bessemer steel production, to design and build the most modern steel plant that money could buy. When new technology appeared, Carnegie scrapped his existing equipment, striving always for machinery that could handle bigger batches and handle them faster, regardless of initial cost. Carnegie once ordered Charles Schwab, his first lieutenant, to tear out a three-month-old rolling mill when Schwab said he had found a design that would do the job more cheaply.

Carnegie's willingness to spend lavish sums of money on new equipment astounded his competitors. They didn't understand the principle of economies of scale. On one occasion, Carnegie recalled, "the older heads among the Pittsburgh manufacturers [criticized my] extravagant expenditures . . . on . . . new-fangled furnaces. But in the heating of great masses of materials, almost half the waste could sometimes be saved. . . . The expenditure would have been justified even if it had been doubled. . . . In some years the margin of profit was so small that the most of it was . . . from savings . . . from the improved furnaces."

Another way to reduce the cost of each ton of steel manufactured was to accelerate the production process by the old Pennsylvania practice of "hard-driving," that is by getting the maximum output of steel in the shortest possible time, regardless of wear and tear on men and machinery. Cost accounting showed that the expense per ton of iron manufactured thus was less than if the equipment were coddled, as was the British practice. The money generated by faster production more than paid for a new furnace.

Watching the hard-driving techniques that raised production at one Carnegie blast furnace from 13,000 tons to more than 100,000 tons a year, Sir James Kitson, president of the British Iron and Steel Institute, predicted "it won't last. . . . The continual work at high pressure does not pay in the end." Kitson's mistake reflected tradition. This difference in attitudes toward labor and machinery between the United States and Great Britain had been noted by British Industrial Commissions in the 1850s. Cost accounting had few adherents in nineteenth-century British industry (and few enough in the twentieth century); manufacturers planned largely by instinct and custom. Carnegie planned on the basis of evidence. The British method was guesswork that usually kept costs high; Carnegie's produced rational policies that drove costs down. An exchange between English industrialist Sir Lowthian Bell and one of Carnegie's furnace superintendents highlighted the conflict. Bell condemned the "reckless rapid rate" of hard-driving "the furnaces so that the interior of each furnace was wrecked and had to be replaced every three years." The superintendent replied, "What do we care about the lining? We think a lining is good for so much iron and the sooner it makes it the better."

Another English visitor once told Carnegie, "We have equipment we have been using for twenty years and it is still serviceable." "And that," Andy replied, "is what is the matter with the British steel trade. Most British equipment is still in use twenty years after it should have been scrapped. It is because you keep this used up machinery that the United States is making you a back number." This theme Carnegie repeated often, usually also tying America's commitment to industrial progress to the free climate created by its democratic political system. It formed the leitmotif in much of his writing, particularly *Triumphant Democracy* (a self-explanatory title if ever there was one), published in 1886. The book began, "The old nations of the world creep on at a snail's pace; the Republic thunders past with the rush of an express."

Certainly things moved quickly in Carnegie's mills, further savings being gained by rushing materials from one operation to another. The movement of steel ingots from blast furnace to rolling mill was speeded by pouring the steel into molds on moving flatcars. Sidney Gilchrist-Thomas, a British metallurgist, was fascinated by such velocity and volume. He remarked to Alexander Holley (who was guiding him through the plant), "I would like to sit on an ingot for a week and watch that mill operate." Replied Holley, "If you want an ingot cool enough to sit on, you'll have to send to England for it."

Carnegie drove his men as hard as he drove his machinery. From the beginning, he employed supervisors who understood railroad accounting methods, or who could learn them quickly. Holley himself was an authority on railroad costs; he knew just what Carnegie wanted in the way of scales and checkpoints to keep track of production. Carnegie's first superintendent was

W. P. Shinn, former superintendent of the Allegheny Valley Railroad. Carnegie demanded that weekly cost sheets be sent to him no matter where he was. By comparing this week's performance with last week's, or one man's with another's, he kept track of who produced quickly and cheaply and who did not. As one manager remembered, "You [were] expected always to get it ten cents cheaper the next year or the next month."

The system allowed Carnegie to control his firm's complex operations. He could make intelligent decisions about hirings, firings, and promotions even though he had "no shadow of claim to rank as inventor, chemist, investigator, or mechanician" and he did it while spending much of his time away from the mill. Carnegie had little scientific understanding of the new techniques, but he knew when one month's costs turned out lower than another's. He did not need to judge the scientific merits of technical excuses made by managers; he could compare a man's performance with others in the same position. He then demanded explanations in plain English.

Successful subordinates could expect quick promotion. "He may be just the man we need," Carnegie said of one suggested change. "Give him a trial. That's all we get ourselves and all we can give to anyone. If he can win the race, he is our race-horse. If not, he goes to the cart." Racehorses, if they ran long and fast enough, might ultimately be admitted into the firm's partnership. The shares thus won were fractional, but by the 1890s even one sixth of one percent of Carnegie Steel was worth hundreds of thousands of dollars. "Mr. Morgan buys his partners," Carnegie boasted; "I raise my own." Through this arrangement of multiple partnership (a common form of business structure in Scotland, but unusual in the United States, where few partnerships had more than two or three members), Carnegie expected to generate loyalty and results. The system also sometimes fostered jealousy, treachery, bitterness, and despair, but some forty men rose through the ranks to partnership, including at least one immigrant who spoke no English when first employed, and one man who, like Carnegie, began his career as a telegrapher.

Choosing subordinates was a problem that increasingly bedeviled American entrepreneurs in the nineteenth century. Finding competent lieutenants often proved vital to success. When Eli Whitney tried to run his arms business unaided, he nearly destroyed himself and his firm. Cyrus McCormick needed help from the beginning. Carnegie, who had learned on the railroad what round-the-clock operations meant, knew that he had to accept delegation of authority (and the creation of departments and ranks that went with it) in order to achieve cost-based management in his steel business. He nevertheless kept the ultimate authority in his own hands. Manufacturers, then, did not leap from old-style, family management to a full-fledged, modern bureaucratic arrangement; rather, they yielded grudgingly to necessity. The result was a gradual, evolutionary process. Outside of the railroads, the predominant structure remained a hybrid, a mixture of family ownership and operation with the slow turning over of some responsibilities to salaried managers.

Desperate for help, but reluctant to surrender control, businessmen usually exhausted their family's resources before involving outsiders. In 1818, Eli Whitney, whose son had not yet been born, wrote his nephew, begging for help in "getting on with my affairs which have been so numerous, embarrassing, and oppressive that I am almost driven to delirium. I find that it is absolutely impossible for me to accomplish . . . the most pressing necessit[ies]."

Cyrus McCormick, as we have seen, pressed his brothers into service. Carnegie did likewise, dragging his brother Tom into his business, first as a partner, ultimately as general manager. It is an old axiom that the best horses get ridden hardest; in business, this often meant that the most trusted became the most abused. Andrew Carnegie, like McCormick, spent much of his time away from the mill — in the early years, on business, later in global gallivanting and hobnobbing with the gentlefolk. In their absence, these potentates expected their siblings to keep the home fires burning, profitably. "We must work like sailors," Andy exhorted from his European spa, writing to Tom, holding the fort in Pittsburgh. "I'm sure you have had a trying time of it," Andy added, "and often you must have felt disposed to throw up the game [but] the more I find myself drinking in enjoyment, the deeper is my appreciation of your devoted self-denial. . . . It is a heavy load for a youngster to carry," but after all, Tom should realize, "if you succeed, it will be a lasting benefit to you."

Cyrus McCormick, idling away the Civil War in an English haven, accused his brothers, running the firm in Chicago, of "cruel treatment" when production fell below the absent magnate's expectations. He demanded that Leander not neglect the factory while building a new home. Such strains often broke family ties, or broke down family members, as was demonstrated by William McCormick's nervous breakdown, Leander's hatred for Cyrus, and Tom Carnegie's early, bibulous death. Business quarrels shattered many an American family into feuding factions, often hastening the decline of family management.

When relatives proved inadequate in number, talent, or disposition, businessmen usually turned next to friends. Some of Carnegie's enduring partners in the steel business were men he had known since childhood. If forced to turn to strangers, an entrepreneur naturally sought, above all, to find people he could trust, which most often meant people like him. What Tom Scott saw in Carnegie — a reflection of himself when young, poor, bright, and ambitious — Carnegie saw in Charley Schwab. As the scale of business enterprises ballooned, such mentor-protégé relationships proliferated between men of common background and outlook. Ironically, one of them, the alliance between Pierre du Pont and Alfred Sloan, produced the ultimate substitute for family control — the vast shareholding depersonalized bureaucracy of General Motors. Such bureaucracies eventually emerged as a dominant fact of American business life. But the paradoxical reality was that they resulted, in part, from entrepreneurs' struggles to perpetuate family ownership and management in an economy that made such traditional methods increasingly inapt.

Carnegie Steel, while typifying such transitional organizations, functioned better than most. Its blend of traditional ownership and modern, cost-based management gave Carnegie the best of both worlds.

From the 1870s through the 1890s, Carnegie, costs always in

mind, drove his firm relentlessly. He hired a chemist to determine which ores to feed to which furnaces; he built open-hearth furnaces; he bought mines and quarries and coke smelters to supply raw material, and railroads to haul them to his mills; he refused to fix prices, meanwhile undercutting his competitors, and buying many of them out; when the railroad market declined, he shifted some of his capacity to the rolling of structural beams and angles such as those used in the Brooklyn Bridge, in America's first skyscraper, the Home Insurance building in Chicago, and in Chicago and New York's elevated railroads.

Through booms and recessions Carnegie Steel rolled on. By 1900 it alone produced more than the entire British steel industry. As volume rose, costs fell, and profits soared. The first ton of Carnegie steel cost $56 to produce; by 1900 the cost was down to $11.50. In 1888 the firm made 2 million dollars; in 1894, 4 million dollars; in 1900, 40 million dollars. A contemporary observer declared, "Such a magnificent aggregation of industrial power has never before been under the domination of a single man." Carnegie himself cried, "Where is there such a business!"

Carnegie's triumph was made all the sweeter by the fact that he achieved it despite the frenzied efforts of promoters and financiers to defeat him. By the 1890s, the capacity of the American steel industry exceeded the market. In other industries confronting this situation, financiers like J. P. Morgan tried to stabilize prices by controlling production. They set up holding companies that ended competition by merging the capital and control of the most powerful competitors. The trust (as holding companies were popularly called) traded its certificates for the stock of members; its total capitalization usually depended much less on the aggregate earning power of its constituent parts than on the total sum necessary to induce all the proprietors to sell.

One by one, manufacturing trusts lumbered into the field in the late 1890s. Several made overtures to Carnegie's firm. When some of Carnegie's partners, weary of the struggle, wanted to sell out, Carnegie would have none of it. In 1897 Illinois Steel, a Morgan creation, suggested a pool to divide the business in heavy steel. "Our policy in my opinion," Carnegie wrote his

partners, "is to stand by ourselves alone. . . . Take orders East
and West. . . . As for Illinois Steel: if you do arrange with them
you are simply bolstering a concern and enabling it to strike you
in the near future. . . . We have made the fight, the enemy is at
our mercy, now do not let us be foolish enough to throw away
the fruits of victory."

In 1898, another behemoth, Federal Steel, emerged from the
Morgan workshop. Carnegie spurred his partners on to battle.
"Surely my views about going into the trust are well known. . . .
The Carnegie Steel Company should never in my opinion enter
any Trust. It will do better tending to its own business in its own
way. . . . We hope our competitors will combine, for an independent concern always has the 'Trust' at its mercy." In 1899, yet
another trust, American Tinplate Company, threatened to stop
buying Carnegie's steel unless he agreed not to sell to other tinplate manufacturers. Carnegie refused: "In these days of Trusts
and other swindles I do not favor the contract. . . . I do not believe it is legal; I do not believe it is right. I think the Carnegie
Company should keep a pure record. . . . I believe that independent concerns will soon beat the trust." When American Tinplate
and other trusts began to cancel orders for Carnegie's steel in
1899, he wired his partners, "Crisis has arrived, only one policy
open: start at once hoop, rod, wire, nail mills. . . . Have no fear as
to result, victory is certain."

Carnegie's confidence had a solid foundation. He knew that
none of these "paper concerns" could survive in competition
with his efficient, streamlined establishment. It was, as a congres-
sional committee later described it, "a contest between fabricators of steel and fabricators of securities; between makers of
billets and makers of bonds." Carnegie himself described Federal Steel as "the greatest concern the world ever saw for manufacturing stock certificates. . . . But they will fail sadly in steel."
Such a trust, in fact, could survive only in the absence of efficient
competition. Many of Federal's companies had only a creaky
collection of obsolete machinery (some of it dating back to the
Civil War); they were scattered randomly around the country
and they were vastly overcapitalized. National Tube, for exam-

ple, had a capital stock of 80 million dollars on which to try to pay dividends. Julian Kennedy, Morgan's expert on steel works (a Carnegie-trained man), told Morgan that National Tube's 19 plants had a real market value of only 19 million dollars.

In 1900, Carnegie prepared to annihilate this upstart. Carnegie's firm owned a patent for manufacturing seamless tubes and designed a tube plant that would employ the closest thing to continuous flow manufacturing yet achieved in the steel industry. "How much cheaper, Charley, can you make the tubes than the National Company?" Carnegie asked Schwab, who answered, "At least ten dollars per ton." "Well," said Andy, "go and build the plant then."

When Carnegie announced his plans to build a tube plant, "he became an incorporated threat and menace to the steel trade of the United States," according to one of Morgan's partners. Morgan, capitulating, asked Carnegie to name his price. Carnegie, satisfied with his victory, anxious to undertake his long-delayed plans for philanthropy and self-improvement, and having no son to whom he could pass on the business, was finally ready to retire. When he sold out, he apparently had little faith in the future of the newly formed United States Steel Corporation, for he insisted on his payment in gold bonds, thus acquiring a mortgage that insured his right to reclaim his property should the trust fail. He had beaten the trust once and was ready to do it again if need be. "I believe you would have captured the steel trade of the world if you had stayed in business," a Congressman remarked to him later. "I am as certain of it as I can be certain of anything," Carnegie replied. Elbert Gary, who became chairman of United States Steel, observed, "If the management that was in force at the time had continued, the Carnegie company [might] have driven entirely out of business every steel company in the United States."

So Carnegie retired to a life of philanthropy and promotion of peace. Looking back on his career, he could savor many triumphs: his rise to wealth through hard work amd shrewd investment; his triumphant return to Dunfermline in 1881, when he and his mother had ridden in a palatial coach and four in triumph through the town they had once fled in poverty, passing under banners reading "Welcome Carnegie, generous son"; his friendship with luminaries such as Herbert Spencer, Matthew Arnold, William Gladstone, and Woodrow Wilson; his successful marriage and the daughter it produced; and, last but not least, a bulging file of letters that he labeled "Gratitude and Sweet Words." He had also known his share of disappointment and tragedy: the failure of his father; the alcoholic death of his brother; and, above all, the catastrophe of the Homestead strike, which his callousness had precipitated. But he had fashioned a philosophy that gave him peace. Years before, he had read Herbert Spencer and found an explanation of the fundamental life process that made sense to him in light of his own career:

Light came in as a flood and all was clear. Not only had I got rid of the theology and the supernatural, but I had found the truth of evolution. "All is well since all grows better" became my motto, my true source of comfort. Man was not created with an instinct for his own degradation, but from the lower he had risen to the higher forms. Nor is there any conceivable end to his march to perfection. His face is turned to the light, he stands in the sun and looks upward.

Buttressed by Spencer's philosophy, Carnegie could endure his mistakes and rejoice in his successes secure in the belief that by following his own star he helped move society as a whole toward its bright destiny. Finally, he justified his fortune by giving it all away. He saw himself as the trustee of wealth, not its owner. "The man who dies rich, dies disgraced," he wrote in 1889. After retiring he lived up to his own creed.

If Andy could see United States Steel today, he probably would think things had gone to hell since he left the business. But if he looked elsewhere in the American economy, he'd probably feel better, for wherever efficient manufacturing goes on in the United States, the Carnegie heritage lives.

Edison at work in his laboratory.   The table often served as a bed.

5

The Most Useful American Thomas A. Edison

TRAVEL has a lot of advantages, including the opportunity to engage in a variety of social analyses, ranging from the acute to the crackpot. To the latter category I add my superficial observation that a higher percentage of habitual airplane passengers send their children to college than do people who ride trains. When I flew a great deal, I met lots of college parents and spent considerable time arguing that when the fate of the universe passed into the hands of their children things could be expected to improve rather than collapse. I admire my students; I think they comprise the most decent generation of people this country has yet produced. I am not alarmed that they watch a lot of bad TV; their parents passed through childhood reading terrible books and wasted many a Saturday afternoon gazing rapturously at movie screens filled with unimaginably puerile nonsense.

It's stylish to bemoan young people's supposed inability to read, write, or conjure with numbers and then predict dire consequences ahead. The Cassandras usually document their auguries with statistics that show declining scores on standardized tests that supposedly measure a student's aptitude for college, graduate school, medical school, law school, business school, and I know not what all else. None of this apparatus nor the results it produces impresses me, although I personally have benefited enormously by it. The tests prove little except how well a student does on the tests, and no one has the vaguest idea what any of it means in any other context, despite elaborate pretensions to the contrary. One potent precedent for my skepticism was established long ago by Thomas Edison, who thought such tests absurd, and mockingly devised one of his own entitled the "ignoramometer."

It simply isn't true that today's students cannot read. Students in fourth-rate colleges today read more than students in citadels of intellectuality did a generation ago, and while the worst of them can't write any more than the worst of them ever could, the best of them write so well that I'm repeatedly dazzled by their skills. If in fact, they know no arithmetic (and I personally couldn't care less; calculators are dirt cheap), the fault lies far more with those who inflicted the "new math" upon them than on the students themselves. If every student in the United States rose up and refused categorically to submit to any further standardized testing, we'd all be better off. Today's college students simply come prepared in a different way from the generations that preceded them. Not worse, different. Calling them uneducated is silly. As I told one of my sneering colleagues, it's all very well for us to rejoice in the elegance of our intellectual preparation, but Coleridge would have dismissed us as barbarians.

My students have provided me with a lot of rewarding surprises, not least of which has been the discovery that many of them truly love history for its own sake. Among the more passionate I've encountered was one who worked as a guide at the Greenfield Village and Henry Ford Museum in Dearborn, Michigan. Among other relics of the American past, Henry Ford had Thomas Edison's Menlo Park laboratory brought intact to Greenfield Village. And I do mean intact: every plank, every nail, every bottle, every machine, indeed the very earth on which it sat was dug up, and the whole collection brought to Michigan. When Ford triumphantly presented his handiwork to Edison, the inventor, who had not seen the laboratory in forty years, said, "You got it ninety-nine percent perfect." "What's wrong with it?" asked the crestfallen Ford. "We never kept the floor this clean," replied Edison.

My student, whose sense of the drama of the past together with her considerable thespian abilities made her a favorite with the visiting throngs, particularly liked to show people through Edison's laboratory. Steering her charges through the labyrinth of mysterious apparatus, shelved chemicals, and workbenches and tables on which Edison had often napped, she would sometimes abandon the prepared script, carefully researched by the Museum's staff, in favor of an extemporaneous discourse, the author of which, or so she claimed, was Edison himself. The living Edison, blunt, cranky, and deaf, had relied heavily on shouts and obscenities when communicating to his subordinates; however, his pneuma displayed both a gentler temperament and more subtle methods, inspiring his cicerone by spiriting his thoughts into her mind. Fascinated visitors often asked their guide what use Edison had made of this or that mysterious apparatus, now squatting obscurely in some dusty nook or cranny. Invariably, she rendered an explanation, often in elaborate detail, only afterward realizing that she had never noticed the relic before and had no personal knowledge of it whatever.

So where did she get her information? "From Edison," she told me; "I'm just his amanuensis." Well, who's to say otherwise? In 1920 Edison, then in his seventies, explored the possibility of communication between the quick and the dead. The subject generated widespread interest in the era following a war that had killed millions. Edison, having tried nearly everything else (and perhaps thinking that he himself would need celestial contact in the near future), began searching for an appropriate technology. "I don't claim," Edison told a reporter from *Scientific American,* that:

Our personalities pass on to another existence or sphere. I don't claim anything because I don't know anything. . . . But I do claim that it is possible to construct an apparatus . . . so delicate that if there are personalities in another existence or sphere who wish to get in touch with us . . . this apparatus will at least give them a better opportunity to express themselves than the tilting tables and raps and ouija boards and mediums and the other crude methods now purported to be the only means of communication.

One of his assistants, Edison observed, had died while working on the apparatus, and "he ought to be the first man to use it if he is able to do so."

If Edison ever received news from the other world, he kept it to himself. The whole business may have been a hoax, for Edison's character included a wide streak of perversity. Genuinely iconoclastic in scientific matters, Edison enjoyed spreading consternation in other areas as well. The fundamentalist clergy and their fervent followers formed a particularly attractive target, since Edison, like many another inventor before and after him, had often stirred the wrath of the faithful by carrying worldly business into the precincts of the Heavenly City. Samuel Morse's telegraph, for instance, had provoked many a sermon and letter to Congress on the lines of "If God had intended words to be sent over wire, He would have . . ." This opposition Morse tried to negate through his choice of "What hath God wrought" as the first official message.

In 1910, when asked what a personal God meant to him, Edison replied, "Nothing," a statement he repeated at suitable intervals. What he really believed is anyone's guess, but he unquestionably enjoyed spreading distress among archenemies of the inventive mind. Suggesting the possibility of an apparatus delicate enough to communicate with the departed may have been just another excursion in provocative posturing. But maybe not. He didn't get the job done in his lifetime, but Edison the ghost may have finished what Edison the man began. If so, it wouldn't be the only time that Edison succeeded where others failed, and it wouldn't be the only revolution Edison ever facilitated.

Americans have evinced an ambivalent view toward things revolutionary. In the political sphere we have embraced the notion that the first revolution did the job so well that there has been neither excuse nor justification for one since; consequently, we've neither wanted, needed, nor had any more.

While steadfastly resisting political overturn in either thought or deed, however, Americans have celebrated the interrelated revolutions in transportation, communication, and energy that remade their society. As technological advancements broke the shackles that had limited transportation and communication to the velocity of wind and water and accelerated them to the speed of sound and light, most Americans rejoiced and called it progress. Fundamental to this change and to the expansion of manufacturing capacity, was a two-stage revolution in the ways by which man converted potential energy to power. In the first stage, steam supplanted human and animal muscle, wind, and water as the source of power to drive tool and machine; in the second, electricity and the internal combustion engine took over. In retrospect these momentous changes seem easy, logical, and even inevitable to most Americans, a smug perspective reinforced if one restricts one's travels to those countries favored by American Express Company tours, but quickly shattered by a detour to Niger or the Panamanian outback.

American industry has thus developed in three distinct periods, demarked by the prevalent energy source of the time. Eli Whitney belonged to the first era. The first cotton gin was a machine "which required the labor of one man to turn it" and could also "be turned by water or with a horse." On the other hand, manufacturing cotton gins, muskets, or anything else in volume, required "machinery moved by water," and this imperative dictated the location of his works where there was "a good fall of Water in the Vicinity." Above all, in the early days these waterfalls had to be in close proximity to the point where the stream became navigable to the sea, for only water transportation was economically feasible for heavy materials. It also greatly facilitated matters if these riparian resources could be found near settled areas where labor and markets were available.

In Whitney's day this happy combination could best be found on rivers from the Susquehanna northward. There the mountains lay close to the sea and ribbed the land between with rocky spines that eroded into a staircase of waterfalls ideal for powering machinery. Many rivers compressed a great vertical fall into a short lateral distance. In twenty miles of Pennsylvania and Delaware countryside, for example, the Brandywine River has a bigger drop than Niagara Falls. In some cases — the Brandywine at Wilmington, Delaware, the Passaic at Paterson, New Jersey — the last fall drops into tidewater. South of the Susquehanna, the fall line lies hundreds of miles from the coast in a region that was, in Whitney's time, largely a wilderness. From there to the ocean the rivers flow lazily through soft southern soil and limestone.

Since American manufacturing was born in this era of water power, its cradles were the valleys of the Brandywine, Connecticut, Merrimack, and other rivers of the north, not the James, Cape Fear, Savannah, or Chattahoochee. Southern cotton became cloth at mills in Lowell, Waltham, and Chicopee, Massachusetts, far removed from the raw material source, and Whitney, retreating from Georgia to a suitable locale familiar to him, manufactured cotton gins and muskets in New Haven, Connecticut, for markets that lay far away.

Steam power liberated Cyrus McCormick and Andrew Carnegie from some of these locational restrictions. Although both men situated their works on navigable waterways and used them to transport raw materials and finished products, the railroads played a crucial role in their firms' massive expansion. Railroads created much of McCormick's market, carrying settlers to the land and their produce away from it, while making it possible for McCormick to distribute his machines in the huge landlocked regions of the wheat belt. Carnegie Steel used railroads so extensively to bring raw materials in and carry finished products away that it became the largest single railroad customer in the world.

In deciding where to build his plant, neither McCormick nor Carnegie had to consider access to water power. Steam engines worked anywhere you could get fuel to them, and Chicagoans rightly regarded McCormick's steam-powered plant as a symbol of the new industrial age. A visit to McCormick's factory in 1851 moved a local newsman to a baroque burst of rhetorical elegance:

An angry whir, a dronish hum, a prolonged whistle, a shrilled buzz, and a panting breath — such is the music of the place. You enter — little wheels of steel attached to horizontal upright and oblique shafts, are on every hand. They seem motionless. Rude pieces of wood without form or comeliness are hourly approaching them upon little railways, as if drawn thither by some mysterious attraction. They touched them, and *presto,* grooved, scalloped, rounded, on they go, with a little help from an attendant who seems to have an easy time of it, and transferred to another railway, when down comes a guillotine-like contrivance — they are sawn, bored, and whirled away, where the tireless planes without hands, like a boatswain, whistle the rough plank into polish and it is turned out smooth shaped and fitted for its place in the Reaper or the Harvester. The saw and the cylinder are the genii of the establishment. They work its wonders, and accomplish its drudgery. But there is a greater than they. Below, glistening like a knight in armor, the engine of forty-horse power worked as silently as the "little wheel" of the matron; but shafts plunge, cylinders revolve, bellows heave, iron is twisted into screws like wax, and sawed-off at the rate of forty rounds a second, at one movement of [the engine's] mighty muscles.

There, in Cyrus McCormick's factory in 1851, with its power tools turning out interchangeable parts and its "little railways" moving components from one operation to another, stood a fulfillment of the system of manufacturing that Eli Whitney had envisioned. Driven by its power plant that could be erected almost anywhere, McCormick's establishment was a rudimentary but unmistakable prototype of the modern factory that lies at the heart of American industrial productivity. Carnegie's Edgar Thomson steel works, which opened a quarter of a century later, carried the evolution one step further. Steam-powered machinery made it possible to expand volume and speed up production so much that by the end of the nineteenth century Carnegie's mill produced as much in one day as an 1850 Pittsburgh establishment could produce in a year. Steam drove the fans that put the blast in the hard-driven furnaces; steam-powered rollers shaped the rails and beams; steam cranes and locomotives moved the material from one operation to another and from the plant to its customers.

Outside the factory, however, the world progressed more

slowly. For all the impact they had on American business, steam engines had little effect on life in the American home, whether city or farm. There, human muscle and horseflesh, as always, supplied the power that got the chores done. Before electricity most urban Americans lived dark, smelly, tattletale gray, washed-by-hand lives in the homes and streets lit by guttering wicks and flickering gaslamps, suffused with the reek of coal smoke, human excretion, and horse manure. Farm families, enduring numbing toil and embittering isolation, struggled with the realities of an existence far removed from the romantic Jeffersonian myth of the happy yeoman, an existence starkly chronicled in the novels of Willa Cather and Ole Rölvaag, and graphically depicted in *Wisconsin Death Trip.*

How much impact Edison's work had on these daily American lives is suggested by a partial list of the projects in which he involved himself as inventor, manufacturer, perfecter, or promoter. These included: the electric light and all the associated apparatus needed to generate and distribute electricity, first for lighting and then for the whole paraphernalia of electrical appliances; the phonograph; motion pictures; electric traction motors and storage batteries that powered streetcars and delivery wagons and got horses and their droppings off the streets; the "Edison effect," the phenomenon that led to the vacuum tube, the keystone of wireless telegraphy, radio broadcasting, and television. Small wonder that the public acclaimed Edison as the "most useful American."

Edison also contributed directly and significantly to America's industrial development by perfecting a system to send multiple telegraph messages in both directions over the same telegraph wire, by lighting up factories as well as homes, by devising new methods to manufacture and pour cement, by developing the prototype of the modern industrial research laboratory, by inventing the mimeograph machine, and by innumerable other contributions to technology. So active was Edison that, on the average, he produced a patentable device every two weeks of his adult life. Together he, his colleagues, his rivals, and his imitators literally and figuratively electrified America by devising a power source, driven by falling water, steam, or the internal combustion engine to generate a cheap, flexible energy whose voltage could be stepped up to drive the heaviest industrial machinery, or down for every household.

Edison, along with those who perfected the internal combustion engine, thus presided over the last energy revolution we have so far had, though he suspected that others lay ahead. Today, groping for new sources of energy, we travel paths that Edison surveyed speculatively long ago. In 1922, he noted in his diary the possibility of atomic energy: "It may come someday. As a matter of fact, I am already experimenting along the lines of gathering information at my laboratory here. . . . So far as atomic energy is concerned there is nothing in sight just now. Although tomorrow some discovery might be made." On this subject, as on many others, Edison displayed his uncommon faculty ("a pipeline to God," some called it) for sensing that a thing might be done without at the moment seeing how. Some of his visions — helicopters and hovercraft, for example — remained just that, visions, in his lifetime. But many became realities that changed American life; indeed, few men could claim to have witnessed so much change or to have contributed so much to the process.

When Thomas Edison was born in 1847, James K. Polk was President; there were 29 states containing 21 million people (85 percent of them living in rural areas), served by 5,000 miles of railroad. When he died in 1931, Herbert Hoover was President; there were 48 states, with a population of 124 million (56 percent of it urban), and 430,000 miles of track. In addition, industries unheard of at Edison's birth had reshaped American lives by the time of his death. In 1931, 26 million motor vehicles traveled 216 billion miles over 830,000 miles of paved highway; scheduled airlines flew 43 million revenue miles; Americans had 20 million telephones and made 83 million calls a day on them; 17 million families had radios, and there were 612 broadcasting stations; 68 percent of American households had electricity and had purchased more than 300 million dollars' worth of electrical appliances and radios every year since 1925; altogether, Americans consumed 110 billion kilowatt hours of electricity, almost half of it in factories, where electric motors furnished more than half the total horsepower used.

Almost at its beginning Edison's life was buffeted by the tempest of change stirred by the introduction of steam power. He was born in Milan, Ohio, a town that owed its prosperity to a canal that carried Ohio farmers' produce to Lake Erie and thence to eastern markets. In 1854 the Lake Shore Railroad, building west, bypassed Milan. The canal dried up and the town with it; Edison's father's timber business collapsed. Samuel Edison removed his family to Port Huron, Michigan, set up a new business and sent his son off to school. The local schoolmaster (no Eli Whitney he) pronounced young Thomas "addled," enraging Edison's mother, who declared the teacher a fool and carried the boy home determined to teach him herself (a temptation I've often resisted). This exercise of parental discretion which, in our more enlightened age, would, unless excused on grounds of religious idiosyncrasy, land its perpetrator in the hoosegow, or worse, in the arms of a lawyer, rescued Edison from a style of learning he found "repulsive."

Under his mother's supervision Edison escaped from the rote learning of the schoolhouse to an early exposure to classics like Gibbon and Shakespeare. He read Thomas Paine and experienced a revelation similar to Carnegie's encounter with Spencer:

It was a revelation to me to read [Paine's] views on political and theological subjects. Paine educated me then about many matters of which I had never before thought. I remember very vividly the flash of enlightenment that shone from Paine's writings. . . . I went back to them time and time again, just as I have done since my boyhood days.

Newton's *Principia,* however, proved heavier going; young Edison soon found himself lost in "the wilderness of mathematics," for which he developed "a distaste . . . from which I never recovered." In fact, mathematics roused his perversity throughout his life and he continued to dismiss it as merely a necessary adjunct to his trade. "I look upon figures as mathematical tools," he declared, "which are employed to carve out the logical results of reasoning, but I do not consider them necessary to assist one to an intelligent understanding of the result." Later he added, "I am not a mathematician, but I can get within ten percent in the higher reaches of the art." Besides, he concluded with savage satisfaction, "I can always hire mathematicians, but they can't hire me." (Stung by the truthful arrogance of these and other sallies, his critics coined the pejorative term "Edisonian" to denote the trial and error methods forced on Edison and others by their lack of theoretical background.)

The books that most fired young Edison's imagination, however, were Richard Parker's *Natural and Experimental Philosophy,* and a *Dictionary of Science.* Spending all his pocket money on chemicals, bottles, and other apparatus, Edison lay below stairs to carry out the experiments described in these magical books. According to his father, Edison "never knew a real boyhood like other boys" because "he spent the greater part of his time in the cellar." Like most sorcerers' apprentices, Tom produced some jarring results, leading his father to predict, "He will blow us all up!" Edison's mother, like Carnegie's, stood behind him. "Let him be," she urged; "[he] knows what he's about." "My mother was the making of me," Edison later recalled, "She understood me; she let me follow my bent."

In 1859 fate in the form of the railroad boom once again took a hand in young Edison's life. It found him, like Carnegie, toiling away in his cellar. The Grand Trunk Railroad, building a line from Portland, Maine, through Canada and across Michigan to Chicago, reached Sarnia, Ontario, across the St. Clair River from Edison's hometown, Port Huron. The railroad established a car ferry to shuttle its trains across the river and built a branch line from Port Huron to Detroit. Finding himself this time squarely in the path of railroad-borne progress, young Edison swiftly climbed aboard.

Declaring himself grown and independent at the age of twelve, Edison became a "train butcher," selling candy, fruit, and vegetables on the morning trip from Port Huron to Detroit and the evening Detroit newspapers on the return journey. This was no commuter train, bounding from stop to stop as quickly as possible so as to get workers to and from suburbs and city, but rather a now-extinct species known as the "way passenger train." The train left Port Huron at 7 o'clock in the morning and took 4 hours to cover the 63 miles to Detroit; in the evening it left Detroit at 5:30 P.M. and arrived back at Port Huron at 9:30. The train paused at each station, loading and unloading passengers, baggage, and express parcels before sauntering on down the line.

Thus at an age when, nowadays, children are thought capable of little more independent action than flicking on a television set, Edison developed the pattern, continued throughout his life, of working sixteen-hour days and making the most of them. In Port Huron he set up a garden and hired boys to tend it to supply him with produce to sell on the train. In Detroit he used the six-hour layover to peruse the scientific volumes in the Detroit library. In the train baggage car he set up a printing press and published a sheet called the *Grand Trunk Herald,* containing local news and gossip, which he peddled to the passengers. In 1862 he found a way to enlist the telegraph as an aid to his entrepreneurial energies. Hearing that a bloody battle had been fought at Shiloh, Edison persuaded the editor of the Detroit *Free Press* to supply him with 1,500 newspapers on credit. He then cajoled the railroad's Detroit telegraph operator into sending the headlines to all the stations down the road, where the stationmasters chalked the bulletins up on the train board. As the evening train worked its way north, Edison found a mob at each station so eager to buy his newspapers that he was able to raise the price from five cents to a quarter and sold out his entire stock. "You can understand," he recalled, "why it struck me then that the telegraph must be about the best thing going, for it was the telegraphic notices on the bulletin boards which had done the trick. I determined at once to become a telegraph operator."

The chance came through an incident worthy of Horatio Alger's imagination. Standing on the platform at Mt. Clements, Michigan, Edison saw that the station telegrapher's son was about to be run over by a passing freight train. Edison, the boy's father remembered, threw

his papers ... upon the platform, together with his ... cap, and plunged to the rescue, risking his own life to save his little friend, and throwing the child and himself out of the way. . . . They both landed face down in sharp, fresh gravel ballast with such force as to drive the particles into the flesh, so that, when rescued, their appearance was somewhat alarming.

Unlike Alger's characters, the relieved father had neither fortune nor daughter to bestow upon his benefactor, but he gave what he had, teaching Edison the telegrapher's art.

Soon mastering the rudiments of the craft, Edison easily secured a regular job because operators left the railroads and telegraph companies in droves for the higher pay and greater excitement of the Military Telegraph Corps. In 1863 Edison began an eight-year career as a "boomer," an itinerant telegraphist who, like similar-minded brethren among railroad brakemen and locomotive firemen, worked for a while at one place and then restlessly moved on to another, motivated by an independent spirit that Jimmy Rogers, Leadbelly, and others wove into American folklore:

I went down to the depot and I looked up on the board;
It said, "There's good times here, but there's better down the road."

Joining this mobile brotherhood (also, like the passenger train, now largely extinct), Edison traveled far and wide, working in Louisville, Nashville, Memphis, New Orleans, Fort Wayne, Indianapolis, Cincinnati, Detroit, and a dozen other, smaller towns in the United States and Canada. Serving a variety of railroads and telegraph companies, Edison became a first-class operator and developed a style of his own. One of his colleagues later recalled that

a memorable experience of this episode [of my life] was to listen to what might be called the autograph of a certain operator . . . at Indianapolis named Edison. The telegraphic style of the great inventor that was to be was unique, and was detected by its lightning-like rapidity. It was the despair even of expert telegraphers, who often had to break into his narrative to ask him to repeat.

Like most boomers, Edison had idiosyncrasies that made him something less than an ideal employee and often got him fired.

For some, the weakness was drink; for others, a tendency to leave the apparatus unattended while they pursued gambling or more pernicious weaknesses of the flesh. For Edison the snare was his scientific curiosity, which often led him to conduct experiments on the telegraphic apparatus itself, or to be involved with his bottles and chemicals when he should have been dispatching trains or forwarding telegrams.

Finally, in 1868, Edison wandered to Boston, where he took a job with the Western Union Telegraph Company. Now twenty-one and wise in the ways of the road (though woefully naïve about cities and the business carried on in them), Edison manifested personal traits that never subsequently changed: slovenly dress, a tireless indifference to night and day that made his work habits the despair of those who tried to keep up with him, a gaudy vocabulary (as essential as good eyesight to survival around a railroad, as Carnegie also had learned), and a national reputation for his skill matched only by his cockiness. Ace telegraphers, like gunfighters, confronted challenges at every turn, but Edison, who could send faster than anyone else could transcribe and transcribed faster than anyone else could send, proved hard to shoot down.

On his first night in Boston, his fellow operators manipulated their assignments so that Edison had to take a message from "the fastest man in New York." The New Yorker began slowly, but "soon," Edison said,

the New York operator increased his speed, to which I easily adapted my pace. This put my rival on his mettle, and he put on his best powers, which, however, were soon reached. At this point I happened to look up, and saw the operators all looking over my shoulders, with their faces shining with fun and excitement. I knew then that they were trying to put a job on me, but kept my own counsel and went on placidly with my work, even sharpening a pen at intervals by way of extra aggravation.

After some minutes of this, Edison "thought the fun had gone far enough ... [so I] opened the key and remarked: 'Say, young man, change off, and send with your other foot.'"

Working at night, studying in the daytime, Edison delved into Michael Faraday's *Experimental Researches in Electricity.* Bristling with confidence, armed with a thorough knowledge of the practical and theoretical aspects of telegraphy, Edison decided to become an inventor. Logically enough, he looked for some situation in which the application of telegraph technology might improve the status quo. In the factory of Charles Williams, who later made Alexander Graham Bell's first telephone, Edison devised an apparatus to record votes in legislative assemblies instantaneously. To his amazement he soon discovered that his potential customers, both in the Massachusetts legislature and the federal Congress, reacted with horror to this device that threatened to accelerate the traditional, glacial pace of their proceedings. "Young man," they told him in Washington, "if there is any invention on earth that we don't want down here, it is this." With his feathers thus singed, Edison determined to waste no further time inventing things that, however useful, did not have an immediate commercial application.

The incident of the automatic vote recorder taught Edison a lesson often disregarded by otherwise prescient individuals before and since: the man who deals in ideas that are ahead of his time is destined for oblivion, not success. Success most often goes to those who perfect innovations that are long overdue. After his first failure, Edison concentrated his efforts on developing equipment to improve telegraphic services where they had already proved useful and profitable. In January, 1869, he placed a notice in *The Telegrapher* announcing that "T. A. Edison has resigned his situation in the Western Union office, Boston, and will devote his time to bringing out inventions." The first of these was an improved stock ticker that supplied current market quotations to brokerage houses. This device found a ready market and made Edison some money, which, establishing another lifelong pattern, he immediately plowed back into other experiments. When these new enterprises failed, Edison decided to emulate the American capital market and migrated from Boston to New York, arriving, penniless, in May, 1869.

In New York, Edison for a time fell upon lean days, existing largely on a diet of apple dumplings until fate once again rescued him. Poor but not unknown in his own field, Edison was befriended by Franklin L. Pope, chief engineer of the Laws Gold Reporting Company, one of two firms that had a stranglehold on the lucrative service of furnishing gold and stock market quotations to brokers in New York. Pope let Edison sleep on a cot in the company's battery room. Edison thus chanced to be on hand one day when the central transmitting machine broke down. Pandemonium at once ensued as runners from dozens of brokerage houses rushed into the office demanding instant information. Both Pope and Dr. S. S. Laws, the firm's proprietor, succumbed to the hysteria of the moment. Edison, keeping his head, located the trouble and soon repaired it. Impressed and relieved, Laws hired Edison at a salary of $300 a month, two and a half times his wage as a first-class telegraph operator. But Edison, who had no more mind than Carnegie to restrict himself to the "narrow field" delineated by "the beck and call of others," soon resigned and set up a partnership with Pope. Pope, Edison & Company advertised its services as electrical engineers, specializing in "the application of electricity to the Arts and Sciences." Edison offered to design instruments "to order for special telegraphic services," and to perfect "the application of Electricity and Magnetism for Fire-Alarms, Thermo-Alarms, Burglar-Alarms, etc."

Despite this grandiose advance billing, Edison in fact continued to concentrate on a narrow range of telegraphic instruments. By this time the principle had become well established that patents were something that capitalists either bought or evaded. As a man whose fertile mind spun off a series of practical improvements for an industry embroiled in cutthroat competition, Edison soon found himself courted by the emerging titans of telegraphy, particularly the moguls at Western Union, who wanted nothing less than a monopoly of the industry in the United States.

It was easier to plan such a monopoly than to accomplish it, even for Western Union, masterminded by Ezra Cornell and

Amos J. Kendall, and backed by the vast financial resources of a Vanderbilt-Morgan syndicate. An industry that offered glittering prospects for profits, a national market of continental dimensions, plentiful supplies of capital, and new technology that improved almost daily, invited competitors. They appeared from far and wide to challenge Western Union's hegemony. Western Union mounted a two-handed counterattack, gathering in existing rivals with one hand while reaching out with the other to snap up new inventions before they could help the competition. Thus, when Edison designed an improved stock printer and organized a service to rent it to subscribers, Western Union bought him out for $5,000. The company then proceeded to add Edison to its stable of inventors, which included among others Elisha Gray (who subsequently created a working telephone simultaneously with Alexander Graham Bell).

Edison did not become a formal employee of Western Union, but General Marshall Lefferts, one of Western Union's executives, gave him a series of practical problems to tackle and supplied the money to finance his research. With the money from the sale of his stock ticker supplemented by Western Union's subsidy, Edison could afford to become a free-lance inventor, a scientific soldier of fortune, free to pursue any problem that intrigued him, as well as to accept specific assignments from Lefferts. While Edison operated under an informal understanding that Western Union would have first refusal on any patents he might obtain, he could in fact double-cross his patron by selling his inventions to anyone he chose.

Some months and several inventions later, Lefferts called him in and offered him $40,000 for the work done so far. Edison accepted and, knowing nothing of banks (or so his version of the story goes), sat up all night in his Jersey City boardinghouse, fearful that some footpad might relieve him of his new-found wealth. The next day, with a friend's help, Edison penetrated the mysteries of banking sufficiently to open a deposit account, but to his dying day he retained the deep-seated suspicion of bankers and banking that characterized many Americans (Henry Ford a spectacular example) of rural midwestern origins.

Now possessed of more wealth than he had ever dreamed possible, Edison moved across the river to Newark, New Jersey, and opened a factory to manufacture the new stock tickers for Western Union. Earlier, when he had received the $5,000, Edison had written home to his irascible father, "Don't do any hard work and get mother anything she desires. You can draw on me for money. Write me . . . how much money you will need . . . and I will send the amount on the first of [the] month." Old Sam's astonishment at finding his vagabond son rich enough to pension off his parents increased when Thomas, now ensconced in his Newark factory, wrote, "I have one shop which employs 18 men and am fitting up another which will employ over 150 men. I am now what you Democrats call a 'Bloated Eastern Manufacturer.' "

Between 1869 and 1875, the inventor-cum-bloated-manufacturer continued to improve the telegraph. Financed by Western Union and by the Mephistopheles of late nineteenth-century American finance, Jay Gould, Edison churned out improvements, patented them, and then set up factories to produce the equipment. Inevitably he became embroiled in the suits and countersuits with which the corporate rivals battered one another. He had to endure character assaults in and out of the witness box, hearing himself branded as a man who had "basely betrayed" his Western Union patrons, as a "rogue inventor," a "professor of duplicity and quadruplicity," and as a "young man [with] a vacuum where his conscience ought to be."

Since Edison sometimes accepted support from several companies simultaneously to work on the same problem, and then sold the results to the highest bidder, some of these accusations bore an element of truth. Since he considered himself more swindled than swindling, Edison's conscience emerged relatively unscathed. "Everybody steals in commerce and industry," he reflected. "I've stolen a lot myself. But I knew *how* to steal. They don't know *how* to steal — that's all that's the matter with them." His excursions into the freebooting world of high finance, which included a fleecing at the hands of Gould and a particularly ferocious courtroom denunciation by a master of legalistic histrionics, Roscoe Conkling, did, however, persuade him that the denizens of Wall Street were an even more rascally lot than small-town bankers, a view later vehemently espoused by his disciple, Henry Ford.

However reprehensible these characters might have been, Edison had to deal with them, for in the late nineteenth century technology became so complex and so expensive that no inventor could hope to progress far without access to capital markets and the men who manipulated them. The day when an Eli Whitney could create a revolutionary machine using hand tools to shape bits of wood and wire, and could then test his creation by turning a crank, had not entirely passed, as Edison later proved with the phonograph. But most electrical apparatus required months of experimentation to perfect expensive, precision equipment to manufacture, elaborate facilities to test (the only way to try a system of long-distance transmission was to have a far-flung network to transmit on), and a well-financed factory to manufacture. Consequently, Edison and other inventors found themselves clutching at financiers, however distasteful the embrace.

Many brilliant inventors had a business sense that would have embarrassed children. Edison, who started shrewdly enough in his days as a railroad vendor, apparently lost his somewhere along the way. For years, he admitted, he kept nothing but payroll accounts. "I kept no books," he said. Sometimes he simply handed clerks fistfuls of cash with which to pay bills, but usually he settled his debts with personal notes. When the notes came due he "had to hustle around and raise the money." This chaotic system avoided "the humbuggery of bookkeeping, which," he said, "I never understood." Later, when his empire grew so large that some form of financial organization became unavoidable, he put his affairs in the hands of Samuel Insull, a bounder with ideas so original that in later life his handiwork helped precipitate the Great Crash of 1929 and inspired a whole new category of preventive legislation.

In the wide-open booming economy of the late nineteenth century, fortunes could be made by alliances of capitalists and technicians. The prospects were alluring enough to bring forth an endless stream of innovations across the whole spectrum of business activity. Unsurprisingly, the inventors often came out on the short end; promoters Ezra Cornell, Theodore Vail, and J. P. Morgan made fortunes out of the telegraph, the telephone, and the electric light that dwarfed the returns to Samuel F. B. Morse, Alexander Graham Bell, and Edison, who invented them. As the golden stream flowed by, Edison did, however, manage to siphon off enough to finance projects that filled even his monumental working hours. On an upper floor of his Newark factory, Edison established a laboratory, filled it with apparatus and staffed it with technicians. Their enthusiasm for the work, or for Edison himself (some of his most talented associates migrated to Newark specifically to associate themselves with the great man), was such that they thrived on working conditions that Edison himself summarized by saying, "We don't pay anything and we work all the time."

Work all the time they did, as Edison, driven by inspiration or financial necessity, turned his team onto one project after another. Some of these quests were original, including one that produced the first mimeograph machine. (These personal projects gave him special satisfaction. After completing one of them, he noted in his journal that it was "invented by & for myself and not for any small-brained capitalist.") Some involved improving upon the work of other inventors, such as the automatic telegraph, invented by George D. Little and brought to Edison by Edward H. Johnson, an entrepreneur who had bought Little's patent. Others, including the telephone, were suggested by corporate sponsors like Western Union. Whatever the inspiration, the approach was the same. Rounding up everything known on the subject, Edison listed all the alternatives that he and his staff could conjure up, then set his team to work creating the apparatus necessary to test them all. Edison was a driving master of the hunt. Once, when confronted with a breakdown in a new model stock ticker, Edison summoned his staff: "Now, you fellows," he told them, "I've locked the door, and you'll have to stay here until this job is completed." It took sixty hours, and while this admittedly was an extreme case, Edison commonly expected his men to work until they could work no more, then nap on a workbench, the floor, or in some out-of-the-way corner until they could rouse themselves enough to work again.

The employees tolerated this regimen because the boss worked as hard or harder. In addition, his charismatic, pyrotechnic character generated excitement and kept the staff entertained. "Mr. Edison had his desk in one corner," one of his workers said, "and after completing an invention he would jump up and do a kind of Zulu war dance. . . . He would swear something awful. We would crowd round him and he would show us the new invention and explain it to the pattern maker and tell us what to do about it." Once, returning from a day spent in negotiations with New York lawyers and capitalists, who used a language Edison described as "as obscure as Choctaw," he rushed into "the workshop with a whoop, fired his silk hat into an oil pan, and was preparing to send his fine coat after it, when someone laughingly pinned him down." Edison then gladly resumed his normal persona, "as dirty as any of the other workmen, and not much better dressed than a tramp."

By 1876, America's centennial year, Edison's combined labors as inventor and manufacturer brought him solvency, even modest wealth. The hard-won principles of modern manufacturing — repetitious reproduction of undifferentiated components, constantly monitored by cost-control accounting — always bored Edison. Nevertheless he understood them and applied them to his own enterprises, despite his public pronouncements on the boredom of bookkeeping. Even the magic of economies of scale, which Andrew Carnegie, across the mountains in Pittsburgh, was about to teach the iron trade of the world, held no mystery for Edison. When he first began to manufacture light bulbs, for example, they cost $1.40 each to produce, but Edison priced them at 40¢, knowing that volume production would soon bring costs down.

But manufacturing, which demanded constant attention to a single project, could not long absorb a man with Edison's cast of mind: "I never think about a thing any longer than I want to," he said. "If I lose my interest in it, I turn to something else. I always keep six or eight things going at once, and turn from one to the other as I feel like it." In 1876, therefore, Edison abandoned his manufacturing ventures, moved his equipment and his staff to the hamlet of Menlo Park, New Jersey, twenty-five miles south of Newark and then a remote spot. At the Menlo Park laboratory, Edison institutionalized his role as creative inventor, establishing what amounted to an invention factory, where he planned to produce technology to order while simultaneously pursuing his own interests.

At Menlo Park, Edison continued to restrict his organization to projects that promised to make money and make it quickly. As one commentator observed, Edison was "the first great scientific inventor who clearly conceived of inventions as subordinate to commerce." By adhering to this maxim, Edison became, as German economist Werner Sombart observed, "the outstanding example of a man who made a business of invention itself." As such he contributed to the dynamic blend of technology and capital that drove American manufacturing to world prominence in the late nineteenth century.

Edison himself made no bones about his role:

I do not regard myself as a pure scientist, as so many persons have insisted that I am. I do not search for the laws of nature, and have made no great discoveries of such laws. I do not study science as Newton and Faraday and Henry studied it, simply for the purpose of learning truth. I am only a professional inventor. My studies and experiments have been conducted entirely with the object of inventing that which will have commercial utility.

He insisted upon a similar focus among the members of his staff. Criticizing one of his subordinates, Edison said:

I set him at work developing details of a plan. But when he [notes] some phenomenon new to him, though easily seen to be of no importance in this apparatus, he gets sidetracked, follows it up and loses time. *We can't be spending time that way!* You got to keep working up things of commercial value — that is what this laboratory is for. We

*Edison in 1888 after a nonstop seventy-two-hour
stint on the phonograph*

can't be like the old German professor who as long as he can get his black bread and beer is content to spend his whole life studying the fuzz on a bee!

At Menlo Park this pragmatic formula brought dynamic results and considerable income, which Edison, as always, reinvested in new apparatus and further research. He continued to enjoy corporate patronage. Western Union, for example, concluded in 1876 that the telephone was not just a gadget but a dangerously competitive form of communication. It once again engaged Edison, this time to create a system that evaded the patents held by Alexander Graham Bell and his backers. Edison soon produced one that, after the inevitable, protracted legal wrangles, brought him $300,000. It also required a second trip to England (he had gone once before in an unsuccessful attempt to sell his telegraphic apparatus to the British post office), where he supervised its installation and testing. Unlike so many of his countrymen — McCormick, Carnegie, T. S. Eliot, Henry James, to name a few — who found European society sophisticated and invigorating, Edison thought the English slow and unimaginative. "The English," he said, "are not an inventive people." This shortcoming he explained by one of the crackpot formulas that so endeared him to the American press and public: "They don't eat enough pie. To invent, your system must be all out of order, and there is nothing that will do that like good old-fashioned American pie."

The phonograph, which Edison and his helpers constructed late in 1877, exemplified Edison's dedication to the profit motive. The talking machine excited the public imagination, bringing newspaper reporters, scientists, and other interested parties on pilgrimages to the wilds of New Jersey. Edison enjoyed showing visitors around and performing parlor tricks to convince the many skeptics that his apparatus did not depend on some chicanery like ventriloquism, but actually reproduced the human voice. Arthur Clarke, coauthor of *2001: A Space Odyssey,* a man who predicted communications satellites twenty years ahead of time, claims that "any sufficiently advanced technology is indistinguishable from magic." The public reaction to the phonograph certainly mirrored such a viewpoint. Edison was dubbed "the Wizard of Menlo Park," a title reaffirmed in the public imagination by subsequent sorceries, particularly the electric light.

Edison basked in the publicity generated by the phonograph, but didn't let it blind him to the needs of his purse. He set the phonograph aside for some years in favor of the telephone and the electric light, which offered superior commercial possibilities.

The invention of the incandescent electric light, which brought Edison enduring, worldwide fame, resulted from his belief that electricity could be harnessed to tasks other than communication. Steam engines could generate plenty of power, but it was not easily transmitted beyond the confines of a factory. In addition, the country contained many remote areas, where a shortage of fuel or a small market made steam power uneconomical. Edison thought that electricity, which flowed through wires like water through pipes, might be generated at a central location and then transmitted to operate branch-line railroads, or to do the heavy work at isolated mines and quarries. Edison turned his attention to the potential of electric lighting during a visit to the workshop of William Wallace, a dynamo manufacturer in Ansonia, Connecticut. After watching Wallace's experiments with arc lights, Edison left Wallace with this parting shot: "I believe I can beat you making electric lights. I don't think you are working in the right direction."

Edison's boast flowed from one of his intuitive perceptions. The arc light had been in use since the 1850s, illuminating streets and lighthouse beacons, but had inherent disadvantages — glare, obnoxious fumes, and the need for frequent adjustment — that made it impractical for use indoors. Inventors on both sides of the Atlantic struggled to eliminate these quirks, but Edison's nimble mind leapt to another track altogether. He would make light not through an electrical arc — that is, passing a current across a gap from one conductor to another — but by incandescence: that is, passing a current through a continuous conductor of sufficient resistance to glow. Other men had tried this idea before and were trying it then, but none so far had succeeded in overcoming the practical problems involved. Edison returned to Menlo Park and set to work at once, for here lay an idea with a huge and waiting market.

When Edison started his search, indoor lighting depended on the burning of candles, coal gas, or kerosene. Only the latter two were economical on a large scale, but both had objectionable features. They shed a feeble light and smelled. Both were fire hazards. The business of distributing gas, furthermore, had been cartelized by a combination of local companies. This aroused the traditional venomous American response to such situations and opened a lucrative market for kerosene that John D. Rockefeller was busily exploiting in the interests of his own growing monopoly. Kerosene refiners, moreover, had access to a large market where no competition existed, for kerosene lanterns could be carried to the darkened dwellings of rural America, where half the population lived and where no gas company, not even a monopoly, could operate profitably. Nowadays, our reflexive association of petroleum and the automobile obscures the fact that Rockefeller built his empire and his fortune on kerosene, not gasoline, that the United States was the Saudi Arabia of the nineteenth century, and that Rockefeller's machinations excited hostile suspicions around the world ("that greedy little prune-faced peasant," one Frenchman called him) as great as the trepidations with which we now await the latest bulletin from the Organization of Petroleum Exporting Countries.

So, the market was there and Edison went after it. Difficulties there were in plenty: the right-shaped bulb had to be found; a filament that would glow without breaking had to be perfected; pumps had to be developed to create a near-perfect vacuum in each bulb. Once successful, laboratory methods had to be translated into manufacturing practice that would permit mass production. A system to supply electricity had to be developed from scratch. Not a single generating station existed; not a foot of wire had been strung.

Edison confidently predicted that he would succeed "in six weeks." But the weeks became months and, as time and equipment ate up money, Edison had to seek outside help. In the fall of 1878 the Edison Electric Light Company was founded to finance research, take out patents, and license their use. Among the new firm's backers were Western Union and, almost inevitably, a Morgan partner. With adequate financial backing, and with the marathon labors of his laboratory team guided by the calculations of a theoretical mathematician, Francis R. Upton, whom Edison had grudgingly hired, the Wizard ultimately fulfilled his own prophecy. In the last week of 1879, Edison put on a spectacular display of incandescence at Menlo Park, lighting the grounds and the laboratory with long strings of bulbs. Special Pennsylvania Railroad trains brought newspaper reporters and throngs of pilgrims to witness the miracle.

Electricity went on to light much of the world, but that week in December, 1879, was the high point for Edison. Thereafter his own role in it declined. The tremendous amount of capital required to manufacture equipment, generate electricity, and distribute it forced Edison to yield more and more control of his electrical company to financiers like Morgan. In addition, his initial demonstration of electricity's potential led to a swiftly ramifying technology so complex that Edison could not keep up with it. Hundreds of other experimenters were attracted, one of whom, George Westinghouse, developed a system of alternating current that supplanted Edison's direct-current method. Within a few years, Edison's technical skills no longer had any relevance to the booming American electrical industry.

J. P. Morgan soon combined the bulk of American electrical manufacturing firms (most of which bore Edison's name in some combination) into one of his pet behemoths. He called his new creation "General Electric," thus erasing even the inventor's name from the masthead. A few weeks later Edison exposed his bitterness when his secretary, Alfred Tate, asked him a question about electricity: "Tate," Edison replied, "if you want to know anything about electricity, go out to the galvanometer room and ask [Arthur] Kennelly. He knows far more about it than I do. In fact, I've come to the conclusion that I never did know anything about it. I'm going to do something now so different and so much bigger than anything I've ever done before, people will forget that my name ever was connected with anything electrical."

People of course did not forget, nor did Edison do anything much bigger than he'd done before, but he kept trying. The fortune he made in electricity disappeared into a fruitless attempt to separate low-grade iron ore by magnetism. When the money was spent, he said, "Well, it's all gone, but we had a hell of a good time spending it." Undiscouraged, he returned to the phonograph, perfected it, made another fortune, and yet another in motion pictures. He devised a practical electrical storage battery, which he manufactured profitably. Although he continued his driving pace at work, he found more time for his personal life. His first marriage, in 1871 to Mary Stilwell, a worker in his Newark factory, suffered from his neglect; it produced three children, two of whom came to unhappy ends. In 1884, his first wife died of typhoid fever. Two years later he remarried. His new bride, Mina, though only nineteen (Edison, like Whitney, McCormick, and Carnegie, apparently preferred young women), was made of sterner stuff. She forced Edison's life into a semblance of order, demanded companionship, and insisted that he fulfill his family responsibilities, a regimen that he increasingly enjoyed as the years passed. In these more normal family circumstances, the children of the second marriage thrived. (One of them, to Edison's wry amusement, became a theoretical physicist.)

As the first quarter of the twentieth century passed, Edison found himself revered as an American folk hero, a role he relished. Newspapermen, as always, found him excellent copy. Like Carnegie, he was almost always good for some iconoclastic statement. When a clergyman asked him if he should install lightning rods on his church spire, Edison answered, "By all means, as Providence is apt to be absentminded." Edison also supplied reporters with quotable aphorisms: "Genius is one percent inspiration and ninety-nine percent perspiration."

In his declining years, Edison found an increasing fascination in nature's miraculous powers. He gloried in the perfection of an oak leaf and enjoyed showing a burned thumb that had healed perfectly, observing that "the life entities rebuilt that thumb with consummate care." He enjoyed camping trips with Ford, Harvey Firestone, naturalist John Burroughs, and the entourage of reporters that accompanied their caravan. Tutored by Burroughs and encouraged by Ford and Firestone, Edison developed a strain of giant goldenrod, searching for a source of raw rubber that could be raised in the United States. As he grew older, the driving force of creativity wound down into more relaxed forms of puttering and rumination. When asked, as he often was, when he planned to retire, he usually responded, "When the doctor brings in the oxygen tank." After the First World War, however, he retired in fact, if not in name.

When he died in 1931, the world mourned the passage of an original mind and Americans the loss of their "most useful citizen." During his lifetime, theoretical scientists had deprecated the contributions of men like Edison and Alexander Graham Bell. The latter had been caustically described by theoretical physicist James Clerk Maxwell as an elocutionist who "to gain his private ends [became] an electrician." Professor Emory A. Rowland of Johns Hopkins University said that "he who makes two blades of grass grow where one grew before" might do mankind some good, but "he who labors in obscurity to find the laws of such growth is the intellectual superior as well as the greater benefactor of the two." Perhaps, but in Edison's lifetime and to a large extent through the force of his own efforts, practical science became inextricably intertwined with American industry, nourishing its growth by the constant infusion of updated technology. Edison's example persuaded progressive corporate managers that their firms must have "invention factories" of their own. From General Electric, the Bell System, and Du Pont, the idea of integrated research facilities spread across the spectrum of American industry and ultimately into the government. With its complex of individual, corporate, and government-sponsored facilities, the American economy has channeled a higher percentage of its income into research and development than any other in the world. Science tied to industry has facilitated prodigious (if often wasteful) growth, created terrifying weaponry, and given mankind a powerful ally in its eternal combat with darkness, isolation, and hunger.

Today we ponder these awesome consequences with mixed emotions, but our predecessors welcomed the convergence of science and industry, seeing it as evidence of America's superior contribution to the elevation of mankind. Scientific change meant human progress, and practical scientists were American heroes. Americans needed no Kants or Spinozas to transcribe the music of the spheres, but practical men who could

> *Bring the balloon of the mind*
> *That bellies and drags in the wind*
> *Into its narrow shed*

where it could do some useful work.

In the tradition of earlier Americans who had dubbed a mechanic "the artist of his country" and a reaper manufacturer a "hero in the classical mold," one of Edison's contemporaries celebrated a society in which "the chemist, the mineralogist, the botanist, and the mathematician are fellow laborers with the practical farmer and the manufacturer," and "vain and unprofitable theories no longer engrossed the attention of men of science." Other peoples might view "an active and feverish imagination . . . as [a] distinguishing mark of [the] philosopher," but not hardheaded Americans. For them, "philosophers are businessmen," and Edison, who made invention a business, was repeatedly named "America's most useful citizen" by his countrymen.

It was said when Edison died, and it has been said often since, that the world would never see his like again. In a world run by huge bureaucracies and staffed by scientists trained for years in arcane disciplines, so these lamentations go, such individualists have no place, and useful scientific perceptions are beyond the reach of minds not formally trained. I think such obituaries for individualism were and are premature. On April 17, 1978, *Newsweek* magazine carried a story about an obscure inventor named Stanford Ovshinsky. In 1968, Ovshinsky had predicted that the use of solar energy would eventually become feasible through the development of cheap, electronic switches that would convert the sun's heat into electrical current. "Electronics experts," *Newsweek* reported, "were highly skeptical on two counts. Theorists could not imagine how the amorphous semiconductors could possibly work. And they and others regarded Ovshinsky as a scientific outsider. He had no college degree, let alone one in physics; his only apparent talent seemed to be publicizing [himself]. Ten years later, Professor David Adler of the Massachusetts Institute of Technology admitted, 'Almost every statement Ovshinsky made in 1968 has now turned out to be true.' " The role of individuals in the making of history, even scientific history, may not have died with Thomas Edison.

The Edison heritage surely lives on, most obviously in the American lifestyle, which he transformed, but equally dynamically (if less visibly) in American industry. During Edison's lifetime, and partially because of his work, applied science became a permanent component of American manufacturing. Like so many of the techniques developed by nineteenth-century individualists, systematic industrial research has been bureaucratized by big business, which created research and development departments and sequestered them in places like the Bell System Laboratories and the Du Pont Experimental Station. But, as we shall see in the case of Edwin Land, here and there Tom Edison's notion of an "invention factory" has survived and waxed mighty.

*The tinkerer turned debonair: Henry Ford at the tiller
of his first automobile*

6

The Insolent Charioteer Henry Ford

MY paternal grandfather looked just like Henry Ford, which was fitting, because Ford was one of his folk heroes. Sometimes after Sunday dinner, he would take me by the hand and together we'd sit in the willow tree swing to "watch the Fords go by." Just as Carnegie's ancestor told him wondrous tales of the deeds of Scotland's champions, so mine filled me with the marvels of Henry Ford and the cars he built.

They had a lot in common, these two septuagenarians, enough so that my grandfather could identify with his hero, finding in both their lives much of what was right and good in America. Both had hated the farm with its confinement and drudgery; both had gone to the city and made good, though my grandfather's post on the L & N Railroad surely represented a more modest order of success. To Grandfather, Ford was a simple man, an honest man, whose virtues were manifested in the products he made: plain, cheap, durable, and simple enough to be repaired by any man with a simple set of tools and an ample supply of elbow grease. Wealth, moreover, hadn't changed Henry at all. In his Dearborn mansion he still square-danced with his wife; he sponsored the "Ford Hour" on the radio, which played only "good music, not trash."

Above all, Ford bristled with that cherished American trait, individualism, which caused him to despise all the right things. Ford hated bureaucrats and statistics and had personally led a

raiding party, armed with crowbars, that had routed the statisti-
cians and smashed the machines in a bureau someone had
created behind his back. He hated interference in his affairs and
allowed no one to tell him what to do. When his stockholders
had meddled, he'd bought them out. When Roosevelt and the
NRA had tried to tell him what he could make and how he must
sell it, he'd told them to go to hell and made it stick. When labor
unions had tried to organize his plant, he'd turned guards and
dogs and fire hoses on them to beat them and drive them off, not
because he hated workers (after all, hadn't he paid them $5 a day
when the going rate was $2?), but because he wouldn't let outside
agitators tamper with his freedom or his workers! "What can a
union give them," he asked, "that they don't already have?"
Unions, Ford declared, were a hoax, perpetrated on the workers
by union leaders interested only in levying a tax, in the form of
dues, on the workers' hard-earned wages. The dues then financed the leadership's "union salaries[,] liberating them from
the necessity of work so that they can devote their energies to
subversive activities."

Best of all, Ford detested bankers and Wall Street. He, like his
hero Edison, had never trusted them, had dealt with them only of
necessity and with great reluctance, and had rejoiced at the day
when his wealth put him beyond their reach forever. As far as
Ford and my grandfather (who kept his money hidden in jars in
the cellar) were concerned, Andrew Jackson and all his legatees
in the populist American tradition had been right. Bankers *did*
conspire to defraud and mystify honest, toiling Americans out of
the fruits of their labor. Bankers made nothing, grew nothing,
and waxed fat swindling those who did. People like Edison and
Ford had given us electric lights and cars that ran; bankers, as
any intelligent person knew, had given us the Great Depression,
then more than a decade old. Too bad more of them hadn't
jumped out of windows; maybe we'd have recovered sooner.

In the virtuous American tradition, Ford opposed monopoly
and by single-handedly defying an early patent cartel, had protected America's most important industry from its clutches. He
was gentle: once he'd used the back door of his mansion for

weeks rather than disturb a nest of robins who'd taken up residence in front. He was kind: he'd built Henry Ford Hospital for the people and spent thousands on special medical care for the daughter of one of his supervisors. He was generous: he'd personally kept the city of Inkster, Michigan (and who knew how many others?), afloat through the Depression by contributing millions of dollars of his own money to the city's coffers.

Of course there was another side to the great man, a side I didn't hear about in those Sunday afternoon sermons. He had other hatreds, less appetizing, though no less in the American tradition, including a loathing for Jews, whom he saw as the mainspring of the international bankers' conspiracy. His gentle traits were counterbalanced, perhaps overbalanced, by a core of meanness, savagery, and cruelty. He belittled, humiliated, and destroyed his only son and heir, Edsel. He hired a thug, Harry Bennett, as a bodyguard for his grandchildren, admired Bennett's ruthlessness, made him second most powerful man in the company, and sanctioned his creation of a private Ford Gestapo to bludgeon maverick workers into line or off the property. He ordered old, trusted associates (some with forty years' service) fired for quixotic reasons and hid from them afterward.

He was, in fact, a man studded with paradoxes, as I learned in schools far removed from my grandfather's front-yard swing. A pacifist who, like Carnegie, genuinely despised war and spent freely to oppose it, Ford nevertheless accepted the Grand Cross of the Supreme Order of the German Eagle from Adolf Hitler. The presentation came on Ford's seventy-fifth birthday, July 30, 1938, by which time the Nazi dictator clearly presented the most ominous threat to the peace Ford cherished. Himself a reclusive man who resented intrusions on his privacy, Ford authorized the creation of a "Sociological Department" to Americanize his foreign workers and teach all of them habits of thrift, as well as to educate their families in proper marketing, hygiene, and housekeeping. Run by a tame clergyman, Dean Samuel Marquis, the Ford Sociological Department, as bureaucratic agencies will do, extended its franchise, dictating the workers' private behavior in molds that Ford himself endorsed — temperance, abstinence from tobacco, fidelity for the married and continence for the single — and maintaining a Big Brotherish vigilance to ferret out transgressors.

None of this intruded on my child's delight in such a fabulous character. A more balanced view came years later; meanwhile, other influences intensified the Ford spell. My grandfather's loyalty to Ford automobiles (unbroken, after a brief, youthful flirtation with Willys) passed to my father (who has never owned anything else to this day) and then (with an occasional, unrewarding apostasy) to me. Where I grew up, and in the southern expanse beyond, Ford was *the* car: it was tough; it had character, and above all it was fast; nothing could keep up with a Ford V-8. Moonshiners, bankrobbers, and honest folk all sang a popular hillbilly anthem:

> *We're Ford men and we all know*
> *Ford's a good car and really will go.*

My first car was a 1935 Ford with a rumble seat, and I've owned a lot of others since. Older, wiser, and in some ways sadder, I have a more balanced view of Messrs. Ford and their cars, but old loyalties die hard. I wouldn't buy a foreign car or a Chevrolet under any conceivable circumstances, and when Ford gas tanks explode or Ford transmissions slip from Park to Reverse, I have the urge to confront the current Ford as a disillusioned young fan once confronted his hero, Shoeless Joe Jackson of the Chicago Black Sox, and demand, "Say it ain't so, Henry." As a car owner, I guess I'm nothing but a mannish-boy.

As a historian, however, I have surely changed my view of the car's progenitor: I find him less admirable, but his achievements more remarkable. Henry Ford was one of the few men of whom it can be said that he personally changed the face of America. The impact of his career was so gigantic and so paradoxical as to defy comprehension or description. (On the desk where I write are two three-foot stacks of books, each of which has tried to measure some dimension of the man and his work; virtually all claim partial success at best. And this is only part of the Fordiana in print; Ford must rank with Washington, Lincoln, and Franklin Roosevelt as one of the most written-about Americans in history.)

Henry Ford, the man most responsible for twentieth-century America as we know it, was a child of the nineteenth century, with nineteenth-century ideas that held him in thrall throughout his life. Indeed, it might be argued that Ford pushed those ideas to the maximum industrial capacity they could achieve. Like Frankenstein starting with good intentions, however, he created with his skill and ideas a monster that his talents could not control, with consequences that he could not foresee but came to fear. With the right talent and ideas for his time, Ford became the first (and perhaps the last) billionaire on the strength of a company that he solely owned and controlled. As his fortune and fame grew, his countrymen, charmed like my grandfather by his simple and quintessentially American virtues, conceded to him a reputation for profundity he rarely merited outside the workshop.

In Ford, whose intelligence did not expand with his fortune, the foibles of the ordinary nineteenth-century rural American — bigotry, ignorance, mulishness — became dogma, then mania as senility set in. Enamored of his role as homespun sage and proud of his crank notions, he broadcast his quirks to the world through the newspapers and radio stations of his empire and in three books that expanded his philosophy of production into a blueprint for society that rivaled *Brave New World* in its sterility. Together with the decline of his company from the mid-1920s on, Ford's views — ignorant, absurd, despicable — reduced him, in the eyes of many, from Edison's rival as "Most Useful American" to an object of ridicule, distaste, or loathing. "Ford has to his debit," wrote one critic, "more erratic interviews on public questions, more dubious quotations, more blandly boasted ignorance of American history and American experience, more political nonsense, more dangerous propaganda, than any other dependable citizen we have ever known."

Harsh words, but some of them true enough. Ford once admitted under oath that he didn't know who Benedict Arnold was, couldn't explain the Revolution of 1776 or the basic principles of the American government, and dismissed these questions as trivial because all history was "more or less bunk." Later, announcing that he was "very much interested in the future, not only of my own country, but of the whole world," and had "definite ideas and ideals that I believe are for the practical good of all," he bought the Dearborn *Independent* so that he could give his views "to the public without having them garbled, distorted, or misrepresented." Under Ford's aegis, the *Independent* then launched an anti-Semitic campaign that, among other niceties, denounced Bernard Baruch as the "pro-consul of Judah in America," a "Jew of Super-Power," and the head of an international Jewish conspiracy. Seeking an even broader platform for his wisdom, Ford ran for the Senate in 1918, but lost. (The prospect of Senator Ford tickled his friend Edison no end. Ford, Edison opined, would be the first silent Senator in American history: "He won't say a damned word," Edison laughed.) Undaunted by defeat in his campaign for the Senate, Ford then pondered a run for the presidency in 1924 until cooler counsel prevailed.

The list of Ford's personal follies could be (and has been) extended to fill a book, but these tales — comical, unpleasant, or wicked though they were — largely stemmed from the latter stages of his life, long after his place in industrial history had been secured. (When the Dearborn *Independent* launched its anti-Semitic campaign in 1920, Ford was fifty-seven and had already built six million vehicles.) His views, moreover, on society, history, race, politics, and religion had a tiny impact on America compared to the consequences of his major creations: the cheap car "for the great multitude" and the system of production that made it possible.

By succeeding in his declared goal of making

a motor car for the great multitude . . . large enough for the family but small enough for the individual to run and care for . . . constructed of the best materials, by the best men to be hired, after the simplest designs modern engineering can devise . . . so [cheap] that [any man] making a good salary will be [able] to own one . . .

Ford catalyzed the automotive revolution in American life. But that revolution had consequences far beyond any that Ford envisioned or intended. By creating a machine that made it possible for every man to "enjoy with his family the blessings of hours of pleasure in God's great open spaces," Ford enabled his countrymen to break away from cities and rail lines. But many of them moved into suburbs that devoured many of "God's great open spaces" and carpeted them with settlements whose inhabitants suffered alone in their cars the curse of hours of commuting on crowded, narrow highways. Freeing rural Americans from the drudgery and isolation of country life, Ford galvanized an urban economy that caused many a farmer to abandon the land altogether. Hating management bureaucracies, banks, stockholders, and Wall Street, Ford assembled a business so powerful that his rivals at General Motors had to compete by cementing together thousands of stockholders, millions of Wall Street dollars, and an impersonalized, efficient organization into the world's most powerful corporation. Wedded to the traditional concept of family ownership, Ford so fanatically pursued personal control that he nearly destroyed his company and his family's chance to hold onto it. Embracing, indeed personifying, the American creed of individualism, Ford created a system of mass production that stripped his workers of all vestiges of individuality and reduced them to robot machine-tenders. Sentimental to the point of bathos about the charm and simplicity of an earlier America replete with small farmers, simple machines, and tiny shops, Ford shaped an economic society that threatened to obliterate these artifacts of its past. Aghast at the outcome of his own efforts and fearful that these cherished symbols might vanish, he spent millions on a museum designed to preserve them for posterity.

Symbolically he built his museum, as he had built his industrial goliath the River Rouge plant, at Dearborn, Michigan, near the spot where he was born on July 30, 1863. Ford's father, like Eli Whitney's, was a farmer who made a decent, but not a sumptuous, living. By the time Henry was thirteen, his mother and three children had died, leaving his father a widower with five surviving children. Like Whitney, Henry detested farm life and often shirked his chores in favor of tinkering. "Chicken is for hawks," young Henry said. "Milk is a mess." His father, like Edison's, feared that Henry had "wheels in his head." "John and William [the other two Ford sons] are all right," he told a neighbor, "but Henry worries me. He doesn't seem to settle down and I don't know what will become of him."

What became of him was an increasing obsession with things mechanical. From fixing farm tools, Henry moved on to water wheels, turbines, and watches. At sixteen he fled the farm for Detroit, where he got two jobs: an apprenticeship in a shop that repaired steam engines and part-time work fixing clocks and watches. He soon moved on to apprenticeships at Flower Brothers' machine shop and at the Detroit Drydock Company where, at the age of seventeen, he qualified as a journeyman machinist. Up to that point his life had followed a course common to many American boys of his time. Approaching manhood, he had acquired a smattering of the three Rs and mastery of a craft that would furnish a decent living.

Henry Ford, however, had an uncommon gift — he understood the logic of machines. Somehow, he could look at a machine, see its purpose, understand its workings, and imagine ways to improve it. Unlike Edison, who had the same acute mechanical instincts, Ford's mind rarely lent itself to original creation; he was a master at adapting and improving the ideas of others. He was an innovator, not an inventor, "a natural-born mechanic," as Edison described him. Given a task to perform, a problem to solve, Ford himself might not originate a solution, but he knew an answer when he saw one even if, as happened once, it was in a piece of scrap lying in the sand. At a time when he was searching for ways to build lighter cars, Ford went to an automobile race at Palm Beach: "There was a big smashup and a French car was wrecked. . . . After the wreck I picked up a little valve strip stem. It was very light and very strong. I asked what it was. Nobody knew." It was vanadium steel, as Ford made it his business to learn, an alloy that gave three times the strength per weight of ordinary steel. Applied to the Model T, "vanadium steel disposed of much of the weight" and furnished the last of the "requisites for the universal car."

These instincts and a burning ambition to succeed made Ford a man apart. Moving from job to job brought Ford an ever-expanding knowledge of the machines of American industry, including steam and internal combustion engines. He worked for Westinghouse, repairing steam traction engines that powered threshers and sawmills. In 1885, Henry repaired an internal combustion engine at the Eagle Iron works in Detroit. Then, or soon thereafter, he decided that by applying such an engine to a self-propelled vehicle he could fulfill a long-held ambition, "to make something in quantity." While still a boy, he had considered making watches: "I thought I could build a serviceable watch for around thirty cents and nearly started in the business. But I did not because I figured out that watches were not universal necessities, and therefore people generally would not buy them."

Just how Ford decided that automobiles would be "universal necessities" and that "people generally" would buy them is something that Ford himself may not have known for sure. It seems to have derived from his understanding of innate American restlessness (which he himself shared), which manifested itself in the fact that, as Ford said, "Everybody wants to be someplace he ain't. As soon as he gets there he wants to go right back," or as Bill Knudsen, one of Ford's production men observed, "Everybody wants to go from A to B sitting down." In addition, Ford, who had no formal training in economics and laughed at those who did, perceived something that had eluded most of the erudite brethren of the dismal science: the potential buying power of the American public was enormous and would increase as industrialization expanded.

Whatever the source of his insight, it differentiated Ford from all but a handful of the dozens of men experimenting with motor cars on both sides of the Atlantic, most of whom saw self-propelled vehicles as a luxury to be built and priced for the rich. Even in the United States, with its traditional notions of equality, only Ford, Ransom Olds (Oldsmobile), and Billy Durant (Buick, Chevrolet, General Motors) saw the car's potential as a mass consumer product and found ways to make it a reality.

In 1889 Ford married Clara Bryant, a "neighbor girl," and acquired a source of strength and support in a marriage that endured, as all marriages were supposed to, through sickness and health, wealth and poverty. Fifty years and a billion dollars later, the New York *Herald-Tribune* reported:

Clara never dyed her hair purple or had her face lifted or won the prize at the Beaux Arts Ball. Henry . . . had had his share of odd notions [but] never bet twenty grand on a dice game, never had to be psychoanalyzed . . . and has never been reported by the gossip writers as carrying the torch for either a countess or a showgirl. More, they still dance with each other. It may be that, in more manners than one, they are the richest people in the world.

In 1891 Henry took his bride to Detroit, where he got a job with the Detroit Edison Company, rising eventually to chief engineer. In 1896, he met Edison himself, told the great man of his tinkering with a "gas-buggy" and received what Ford later called decisive encouragement: "There is a big future for any light-weight engine that can develop a high horsepower and is self-contained. . . . Keep on with your engine. If you can get what you are after, I can see a great future."

He already had some of what he was after: two months before, in the wee hours of June 4, he had finished his first gas-buggy. Finding it too big for the woodshed door, he broke down a wall and pushed the car into the rainy street. With Clara holding an umbrella to shield him from the rain and a friend bicycling ahead to warn off nocturnal horsemen, Ford started the engine and took his first test drive. The Ford car had taken to the road.

The Ford Motor Company, however, took longer to get rolling; it got under way in 1903, after several false starts. In 1899, Ford left Detroit Edison. Financed by local capitalists, including the mayor of Detroit, Ford established the Detroit Automobile Company. In keeping with an American practice that dated back to the 1790s Rhode Island textile partnership between the mer-

chant capitalist Moses Brown and the mechanic Samuel Slater, *weakness*
Ford paid no cash for his shares, but contributed his designs and
expertise. The company built twenty-five cars and then failed. A
new effort, the Henry Ford Motor Company, appeared in 1901.
Ford owned a one-sixth interest in the company, but soon found
himself at loggerheads with his backers. Ford claimed they
wanted to build expensive cars while he was committed to a
cheap one. The financiers, protesting that Ford wasted his time
and the company's money building racing cars instead of production models, brought in master machinist Henry Leland to
get things moving.

Racing then, as now, furnished a powerful vehicle for an automobile manufacturer to publicize his creations. Ford, who always had an eye for publicity, especially free publicity, certainly
craved fast cars and knew how to build them. In October, 1901,
Ford challenged Alexander Winton, whose car held the American speed record, to a match race and beat him. In 1902, Ford's
famous 999, Barney Oldfield at the wheel ("Who does he think
he is, Barney Oldfield?" my grandfather used to snarl when
someone passed him), set a new American speed record, made
Ford a local hero to Detroiters, and marked him as a comer in
the industry.

Whatever the source of friction between Ford and his backers,
Leland's presence no doubt intensified it. Ford may well have
had a vision of the kind of automobile he wanted to build and
doubtless wanted to build them in quantity, but he was some
distance from knowing how to go about it. The idea of interchangeable parts had not yet enveloped the automobile industry;
like everyone else's, Ford's early cars were custom-made, one at
a time, like firearms before Whitney. Leland, a master machinist
trained in the post-Whitney firearms industry, was committed to
interchangeability, knew how to achieve it, and instructed the industry's pioneers (including Alfred P. Sloan of General Motors,
as we shall see) in the art. In 1908, Leland dazzled the British
Automobile Club (and much of the rest of the automotive world
as well) with an updated version of Whitney's interchangeability
demonstration. Disassembling three Cadillacs into their constitu-

ent bits and pieces, Leland mixed the parts, reassembled the cars, and drove them five hundred miles without a breakdown. That same year, Henry Ford was to demonstrate how thoroughly he had absorbed Leland's doctrine by mass-producing the Model T, but in 1902, the two geniuses clashed. Leland, one former employee observed, "figured he could tell Ford what to do, but Mr. Ford wasn't the type to take it."

As his backers discovered, Ford wasn't a man who accepted tutelage gracefully, particularly along the lines of what he could and couldn't, should or shouldn't do. He never became such a man, either. Charles Sorenson, whose forty years of service gave him the all-time longevity record among Ford's lieutenants, recalled that "Mr. Ford never caught me saying an idea he had couldn't be done. If I had the least idea that it couldn't be done, I wouldn't announce myself on it to him. . . . I always felt the thing would prove itself."

Ford's fixation with cut-and-try methods (a trait that, like anti-Semitism and an obsession with applied technology, solidified his friendship with Edison) was bolstered by a wide streak of perversity. The very fact that some "expert" (defined by Ford as "a man who knows all the reasons why a thing can't be done") told him he couldn't do something often goaded him to prove the contrary. Together these qualities served him well in the pioneering days when success meant doing all sorts of things that no one had done before, but proved a great liability in later years when he refused to emulate the methods by which his competitors overtook and surpassed him. (Ford's perversity took bizarre forms on occasion. He nearly destroyed his English subsidiary by refusing permission to make the Model T with a right side steering wheel to accommodate the English practice of driving on the left-hand side of the road. No need to change, Ford said. The English would come to their senses eventually, and then Ford would have a head start.)

Frustrated in his purposes, whatever they may have been, Ford quit. (Leland stayed to build the Cadillac Motor Car Company, which he sold to General Motors, and then Lincoln, which, ironically enough, he eventually sold to Ford.) With the automobile craze underway and the country prosperous, Ford soon found new capital for the Ford Motor Company, formed in 1903. A. Y. Malcomson, a coal dealer, and Ford each had 25½ percent of the stock. The balance was divided among ten others, including the Dodge brothers, whose machine shop was to supply most of the parts; C. H. Bennett, who had made his money with the Daisy air rifle; and Albert Strelow, who refurbished his Mack Avenue woodworking shop to provide the company with a factory building. Altogether the firm had $28,000 cash to begin with and never raised another penny by selling stock until after Henry Ford died.

The original list of shareowners soon dwindled. Malcomson sold his 255 shares to Ford and another backer for $175,000; Strelow, in what must rank as one of history's great miscalculations, sold his 50 shares for $25,000 which he lost, McCormick-like, in a phantom gold mine. The magnitude of Strelow's mistake was shown in 1920 when Ford bought out his remaining stockholders. Rosetta Couzens, who owned one share that had cost her $100 in 1903, got $262,000 for it. By 1906 Ford owned 58½ percent of the stock and controlled the company. He could now do as he pleased, and did. He got the company off to a blazing start by taking one of his cars out on a measured mile of cinders, laid on the frozen surface of Lake St. Clair, and driving it at just under a hundred miles an hour, surely a hair-raising ride for a man now forty years old. Capitalizing on this feat, Ford's office manager advertised, "Don't experiment — Buy a Ford." Sure enough, plenty of people did just that.

From 1904 through 1908, Ford produced this model and that, striving for popular acceptance through reliability and low price. In the year 1904–1905 Ford sold 1,745 cars. In 1905 the company paid $288,000 dividends on the $28,000 cash investment made just two years earlier. In 1906 Ford, now in control, concentrated on the Model N, a $600 car, overriding the opposition of the minority shareholders. In the year 1906–1907, the company sold a record 9,000 cars and took in $5.8 million. That same winter, in a locked room at the back of the plant, work began on the Model T, the "universal car," for which Ford was certain there existed a huge market, greater than anything that anyone (with the possible exception of General Motors' promoter, Billy Durant) had ever dreamed.

Ford's conception of the mass consumer market, the hallmark of twentieth-century industrial maturity, derived largely from nineteenth-century ideas. A utilitarian man, raised in the cashpoor austerity of rural America, Ford thought consumer demand represented primarily the human drive for necessities. The rich could afford whatever they wanted, but the bulk of the population husbanded their money to buy what they had to have. In a country like the United States, with its vast distances and large rural population (more than half of all Americans still lived in the country when the Model T first appeared), the need for simple, dependable transportation seemed obvious to Ford. Presented with the chance to buy an automobile that met these specifications at a price they could afford, people would seize it. And they'd continue to seize it, for luxury tastes and luxury incomes might come and go, but the common people and their needs went on forever.

In order to make the cars cheap enough, Ford knew he'd have to make a lot of them. That he thought he could do this resulted not only from his growing knowledge of cheap methods of production, but also from a conception of market dynamics he shared with Carnegie and a few other nineteenth-century proponents of efficient mass production. Unlike many of his contemporaries, driven by frustration with fluctuating demand, which alternately taxed capacity or idled facilities, into combinations that tried to allocate markets and control production, Carnegie thought the market was infinitely elastic. That is, he thought that at some price you could continue to sell everything you could produce. "Take orders at any price that keeps the mills running full," Carnegie exhorted his subordinates. If "demand [falls] short of the capacity to produce [and] a struggle . . . ensue[s] among producers for orders," cut the price: "The sooner you scoop the market the better." During recessions the same policy must prevail — undercut the market: "When you want to capture a falling stone," Andy Carnegie declared, "it won't do to

*The Model T and a primitive assembly line
at Highland Park, about 1914*

follow it. You must cut under it, and so it is with a falling market." If such a strategy were not to prove suicidal, costs had to be reduced simultaneously, but that, Carnegie thought (and with reason), could be managed. His policy kept Carnegie Steel profitable through the depressions of 1873 and 1893, the worst the country experienced before Carnegie's retirement.

Ford, like Carnegie, thought that a low enough price would find a market large enough to absorb all his wares. Henry, however, had no intention of waiting for a falling market to force prices down. The market was there, waiting, and he meant to go get it by cutting prices as fast as reduced costs would allow. (Sometimes even faster. On occasion he cut the price below cost and told his subordinates to "find a profit" on the shop floor unless they wanted bankruptcy and unemployment. He himself couldn't have cared less; he and Clara had all the money they needed and then some.)

Ford also perceived sooner and more clearly than most that industrialization not only reaches customers, but also creates them. The men who rolled Carnegie's rails didn't buy them, but automobile workers bought automobiles, as did their barbers, grocers, and garbage men. Some fraction of the wages Ford paid eventually returned as profits, a fact that permitted, even dictated, a policy of high wages, as he explained to those who predicted bankruptcy when he raised thousands of his workers to $5 a day in 1914.

I have learned through the years [Ford said] a good deal about wages. I believe in the first place that . . . our own sales depend . . . upon the wages we pay. If we can deliver high wages, then that money is going to be spent and it will . . . make storekeepers and distributors and manufacturers and workers in other lines more prosperous and their prosperity will be reflected in our sales. Country-wide high wages spell country-wide prosperity, provided, however, the higher wages are paid for in higher production.

The ways in which Ford got his higher production stamped a grim image on the other side of the bright five-dollar coin. The five-dollar day brought a mob of workers to the Ford gates (in the dead of a Detroit winter, as it happened; when the thousands of disappointed applicants threatened riot, Ford guards turned fire hoses on them). Ford could pick and choose among prospective employees and tyrannize his current workers into faster production with the threat of firing. His analysis of the source of effective demand, however, anticipated John Maynard Keynes by two decades — not a bad effort for a man whose monetary and banking theories were a mixture of superstition, paranoia, and populist humbug.

Once he had designed his utilitarian, universal car, Ford "froze" the model to avoid the expenses of retooling and set out to reduce costs by increasing manufacturing efficiency. The result, of course, was the automobile assembly line, first developed by Ford and his aides, Sorenson, Knudsen, Pete Martin, and others, who came to the plant on Sunday so as not to interrupt current production. By trial and error they developed the system of dragging the chassis across the floor to stations where parts, brought by pulley, conveyor, or inclined plane, were bolted on. Ford's detractors tried to show that the assembly line was the brainchild of his assistants, but Sorenson, who participated, said that while individual contributions came from others, Ford "sponsored" the general idea and approved the specific combination of operations. (He got the idea, so one legend has it, while watching the disassembly of hog carcasses as they rolled down a packing plant trolley.)

Unlike the Model T itself, the assembly line evolved slowly, through improvements introduced throughout the car's eighteen-year production run. Ford applied four basic principles to increase efficiency: the work must be brought to the man; the work should be done waist high so as to eliminate lifting; waste motion, human or mechanical, must be minimized; each task must be reduced to the utmost simplicity. The result was a prodigy of production and cost efficiency and the obliteration of skill and the worker satisfaction that went with it:

As to machinists [said one analysis of Ford methods], old-time, all-round men [in other words, men like Ford himself], perish the thought! The Ford Company has no use for experience. . . . It . . . prefers machine-tool operators who . . . will simply do as they are told to do, over and over again, from bell-time to bell-time.

The Ford system, *Fordismus,* as the admiring Germans called it, thus completed the revolution in production methods begun by Eli Whitney. The skill of shaping wood and metal, once an art as individualized as the fingers that practiced it, was drawn from artisans' hands and lodged in machine tools, leaving the workers with tasks as repetitive and uninspiring as a metronome's.

The system also produced cars (fifteen million of them by 1927), sales volume ($7 billion), and profits (in twenty-four years the company's net worth rose from the original $28,000 to $715 million, including a cash surplus of $600 million). The company outgrew one plant after another, moving from Mack Avenue to Piquette Avenue to Highland Park to, finally, River Rouge. With each move Ford expanded his capacity to manufacture his own parts, cutting out dependency on outside suppliers. This process culminated in the fully integrated behemoth at River Rouge, supplied by an empire that included ore lands, coal mines, 700,-000 acres of timberland, sawmills, blast furnaces, a glass works, ore and coal boats, and a railroad. The Rouge poured out parts that supplied its own assembly plants, as well as a network of others scattered around the United States.

The Rouge concept appealed to Ford's individualism by making him nearly self-sufficient; moreover, the power and symmetry of it all excited him. The plan also had a hard, underlying economic purpose. Inventory costs had always bedeviled manufacturers; as production capacities increased, inventory costs kept pace until huge amounts of capital were tied up in materials awaiting processing or assembly. Ford intended to reduce this burden to a minimum by projecting the precision timing of the assembly line itself back into the operations that supplied it. If, for example, he could mine and ship each day the iron ore required for one day's car production, he need have none stored anywhere. By organizing all his supply lines the same way, Ford created a system of moving inventory which, when it worked, eliminated the need for warehouses, storage facilities, and stockpiles. Even with a final product as simple, unchanging, and undifferentiated as the Model T, the arrangement demanded a marvel of scheduling and performance. It produced such savings, however, that his competitors at General Motors adopted it, ramified it to accommodate the geometric complexities introduced by annual model changes and proliferating options. They also improved it by forcing suppliers, at their own risks, to conform to production schedules, thus avoiding the fixed costs and diverse management problems of an enterprise integrated all the way back to the raw materials. Ford's successors at his own company have since developed the "moving inventory" into a computerized, global art, scheduling, for example, the arrival of parts from fourteen countries around the world to match production schedules in Thailand.

In his own time, *Fordismus* achieved marvels of cost-reduction and production. The price fell steadily from the original $850, finally reaching a low of $263 in 1927. Through 1926 Ford sold half the new cars made in the United States, while producing one every 45 seconds for years and years.

And what a car it was! With its high clearance and planetary transmission, the Tin Lizzie went anywhere, through mud and snow, on roads or off them. Drummers hauled their wares in it; farmers plowed with it, or jacked up one wheel and used it to drive threshing machines. It inspired poems:

> *Yes, Tin, Tin, Tin,*
> *You exasperating puzzle, Hunka Tin,*
> *I've abused you and I've flayed you,*
> *But by Henry Ford who made you,*
> *You are better than a Packard, Hunka Tin.*

jokes:

> *"Why is Henry Ford a better evangelist than Billy Sunday?"*
> *"Because he's shaken hell out of more people than Billy ever did."*

"Lizzie Labels" that festooned the car with:

"Barnum was right"

"You may pass me, bigboy, but I'm paid for"

"Follow us, farmer, for haywire"

"Girls, watch your step ins"

and great tales of running repairs made with chewing gum, bobby pins, and baling wire.

The car could, in fact, be disassembled with the tool kit of pliers, screwdriver, and adjustable wrench that accompanied it from the factory. Once located, the defective parts could, like parts from McCormick's machines, be taken to the dealer and exchanged for new ones. The Model T thus not only established the peculiar American tradition of the automobile as personal billboard (only in America are bumper stickers a commonplace), but also made a rudimentary knowledge of automobile mechanics part of the socialization process undergone by virtually every American male. (A former World War II German *Landser* once told me of his amazement at learning, when taken prisoner by the American army, that nearly every G.I. was mechanic enough to keep jeeps and trucks moving. In his unit, broken-down vehicles had sat for days waiting for the mechanic to arrive.)

On a weightier plane, the Model T called whole industries into being to build highways, vulcanize tires, and refine gasoline. Auto workers' wages, as Ford predicted, nourished service businesses and helped create a market for other mass-produced consumer goods — washing machines, refrigerators, electric irons, indoor plumbing, sewing machines. No wonder that Edison, asked by the New York *World* to comment on the $5 a day, replied, "Let the public throw bouquets to the inventors and in time we will all be happy."

Ford himself, of course, grew wondrously rich and persuaded of his wisdom in all things. The best thing about his system, he frequently boasted, was that making money was an inevitable by-product of the company's main purpose, "to do good." "Your controlling feature," he was once asked, "since you have all the money you want, is to employ a great army of men at high wages, to reduce the selling price of your car so that a lot of people can buy it at a cheap price, and give everybody a car that wants one?" "If you can do all that," Ford declared, "the money will fall into your hands; you can't get out of it."

It could not, of course, go on forever. By 1927 the Model T had saturated the market for utility cars at any price. The very prosperity that Ford had done so much to generate had created a new kind of market that he didn't understand, a market made up of people who could afford to buy cars with features they wanted, whether they needed them or not. More and more people demanded warm, closed cars, with self-starters and soft seats, in a variety of colors. Those who would settle for less had an enormous supply of used Model T's to draw on. General Motors, guided by Alfred Sloan's clear perception of this new demand, supplied it and stimulated it, presenting Ford with a challenge to which he could not, or would not, muster an adequate response.

The Henry Ford of 1927 was not the Henry Ford of 1903. The man was now sixty-four years old, wealthy beyond impoverishment, and rigidly set in his ways. He professed not to know what Chevrolet was doing. "What's more, I don't care," he added. In 1927 he closed down River Rouge for a year while he designed a new car, the Model A, and retooled his plants to produce it. The shutdown presented his competitors with the entire automobile market, including the lowest priced segment, which Sloan had hitherto conceded to Ford for years to come, if not for perpetuity.

The Model A regained some of the lost ground, but its fixed design soon fell back in the market under the onslaught of the annual model changes adopted by General Motors and Chrysler. In 1932, Ford brought out the V-8, his last significant innovation. By that time his company had fallen to third place, and the country had descended to the depths of the Depression. Sales, which had reached 1.7 million Model T's in 1923 and 1.4 million Model A's in 1929, fell to 325,000 V-8's in 1933. At this sales level, the massive, vertically integrated structure, efficient only when car production ran full blast, became an albatross of costs that obliterated profits. Between 1927 and 1933, Ford lost almost $85 million.

The Depression bewildered Ford. The time-honored strategy of combating falling demand by cutting prices had always worked during previous slumps, including one in the year 1920–1921 that nearly bankrupted General Motors. Now it brought only more losses. Nothing in Ford's experience had prepared him for such a market, and he could think of no way to deal with it (he had, of course, plenty of company in his perplexity). Flailing about, he blamed the hard times on bankers' conspiracies, the laziness of the unemployed; then, aping Hoover's Secretary of the Treasury, Andrew Mellon, he called the Depression "a wholesome thing," which he hoped would last a long time, "otherwise the people wouldn't profit by the illness." Finally, he announced that there was no depression: "If we could only realize it," he pontificated, "these are the best times we ever had."

The firm staggered on through the Depression, continuing to lose money, but held together by its $600 million bank account, the loyalty of its die-hard customers, and the quality of the V-8 engine. Remaining old-timers like Martin and Sorenson kept the line running; Harry Bennett and the Depression kept the workers running on the line. Above the shop floor the company was a shambles and an increasingly obsolete one at that. Ford had no cost accounting system worthy of the name, no market research other than dealer comments, no system of product development to meet the fiercely efficient competition mounted by its crosstown rival, General Motors.

Henry Ford presided over the chaos with an iron and capricious hand, his mind lapsing more frequently into the twilight of senility. Even in his lucid moments he devoted much of his energy to projects that had nothing to do with the fundamental weaknesses that sapped his company's strength. He lavished attention on his collections of Americana at the Greenfield Village and Henry Ford Museums; he built airplanes and dabbled with dirigibles; he set up small, water-powered shops at outlying villages in Michigan, where farmers could work in the off season making Ford parts.

When the war came, Sorenson turned the Ford system to the building of bombers, and built thousands of them. The war exacted a heavy toll from the company's dwindling managerial resources. Pete Martin died and, in 1943, Edsel, the son Henry had given a million dollars in gold as a twenty-first birthday present, but could never quite bring himself to entrust with the company, died. In 1944 Ford fired Sorenson, the last of the original pioneers.

Peace found the Ford Motor Company in desperate straits, its plants and products obsolete, its labor force ferociously antagonistic, its management in the hands of a senile octogenarian and the vicious corporal of a goon-squad guard. It also had, as time showed, more assets than met the eye: enormous cash resources, a postwar market willing and eager to buy any car that could be made after a four-year interruption, and, above all, the founder's grandson, Henry Ford II, who saw the company as his legacy and vowed not merely to save it, but to return it to its former glory.

Eventually this combination wrought a resurrection by subjecting the Ford production methods to the organizational disciplines perfected by its rivals. The founder did not live to see the good days return to the Rouge; he died in his Dearborn mansion, Fair Lane, on April 7, 1947. The eulogies that followed dwelt on Ford's epitomization of American qualities. "Abraham Lincoln and Ford," read one, "mean America throughout the world — log cabin to White House — machine shop to industrial empire." "Only in America," declared another, "could he have built an empire of such vast extent. . . . Mr. Ford's eighty-three years give us a vivid, bright example of the opportunity in his lifetime. . . . In [this] one man, with his foibles as [with] his wisdom, is summed up the opportunity and the spirit of America."

Many years before, Ford himself was asked by a hostile attorney, bent on embarrassing him, "What was the United States originally?" Ford, pausing to unlimber a jacknife and commence sharpening it on his leather shoe sole, replied, "Land, I reckon." Whatever it was before him (and who could improve on his answer?), he changed it as much as any man who ever lived in it. After Henry Ford, America was never the same again.

The Patriarchal Powdermaker: Pierre du Pont in 1915

7

The Patriarchal Pioneer
Pierre S. du Pont

ONE day in 1940 my father came home and triumphantly announced that he had gotten a job at Du Pont. Thus ended many years of unemployment, underemployment, and misemployment. It had been a soul-lacerating experience for a man (and there were millions like him) whose self-respect required the opportunity to support his family by practicing his trade of sheet-metal work, a skill of which he was justly proud. It was quite a job he'd found: Du Pont, accepting his credentials as a master craftsman, started him at the top rate for mechanics, more than doubling what he'd earned on his previous job. Better yet, he announced, "Du Pont never lays anybody off. It's a lifetime job." And so it proved; he never lost a day until he retired thirty years later. In the interim he repaid the company's fidelity by going to work through fair weather and foul, in sickness and in health.

Giddy with new-found prosperity, the Livesay family put on a microeconomic demonstration of the power of employment to stimulate business, building a house, buying a car (a Ford, of course), journeying to the supermarket on Saturday night for the week's groceries (meat! butter! ice cream!), then riding around like rich folks, listening to Mark Warno and "Your Lucky Strike Hit Parade." My father, who always had a nice sense of the ludicrous, particularly enjoyed hearing the Metropolitan Opera's Lawrence Tibbett sing "Don't Fence Me In." While I had only a dim sense of the implications of the Depression, I certainly knew that when it ended my father became a lot more fun to live with.

I didn't know it at the time, but we owed our salvation, ironically enough, to Adolf Hitler, whose blitzkrieg had sent the British and French scurrying for massive supplies of gunpowder. Du Pont, as it had twenty-five years before, responded quickly to the call of crowns and pounds and guineas. It threw together a cannon-powder plant in New Albany, Indiana, across the river from our Louisville home. It was a hell of a way to end the Depression and a brutal means of discovering the validity of John Maynard Keynes's theories of government deficit spending to counter recessions, but the Livesays, like millions of their fellow citizens, were in no mood to quibble over what were then abstractions. We were too busy enjoying the upsurge in our fortunes.

The Du Pont presence in my life took a quantum jump after the Second World War. Following his discharge from the U.S. Navy, my father reported back to Du Pont. The demand for gunpowder having dried up and the Indiana plant with it, the company assigned him to its Chambers Works plant at Deepwater, New Jersey. There I found that Du Pont, which hitherto had simply been the place my father worked, now penetrated my entire environment, for the company dominated Deepwater and the neighboring communities as totally as, albeit more benevolently than, any cotton mill ever dominated a southern hamlet or New England town.

Everyone worked for Du Pont, or for businesses that depended on people who did. Social structures and residential patterns were a function of one's position with the company. Adults played at the Du Pont Country Club; children at the Du Pont YMCA. Much of the population lived in company-owned houses. Some boys came to high school wearing street-style safety shoes, bought for them by their fathers at the plant store, a humiliation almost too great to be endured.

The company permeated not only the community's social and economic atmosphere, but also the very air it breathed. Most of the time the area for miles around the Chambers Works was suffused with a stench so monumental that it was often difficult to eat. Complaints — to parents or to local authorities; no one complained to the company — were usually met with a retort on the order of, "You're eatin', ain't ya?"

I soon found that the company also defined the aspirations of most of the boys in high school. (I can't remember that anyone worried about what the girls would do.) All but a handful of the boys expected to go "into the service" or "to the plant," and the company duly absorbed most of each year's graduating class. Du Pont was regarded as a benevolent employer, indeed almost like Japanese firms in providing lifetime security and total care without demanding too much in return. The reputation was deserved. When, on a whim, I went to my twenty-fifth high-school class reunion and asked my classmates what they were doing, most of them replied, "Still messin' around down the plant." They knew they needn't elaborate.

Most high-school discussions about career plans revolved not around whether one would work for the company, but how to avoid certain legendarily unpleasant operations within the plant. Among these were some dye manufacturing operations where, it was widely believed, one's skin gradually turned the color of the product; the tetraethyl lead area, where people sometimes went mad and were spirited away to God-knew-where; and, above all, those operations (no one ever seemed to know for sure just which ones) where workers had to submit to semiannual cystoscopic examinations, rumored to be excruciatingly painful and sometimes to cause impotence.

I escaped this lugubrious lottery by crossing the river into Delaware and going to work for the railroad. My father's lifelong love for trains, unrequited because of the Depression, had passed to me, making me susceptible to the same whistles that had lured Carnegie and Edison. Moving from New Jersey to Delaware was like moving from one of the Duke of Northumberland's coal mines to his hometown, for I found myself surrounded by manifestations of the ducal Du Pont presence. By automobile you could leave Wilmington in three directions, two of them on highways built by Du Ponts. My paycheck said Pennsylvania Railroad, but I deposited it at a Du Pont bank. I read

Du Pont newspapers. I saw plays at a Du Pont–sponsored theatre, listened to the carillon bells on Alfred I. du Pont's estate, strolled among orchids and watched dancing water fountains at Pierre du Pont's botanical garden. The Du Pont Building topped the Wilmington skyline; the best hotel was the Du Pont Hotel. When I went to college, I went to the University of Delaware, itself a recipient of massive Du Pont largesse. Moving on to graduate school, I learned my trade under the masterly and beneficent guiding hand of Alfred D. (for du Pont) Chandler, Jr., whose lifework included systematic analysis of the corporate structures that his family built, structures that had great impact on the broad, sweeping development of American industry and played no lesser role in my own life.

While still in Delaware I myself joined the company for a time, working at night as a laboratory technician at the Du Pont Experimental Station while going to school in the daytime. Edison, although he might have found things too tidy for his taste, would have felt right at home at the Experimental Station, an establishment dedicated to Edison's kind of science — practical, profitable science. The Edison method, however, of having the same team carry a project through from the first glimmering of an idea to the final glow of practical realization had long since been refined at the experimental station. There the labor was subdivided according to type of product and stage of development. Experimental scientists translated ideas into small-scale laboratory processes. If the product looked as though it might have a profitable future, it was taken from the creator's hands and passed on to a team of engineers and technicians, who tried to duplicate laboratory results in factory conditions. If they succeeded, the company acquired the data necessary to make cost projections and to secure patents. With this system Du Pont developed nylon, Orlon, Dacron, Teflon, and a host of other products that kept it in the forefront of the world's chemical manufacturers.

I was personally less intrigued by the company's products than by its personnel policies and the men who carried them out. To a degree that exceeded any example I witnessed before or since,

Du Pont labored continuously to persuade its workers that their fortunes were bound up with the company's, and that the company, big as it was, cared about each of its workers individually and personally. Frontline supervisors carried this policy to the shop floor in two forms: group pep rallies, and conversations with individual workers that invariably began with the boss putting his hand on your shoulder and asking solicitous questions about your personal affairs.

All these theatrics fooled nobody as to their underlying purpose: the company wanted to keep production up and unions out. The workers, nevertheless, tolerated it all with more or less good grace. After all, the company did pay well, never laid anyone off, and fired people so rarely that nobody I worked with could remember when it had happened last. That all this benevolence depended on the company's continuing to make a healthy profit was a fact so obvious that its ceaseless inculcation insulted the meanest intelligence.

In accepting this proposition that their own self-interest and their employer's were identical, my co-workers at Du Pont displayed an attitude characteristic of most American labor throughout the country's history and fundamental to the shape and success of the American business system. Du Pont capitalized upon this attitude, encouraging it with management practices that made their plants more congenial and financially rewarding places to work than the sirocco of a Carnegie Steel mill or the treadmill of a Ford assembly line. Whatever its faults, my colleagues felt, as my father had felt thirty years before, that Du Pont was a company apart, one of the best among American employers.

Certainly the policy that encourages this positive view among its workers is not unique to the Du Pont Company or even unusual today. But in most American industries such policies are relatively recent developments resulting either from employers' learning that enlightened self-interest dictated peaceful labor relations, or from forceful action by labor unions. At Du Pont, in contrast, these policies are as old as the business itself, for they reflect the views of the original founder, Éleuthère Irénée du

Pont de Nemours, who established the company in 1802 as a small powder mill in Delaware. The modern company as I encountered it — huge, diversified — superficially bore little resemblance to the firm in its infancy. But in fact the history of the Du Pont Company involved many continuities besides its personnel policies, the survival of family control foremost among them.

The architect of the modern firm, Pierre S. du Pont, great-grandson of the founder, was a man steeped in family tradition. While transforming the family firm from a powder manufacturer to a diversified international chemical producer, Pierre du Pont created management structures and techniques that were paragons of corporate modernity then and in some senses still are, but he was guided as much by his desire to preserve the good things from the company's past as by his determination to secure its future. Admired, emulated, and studied by practitioners and analysts of the American business system, Pierre's firm remains synonymous with progressive methods in research, development, production, and management.

The company's management itself, at least at the higher levels, retains an awareness of its links to the past. And rightly so, for few firms illustrate more graphically the way in which tomorrow inevitably evolves from yesterday.

The history of the Du Ponts in America began in 1799 when Pierre's great-great-grandfather and namesake, Pierre Samuel du Pont de Nemours, removed his family from the perils of revolutionary France to the haven of post-Revolutionary America. For most fleeing aristocrats emigration meant abandonment of their property and the lifestyle to which it had accustomed them, but the Du Ponts carried with them a portable asset that quickly restored their fortunes in the New World: they knew how to make better gun and blasting powder than anyone in the United States. Both products found a ready and continuing market in a country with a frontier to pacify and mountains to move. The Du Pont powder mill prospered almost from the first day that the original Pierre's son, Éleuthère, opened its doors.

By investing capital, hiring workers, and turning out a needed product, the Du Ponts thus contributed a positive force to the growth of the American economy soon after they arrived. Theirs was not an isolated case; always among the millions of immigrants were many who arrived with talents that could be put to work at once. The newcomers included skilled craftsmen and experienced farmers, as well as technical experts like Samuel Slater and Paul Moody, who brought the secrets of mechanized textile production with them from the mills of old England to those of New England. From its beginnings American industrialization benefited from the presence of these talented immigrants and has continued to do so ever since. By incorporating those who, like Slater and Moody, were drawn by greater personal opportunity, and people like the Du Ponts, who fled political or religious persecution, the American business system acquired at little cost a capital asset of inestimable value. This siphon, which later brought Enrico Fermi and Albert Einstein, among others, to America, continues to flow, as a stroll through the research laboratories of any major corporation will soon demonstrate. (At Du Pont, the man who supervised the project I worked on was an English-born, University of Manchester–trained chemical engineer, who had left England convinced that the doors of British industry would remain forever closed for men like him, the son of a Liverpool bus mechanic.)

Éleuthère du Pont situated his powder mill on the swift-flowing Brandywine at Wilmington, damming the river's flow to supply power for the works. The Brandywine was then, and long remained, one of the centers of American manufacturing. There in the eighteenth century Oliver Evans built the first mechanized, automatic flour mill. Through the first half of the nineteenth century, as business boomed, other mills sprang up along the river's banks, grinding flour and gunpowder, rolling iron plates and paper. Blessed with such a prolific riparian tributary, Wilmington's commerce swelled with firms that furnished shipping, insurance, and banking facilities to the manufacturers upstream, with factories that built mill machinery, and with shipyards that turned the local supply of iron plates to such good advantage that the other Wilmington river, the Christiana, became known as "The American Clyde."

In the heart of this burgeoning valley, the Du Ponts built an enclave of their own consisting of the powder mills, homes for the workers, and, on the high ground above the river, residences for family members. The powder mill community also contained a variety of stores, a doctor, blacksmiths', coopers', and carpenters' shops that made it nearly self-sufficient and independent of its surroundings. Company wagons, shuttling back and forth to Wilmington, provided the necessary connection to the world outside.

Within the company preserve, life developed cohesion and continuity. The company was the family and vice versa. With the exception of a restless handful, male members of the family remained in the valley, knowing from childhood that when the time came, a place in the company's managerial ranks awaited them. The workers' community, too, developed considerable stability as a result of the company's policies. The Du Ponts felt a seigneurial sense of responsibility for their dependents; moreover, powder making required skilled labor to do dangerous work. The company had to be a benevolent employer to attract a labor force and to keep worker turnover low, thereby minimizing loss of life and production. Noblesse oblige thus combined with business pragmatism to dictate the policy of furnishing workers with good housing, providing stores and shops that charged reasonable prices, in addition to the Du Pont practice of paying good wages, providing pensions, and guaranteeing disability or survivors' benefits for the inevitable casualties.

Such self-sufficient communities that centered on a manufacturing establishment were a variation of the centuries-old manorial organization developed in European agriculture and were characteristic of many American manufacturing industries in their formative years. Early entrepreneurs often had to enlist a labor force for their mills and then provide housing and services. The passage of time tended to disintegrate these communities as cities enveloped factories, and urban transportation made it possible for workers to move away from their work. In the nine-teenth century this process overtook the Du Pont community with one exception: the workers moved away from the Brandy-wine enclave, but the family remained — isolated, self-con-tained, relying on each other rather than on outsiders. Pierre du Pont recalled that his father, who was born in 1832 and died in 1885, never had a bank account in all the years he lived along the Brandywine.

Pierre himself was born into this tightly knit community in 1870. Little had changed in the sixty-eight years since the com-pany's founding. Family and firm had expanded, both spreading along the river's banks. The growth of the Brandywine manufac-turing region and the attendant doubling of Wilmington's popu-lation scarcely affected the Du Ponts. Wilmingtonians regarded them as respectable, reclusive, wealthy, and prominent, but by no means the most wealthy or most prominent among Dela-ware's citizens. In fact, among those circles of Wilmington so-ciety whose eminence and wealth dated back to colonial times, the Du Ponts were regarded as parvenus. The community opin-ion was of no consequence to Pierre. Like most Du Pont children before him, he remained within the confines of the family reser-vation, taught by governesses in his home, swimming in the Brandywine, finding his playmates among his cousins and the ten younger brothers and sisters who arrived in rapid succession.

Although some of his uncles and cousins found a life circum-scribed by the family circle confining and broke away, Pierre himself drew comfort and reassurance from the family's solidar-ity. Shy to a fault ("For fault it is," he himself admitted) as a boy, he remained so, reflecting later in life: "I myself have been aware of my shyness since earliest childhood." Although the twists and turns of his career took him far afield, he remained always a Brandywine Du Pont, gravitating toward the reassurance of fa-miliar surroundings; once returned there for good, he labored to perpetuate the environment that had nourished him in child-hood. Even in matrimony he stayed within the familiar circle, marrying his first cousin Alice Belin in 1915.

As the son of Lammot–du Pont, first lieutenant to General

Henry du Pont, senior partner in the firm, the young Pierre had good reason to contemplate the future with equanimity, promising as it did to carry him along the well-worn path to the upper reaches of the company's hierarchy, if not to its very top. In 1880, however, Lammot du Pont burst free of the family cocoon. Convinced that the future lay in the manufacture of dynamite, not black powder, and frustrated in his attempts to convince General Henry to change the company's policy accordingly, Lammot decided to establish his own business, the Repauno Chemical Company, to manufacture the new explosive. By selling his interest in the family partnership, Lammot raised one third of the capital; the other two thirds came from the Du Pont Company itself, and from Laflin & Rand Powder Company, one of Du Pont's friendly competitors. The dynamite works had to be located in an unpopulated area. Lammot chose a site in the swamps of New Jersey, directly across the Delaware River from Chester, Pennsylvania, midway between Wilmington and Philadelphia.

Having removed himself from the company's affairs, Lammot thought it symbolically important to remove his family as well. In the spring of 1881, Pierre's mother told him the family was moving to Philadelphia. The news, which meant that Pierre must soon confront an alien world, came as a shock. "No order of banishment could have been more sorrowfully received," he recalled.

In Philadelphia, Pierre attended Penn Charter School, where he established a record of inconspicuous excellence, earning the nickname "Graveyard" from his classmates. In the Quaker atmosphere that pervaded Penn Charter, Pierre absorbed a tolerance for divergent religious views, a respect for theology as an ethical system, but a profound and enduring skepticism toward all brands of religious mysticism.

In March 1884, the Repauno plant blew up, killing Pierre's father, leaving Pierre, at age fourteen, the male head of the family, a responsibility he accepted gravely and fulfilled for many years. His father's death also brought Pierre under the influence of the man who became his guardian, Alfred Victor du Pont, a resident of Kentucky. Unlike the Brandywine Du Ponts, most of whom considered an apprenticeship at the mill an appropriate and sufficient education for any powder man, Alfred Victor advocated a technical education. Back on the Brandywine, General Henry might rest content with methods that sufficed for generations, but from his better vantage point, Pierre's guardian watched as the fusion of systematic science with manufacturing replaced the rough and ready methods of the past. Alfred Victor's own business interests, which included converting horsecar lines to electricity and manufacturing steel rails for city railways, involved him in industries where science made swift inroads. What Carnegie's chemist Dr. Fricke and Edison's mathematician Francis Upton had done in steel and electricity, others must soon do across the whole spectrum of American industry, making it an example of Louis Pasteur's maxim that "science and the applications of science [are] bound together as the fruit of the tree that bears it."

Persuaded by his guardian's logic, Pierre followed three of his cousins to the Massachusetts Institute of Technology. Quiet and studious, his timidity with strangers eased by the presence of cousins and younger brothers at nearby colleges and prep schools, Pierre did well at MIT, graduating in 1890. Although he left college with some regret, Pierre rejoiced that his long exile was over and he could now launch the only career he had ever seriously contemplated, a job with the family firm.

On September 1, 1890, Pierre went to work at the Upper Powder Yard on the Brandywine, a beginning he regarded as appropriate and auspicious: "This is where my father, grandfather and great-grandfather had entered the company's employ." His mother intensified the sense of homecoming. Delighted to rejoin her family and friends, she moved from Philadelphia, reestablishing the family seat on its original Delaware soil.

Satisfied though he was that the elements of his life had been restored to their proper niches, his experiences at the mill soon raised doubt that swelled to disenchantment. His official duties were light and inconsequential, leaving Pierre free to roam the works. Measuring the firm's equipment with his MIT-trained eye, he found it disconcertingly primitive:

The laboratory, so-called, was in deplorable condition. . . . Equipment was almost nothing. A common kitchen range and one small spirit lamp were the only means of heating for chemical work. No gas or electrical facilities, in a common kitchen sink and one ordinary . . . tap the water supply. Distilled water came from . . . the refinery; the workmen called it "still-water" which referred more to its escape from ill treatment . . . than to any attained purity. Any unusual impurity was accounted for by the words "She must have boiled over." The laboratory contained no chemical reagents for making ordinary tests. Any chemical apparatus was equally deficient in quantity or selection. The chemical balance did not deign to respond to the added weight of a few milligrams, but as it was customary to select weights by hand without the use of forceps the rough operation of weighing powder samples for drying was sufficiently well accomplished.

Everything at the Brandywine mills was "sufficiently well accomplished" to suit the old-line management and was accomplished by equipment that everywhere duplicated the antiquity and obsolescence of the laboratory. Disquieting as Pierre found all these anachronisms, the head of the firm, Eugene du Pont, General Henry's successor, cherished them, as mountaineers did the old-time religion, as "good for our fathers and good enough for me." This complacency derived from the nature of the powder business, for here was no steel industry, no fiercely competitive Carnegie cutting prices to scoop the market. Instead, the powder market of the United States was tightly controlled by a cozy cartel, the Gunpowder Trade Association (one of the few that ever worked in the United States) that set prices and allocated production quotas. As one of the first in the field, and as one of the largest, Du Pont's share had always been big enough to assure prosperity for the firm and wealth for its owners. Du Pont, Laflin & Rand, and other major firms maintained order by buying one another's stock, thereby acquiring a voice in each other's management and access to their books, which made it impossible to violate price and market agreements and get away with it.

With its market assured through control and allocation, Du Pont felt little need of new products or better methods of production. The laboratory was a place for testing, not research; cost accounting could be perfunctory, since a cursory knowledge of costs sufficed. Pierre thus found the powder business, as Carnegie had found the iron business forty years before, a "lump business, run the same way since time immemorial."

The older generation proved unreceptive to suggestions from Pierre and his contemporaries. His younger brother Belin, also an MIT graduate, wrote Pierre in disgust that "even if the [plant] should burn down, they would probably build it up just as it is now or if any changes were made I am sure I would not be consulted." Later, Belin added, "there will be only one way of your doing . . . well with [the company] and that is: eventually becoming the head of the business and changing their entire business methods, so that the business will have a chance of making money as it should."

Pierre's elders could not fathom the restlessness and impatience that afflicted his generation. Younger Du Ponts should do as younger Du Ponts had always done: bide their time and await their inevitable accession to power. In 1899, when he demanded a partnership and an executive position, Pierre reported that "Cousin Eugene simply said that [someday] when things were organized there would be several good places to be filled and thought that I could fill any of them. No special place was mentioned and no salary offered or any mention of giving or selling me an interest in the company."

In the nine years that he had spent with the company, Pierre had made no progress except insofar as his elders had moved inexorably that much closer to their final resting places. His frustrations were intensified by the fact that in the intervening years he had supplemented the skills learned at MIT by acquiring a fundamental understanding of the world of finance and cost-based management methods. These additions had come as a result of his guardian's death in 1893, which made Pierre trustee of his younger brothers' and sisters' estates, a stockholder in Alfred Victor's enterprises, and an associate of his guardian's partners in the steel rail business, Tom Johnson and Arthur Moxham. Johnson tutored Pierre in the mysteries of investment, explaining different kinds of securities and the workings of the stock market, an education Pierre badly needed, for when he had become trustee of his siblings' estates, he recalled, he "hardly knew the difference between a ledger book and leger de-main."

Arthur Moxham, president of the Johnson Company (as the steel rail firm was called) introduced Pierre to the Carnegie method of management. Moxham, Pierre related, "was a master of cost sheets and orderly management. He visited his plant frequently and was interested in details but was always accompanied by the line man in charge through whom every question or recommendation passed. His cost sheets were fascinating. . . ." Part of the fascination stemmed from the fact that Moxham could easily disaggregate the company's gross revenues and expenses, showing what contribution each operation made to the overall result. Nothing like this had penetrated the musty accounting houses on the Brandywine, but Pierre "became hopeful that the business of [the] Du Pont Company could be presented in such clear manner."

Moxham's cost sheets "proved" that the Johnson Company should move from Johnstown, Pennsylvania, to Lorain, Ohio, buy a large tract of land, and erect a new mill. Johnson's choice of location was probably sound enough, for Carnegie and Schwab chose it seven years later as the site for a new pipe mill, but Moxham's plans tripped over the economic stringencies of the Depression of 1893, which confounded normal American optimism by worsening as the years passed.

In January, 1896, the Johnson Company teetered on the brink of bankruptcy, its ambitious plans stymied by the weakness that so often felled fledgling American business, a shortage of working capital. Potentially the firm embodied all the components necessary for long-run success: it had products — steel rails and electric traction motors — certain to be demanded by the booming street railway and interurban industry; it had a new mill and the patents, technical expertise, and management skills requisite to efficient production. These assets augured well for the future, but only if the company could survive the present by finding the cash necessary to pay the current bills. Pierre's cousin, Coleman du Pont, superintendent of construction at Lorain, wrote him that the firm had to find $750,000 and find it in a hurry. Coleman asked Pierre to come up with $100,000 somehow.

With much of his own and his siblings' estates invested in Johnson Company securities, Pierre turned to willingly enough. He found the money at two local banks that did business with the Du Pont Company. For the next two years the two cousins scrambled to keep the Johnson Company afloat, Pierre scurrying about renewing loans in Wilmington, while Coleman tried to raise production and efficiency in Lorain, even bringing in the great guru of the efficiency cult, Frederick W. Taylor, in a vain attempt to wring profits out of minimal production.

Despite these energetic efforts, the future still remained problematical when, in 1898, salvation of a sort appeared in the form of J. P. Morgan's latest Frankenstein monster, Federal Steel. By having his creature devour a large if indiscriminate diet of independent steel producers, Morgan hoped to force-feed Federal Steel into a giant big enough to challenge Carnegie. The Johnson chieftains unloaded their mill on this corporate glutton, retaining only their real estate and an electric railway.

In the transaction, Pierre sustained a financial loss, receiving only $28,000 for securities nominally worth $120,000. But he and Coleman had gained experience that subsequently more than compensated for their misfortune. Pierre had learned the virtues of cost accounting as a management tool and the perils of insufficient working capital; Coleman had run a large industrial enterprise and had learned efficiency engineering from its foremost apostle.

Four years later, in 1902, the cousins got an unexpected opportunity to put their hard-won knowledge to practice on the Du Pont Company. In 1902 Du Pont found itself in a predicament that beset virtually every American family firm at one time or another: the senior partners were weary and anxious to retire, but either had no heirs, like Carnegie, or thought the younger generation ill suited or ill prepared to take over. One younger Du Pont, Alfred I., another of Pierre's innumerable cousins, had acquired a seat on the board of directors and a partnership in the firm, but the senior members had "formed an exceedingly low estimate of Alfred['s] good judgment and business ability." Coleman had the necessary qualifications, but certain family rivalries precluded him. At this critical juncture in their lives family firms usually expired, either selling out to a competitor, as Eli Whitney's heirs sold to Winchester; diluting their ownership by selling large blocks of stock to the public, as Edison's sons did; or succumbing to the ardent advances of trust-builders like Morgan, as did Carnegie and the McCormicks. Whichever course was taken, family ownership invariably receded, and family management usually terminated.

The crisis of succession had come to different families at different times: to Carnegie's after one generation; to McCormick's and Edison's, after two; Whitney's lasted three. At some point, however, the day seemed inevitably to arrive when even the most fecund industrial families could not perpetuate their dynasties. Through one of those fascinating interactions of events that historians love to examine but can rarely explain, an extraordinary number of American business families arrived at this critical turning point simultaneously at the turn of the century. This factor, among others, accounted for the disappearance of more than 2,600 individual firms between 1898 and 1902 and, together with a swelling concern for the consequence to individual Americans of the ending of the frontier and the abuses of big business, contributed to the fin de siècle mentality of despair, rooted in a sense of loss.

The Du Pont Company, which by 1902 could look back on a century of unbroken family domination, presented an unusual case of longevity, but it now seemed certain to join the anonymous multitudes. Despairing of an internal solution, the directors entertained a motion to sell to their largest competitor, Laflin & Rand. Alfred, whose alleged limitations blocked him from succession in his own right, managed to amend the motion so that it called for sale "to the highest bidder." He then announced to his startled colleagues that he himself would buy the business. One of his shocked elders told him that he simply could not have the company. "Why not?" Alfred demanded. "I pointed out," Alfred said later, "the fact that the business was mine by all rights of heritage, that it was my birthright; I told him that I would pay as much as anybody else, and furthermore, I proposed to have it."

This appeal to family tradition rallied Colonel Henry du Pont to Alfred's support: "Gentlemen, I think I understand Alfred's possessive sentiment in desiring to purchase the business, and I wish to say that it has my hearty approval, and I shall insist that he be given the first opportunity to acquire the property." Pulling Alfred aside, he said, "I assume of course, although you said nothing about it, that . . . Coleman and Pierre are, or will be, associated with you in the proposed purchase?" Told that they would, the Colonel added, "With the understanding that Coleman and Pierre are associated with you in the proposition I assent to it most cordially and will do everything in my power to bring it about."

Alfred, whose role in the company diminished almost from the moment the sale was consummated, had planned carefully, struck hard at the appropriate instant, and preserved the company as a family firm. When he had approached his two cousins about joining him in the purchase, Alfred had found enthusiastic allies, but allies whose awareness of Alfred's own limitations as a businessman led them to set certain conditions. Coleman told Alfred that he would participate, but only if he himself got the largest block of stock, assumed the presidency, and could bring in Pierre as treasurer to manage the firm's financial affairs. Pierre, who had left his time-serving job with Du Pont in 1899 to preside over the liquidation of the Johnson Company's remaining assets, and then moved on to buy a street railway in Dallas, jumped at the chance to play a major role in the future of the company that he too considered his birthright. Telling his brothers the good news, Pierre wrote, "The wheel of fortune has been revolving at pretty high speed on the Brandy Wine during the last week or two with the result that Coleman and Alfred and I have made E. I. du Pont & Co., an offer to buy out their property and I today received verbal acceptance of the proposition. . . . I think there is to be some tall hustling to get everything reorganized. We have not the slightest idea of what we are buying, but in that we are probably not at a disadvantage as I think the old company has a very slim idea of the property they possess."

The older generation's pleasure at keeping the firm within the family, and the younger generation's belief that the company had a profit potential far beyond anything achieved by its conservative management combined to facilitate the practical arrangements of the sale. Both parties agreed on a price of $12 million, to be paid by exchanging bonds for the outstanding stock held by family members. Twenty million dollars' worth of stock was then issued and divided among the three new owners. This arrangement promised the sellers a continued income at the established level (as investors they wanted assured income, not return of the principal) and gave the buyers complete control of the company without their having to raise any cash. Whether the young cousins' stock would have any real value depended entirely on their abilities to wring increased income from the property. This they at once set out to do, first taking an inventory to find out just what in fact they had bought. Alfred returned to his accustomed post supervising production at the powder mill. Coleman and Pierre surveyed the company's properties. These by then included additional mills in Iowa, Pennsylvania, Tennessee, and New Jersey, each operating more or less independently of the Delaware facility, with much duplication of effort.

The cousins soon decided to buy up their major competitors, beginning with Laflin & Rand. That erstwhile competitor was in the midst of a succession crisis of its own. The terms of sale followed the pattern established by the original Du Pont transaction: a combination of bonds and stocks that gave the former owners income and the new owners control without any cash changing hands. Once the Du Ponts had their largest competitor, the others fell over like a row of dominoes. Certain opportunists, however, carpentered together new firms overnight, hoping for lucrative sales to the emerging power trust. As one Du Pont executive wryly observed, the belief had become widespread that "there [was] no better investment than to 'sell to the Trust.' " The young Du Ponts assiduously avoided such dubious bargains. Within two years, nevertheless, they had sufficient plant to supply 60 percent of the explosives market. The reason for the 60 percent limit (the same target set for United States Steel by its chairman, Judge Elbert Gary) went beyond mere avoidance of possible antitrust prosecution. Arthur Moxham had at Pierre's behest brought his steel-industry expertise to the new powder company. His explanation of the 60 percent limit reveals the rich Carnegie heritage in American manufacturing philosophy: "If we could by any measure buy out all competition and have an absolute monopoly in the field, it would not pay us." Moxham knew that future demand for explosives might prove highly "variable." Ownership of all capacity would mean that "when slack came [Du Pont] would have to curtail product to the extent of diminished demands." It was better, he continued, to "control only sixty percent of it all and [make] that sixty percent cheaper than the others." Then, when "slack times came we could still keep *our* capital employed to *the full.*" As Carnegie had once urged his subordinates to "cut the price, scoop the market, run full," now Moxham declared, "If you make cheaply . . . you [can] count upon always running full."

The next chore was guaranteeing efficient production. The cousins set about whipping their facilities, which ranged from the efficient to the ragtag and bobtail, into a profitable consolidation. They created a hierarchical, bureaucratic management structure and found people to staff it. Committees and departments specialized in particular functions such as finance, or products such as black powder, dynamite, or smokeless powder. They brought in an auditor from the steel industry to adapt its cost sheets and other accounting devices for use in the powder business. Once developed, such cost sheets soon exposed inefficient plants, which were closed, and inept employees, who were fired.

There were howls of protest from individualists used to doing things their own way in an old-fashioned business. The cousins, confident of their course, steamrolled over all objections. Subordinates who tried to buck the company's new auditors were told to shape up or ship out. To keep the company in the forefront of technological developments, a permanent development department was set up and soon subdivided into three divisions: Competitive Products, Raw Materials, and, most important of all, Experimental. Within two years, then, the cousins had brought off a corporate revolution, one that constituted a unique combination of traditional and modern aspects of American business. As in the past, traditional family ownership continued, but the three principal owners had become corporate managers.

So it was that the accumulated wisdom and experience of America's industrial pioneers was used to transfuse new life into the old company on the Brandywine. With its streamlined organization, standardized, companywide procedures, and updated research and development departments, Du Pont achieved a modernity matched only by firms in the electrical industry. Almost overnight it had metamorphosed from an anachronism into a firm capable of pioneering on its own.

Alfred remained content to limit his horizons to black powder production. Coleman developed a tendency to divert his energies to politics and to outside investments, a proclivity that intensified as the years passed. Pierre came to serve as the chief architect of the company's continuing transformation. Pierre found no contradiction in the combination of traditional ownership with modern management. Indeed, preserving family control remained his first priority. It dictated a policy of conservative financial management coupled with hard-nosed operating efficiency.

The demands of such efficiency soon carried Pierre beyond cost sheets and organization charts. He had to restructure the family's relationship to the firm, retaining the clan as the company's principal capital resource while discontinuing the long-standing practice of automatically promoting family members to management. Not that all the company's top jobs went to talented outsiders. Pierre fiercely believed that a Du Pont should always head the Du Pont Company; moreover, no organization chart, not even Du Pont's, is wholly proof against nepotism. He insisted, however, that a family member's performance on the job, not his family status, should determine his position. Thus the

Du Pont Company would not be headed by the best man around, but rather by the best of the Du Ponts, who, given the family's size, should be more than good enough.

Sidetracking some family members, while drawing from the ranks of numerous Du Pont in-laws, Pierre created a respectable talent pool. Maintaining the family's solidarity behind the firm while reshuffling its members' roles demanded an evenhanded diplomacy for which Pierre's temperament singularly qualified him. A stellar performance from the company itself was also needed, for nothing was so calculated to maintain peace as a steady flow of dividends. A high return on investment with minimal use of outside capital became the guiding principle by which current operations and future projects were judged. Every project had to fortify the company's capital pool by providing for high dividends, as well as substantial retained earnings. Expansion and modernization, as well as diversification into other products, all demanded by Pierre's aggressive subordinates, went forward only as the company and the family together could supply the necessary capital. Even expansion of output required careful planning because of its drain on working capital. Pierre's experience with the Johnson Company had shown him how such a drain could undermine even a solidly based firm. He preferred passing up tempting market opportunities to borrowing short-term capital at ruinous rates. "The impairment of working capital," he told his associates in 1904, "will be credit suicide and the shortest road to financial embarrassment."

Translating such conservative, family-oriented finance into company policy proved no easy task. Demands for capital strained the combined resources of the family and firm. Keeping costs down required not only modernization but also vertical integration to reduce the cost of raw materials, say, by buying nitrate mines and manufacturing acids. Confronted by these and a bewildering array of other demands for capital, Pierre followed a plan analogous to Carnegie's. He and the executive committee delegated the authority over daily operations to department managers and their subordinates, then relied on statistical controls to evaluate the results. The departments had wide and unfettered discretion to solve quotidian problems, including labor disputes. But anything that required a significant capital expenditure required executive committee approval. Such capital demands taken together always exceeded the company's resources. Some method had to be devised to evaluate each. For Pierre, return on investment remained the overriding consideration. This meant that efficiency, not volume, must prevail. The company, Pierre thought, must give preference "to such improvements as will furnish cheaper raw material or cheaper production leaving as a second consideration the actual increase in the volume of business."

By declaring that the company must invest its money where the money would produce the greatest return whether or not an increase in production resulted, Pierre du Pont, so it happened, had arrived at one of the fundamental rules for the survival of a business in a capitalist economy. In the economy as a whole, demands for capital almost always exceed the supply. Consequently, capital flows from areas of low return to more promising sectors. A firm must use its capital to finance efficiency while shutting down inefficient plant or else eventually go under, unless rescued by outside intervention. These days, succor, in the form of the federal government, sometimes arrives to prevent bankruptcy, especially for firms such as Lockheed or the Penn Central Railroad, whose collapse might have unacceptable political, economic, or military consequences. In Pierre's time, no company was thought indispensable, nor was the federal government in the rescue business.

On the contrary, Du Pont faced an indifferent, sometimes downright hostile, government. Du Pont had long furnished most of the powder bought for the United States armed forces. It soon found itself, however, losing the privileged position enjoyed by major arms contractors since Eli Whitney's time. In 1906 the company was branded publicly as the "Powder Trust," and subjected to the same attacks that befell other corporations similarly defined. The next year the government launched an antitrust suit that eventually forced Du Pont to divest itself of significant holdings, in the process creating two new competitors, the Atlas Powder Company and the Hercules Powder Company. In 1908 Congress compounded the threat by authorizing expansion of the government's own powder manufacturing capacity. The government's two-pronged assault against his company hardened Pierre's conviction that every Du Pont dollar must be spent where it would do the most good.

The company's relatively small size invited ever-greater caution. Du Pont's domination of the explosives market made it a dangerous trust in the eyes of both the public and antitrust prosecutors, but in actual size it was a relatively puny member of that despised category. Prior to 1915, Du Pont's capitalization never exceeded $63 million, minuscule compared to the billions of dollars tied up in United States Steel, Standard Oil, American Tobacco, and other giants. As late as 1914, its gross receipts totaled less than the *net profit* made by Carnegie Steel in 1900. The company was in no position to afford unproductive investments. Pierre's strict evaluation of capital expenditures in terms of probable return made good general business sense; it also reflected the realities of his company's situation.

Maintaining investment profitability meant predicting both future costs and prices. Du Pont's cost-accounting techniques and experience in the explosives business allowed the company to forecast manufacturing costs with tolerable accuracy. Forecasting prices, however, was another matter altogether. It required predicting market behavior, an art that to most American business seemed as mystical as voodoo. Carnegie, with no stockholders to placate, had been free to "take [the] orders East and West" that kept his mills "running full" until the market rebounded. Ford, blissfully ignorant of his costs, had pushed production while trusting efficiency to produce profits whatever the price. For Pierre du Pont, cautious by nature and especially about family financial resources, such nineteenth-century attitudes smacked of folly and courted suicide.

Past experience had shown American businessmen the difficulties of controlling the market; antitrust laws had made it an offense even to try. But what could not be controlled, Pierre thought, might nevertheless be predicted. From the outset, Pierre himself prepared forecasts of the company's profits for the year ahead, translating these into estimates of the amount of money available for capital investment. He demanded estimates of future capital requirements from his department heads, assuming that such estimates would rest on predictions of future market behavior. Unsurprisingly, the first efforts were primitive. In 1906, for example, Hamilton Barksdale requested an appropriation to expand the company's dynamite capacity. Barksdale forecast the dynamite market by simply taking actual sales in 1905 and adding a 15 percent increase every year through 1909. Time and practice, however, upgraded market forecasting to a viable management tool, if not to an exact science. Data were collected to test the accuracy of past predictions, and future forecasts revised accordingly. Pierre's insistence made market forecasting an integral tool of Du Pont's management strategy. After the fashion of other successful techniques, it was taken up by other industries to become an important component of the American system of management. Pierre du Pont's obsession with maintaining his family's control had thus led directly to one of the last significant additions to modern American management methods.

Under such guidance the Du Pont Company expanded from its modest beginnings in 1902 to become one of the world's ten largest corporations. It diversified from explosives to the manufacture of hundreds of other products, yet, as generations of managers passed through the company's offices, the carefully estimated rates of return on investment remained their guiding principle. Market forecasting and a management structure that combined centralized financial control with decentralized operations helped Pierre du Pont run a big firm efficiently and profitably in a fluctuating, highly competitive market. Just how big and efficient these firms could become, a subsequent generation would demonstrate at Du Pont and General Motors.

Du Pont, however, under Pierre's restraining hand, grew slowly until the enormous profits of the First World War provided an unexpected infusion of capital. From 1904 to 1912, the company's annual gross receipts rose from 26 to 36 million dollars. In 1913, after the court-ordered dissolution that created Hercules and Atlas, business fell to 27 million dollars. In 1916, the European slaughter multiplied receipts twelvefold, to 319 million dollars. Altogether between 1914 and 1918, the company's sales totaled 1.1 billion dollars: net profits, according to the company's figures, totaled 238 million dollars. (It may in fact have been more; the Nye Committee, which investigated the munitions industry, thought so. Pierre, testifying in 1934, laconically told the inquisitorial senators, "I am not trying to fight the figures, because no matter what the figures are, the profit was very large.") Indeed it was. So large, in fact, that the company's earlier lean capital diet gave way to an investment banquet that vastly exceeded any conceivable needs of the explosives business. Soon Du Pont had a controlling interest in General Motors as well as its own full-scale diversification program.

Pierre met the wartime bonanza with customary wariness. Like most American businessmen, he thought the war not a harbinger of prosperity but an unwelcome interruption to business stability. His view also reflected the company's past experience. Spain's sudden collapse during the Spanish-American War had stuck Du Pont with expanded facilities, warehouses full of unsold powder, and canceled contracts. The outbreak of World War I brought an immediate decline in business. The company sold less in 1914 than it had the year before. The Du Ponts, along with much of the rest of the world, expected the fighting to end quickly. In August, 1914, Pierre's brother wrote an executive of an English dynamite company, "I do hope this unfortunate war will soon be over and appreciate that it must be more of an inconvenience to you than to us." The same month, the company approved the expenditure of a paltry sixteen thousand dollars to expand smokeless powder capacity, stipulating that the money be spent only after "the receipt . . . of large additional orders for Smokeless Powder either from Foreign Governments or our own government."

Even when the war raged on and large orders materialized, Pierre held fiercely to his conservative approach. Sentiment remained secondary to profits; indeed, Pierre declared himself ready to sell to all comers, provided the company's terms were met. In February, 1915, he wrote Coleman that should the Germans become "forward with orders in quantity similar to the orders of the Allied Nations [Du Pont] would be willing to sell." With the Allies, Pierre drove hard bargains to assure a copious return on wartime investment. A French contract for eight million pounds of cannon powder brought one dollar a pound, twice the price charged the United States government. Furthermore, Pierre demanded 50 percent in advance, 30 percent when the powder was ready for the drying house, and the final 20 percent before shipment. Such terms forced the French to supply all capital necessary for expansion while guaranteeing that the company would be paid for all finished orders even if the war ended unexpectedly. Throughout four years of war, though the price declined, the terms remained essentially the same.

The Allies thus financed a massive expansion, not only of the company's facilities, but also of its labor force, particularly among the engineers who designed and built the new plants. Pierre also initiated an aggressive program to insure that the expanded capacity would not be idled with peace. In September, 1915, Du Pont bought the celluloid manufacturing Arlington Company so that after the war it could absorb some of the company's expanded output of solvents and nitrated cotton. As the cash poured in, the company accelerated its diversification, sometimes by buying going concerns, sometimes by acquiring patents for processes its munitions plants could readily adapt. Wartime profits laid a sound foundation for postwar development. When peace came, Du Pont had extended its range of products to include celluloid, artificial leather, dyes, paints, and varnish and owned huge, debt-free plants for their manufacture.

America's entry into the war did nothing to soften Pierre's policies or his demands. He thought it only reasonable that Du Pont should be protected against risk whenever it made a large investment, and he saw no reason to make an exception for the United States government. He demanded contracts that would provide all the capital necessary to build new plants, a suitable profit both on construction and subsequent manufacturing, and sufficient additional funds to pay bonuses to key supervisors. Coleman du Pont, years before, had been impressed with Andrew Carnegie's success in binding the loyalty of key men by rewarding them with shares in the business. Pierre, who had adopted the plan enthusiastically, thought its fine peacetime results made it all the more appropriate in war. That the French and the English had caved in to this demand, Pierre thought, had facilitated the company's prodigies of production and manufacture: "I do not think [it] could have been done without the stimulus of our bonus plan." The U.S. government must do the same, Pierre said, "not only because we would be unwilling to undertake the work [otherwise] . . . but [also] because we could not hold the men in our service unless such outlay be made." (Perhaps the English and French should have tried such bonuses with the Tommies and *poilus*.)

Pierre's demands outraged the public and some government officials, particularly Secretary of War Newton D. Baker, who declared at one point, "We have made up our minds . . . to win this war without Du Pont." One proposed contract led Baker to declare that "his mind could not conceive of the services of anyone being worth such a price." Startled by such hostility, Pierre insisted that his company wanted only "reasonable compensation for [its] services." He planned to argue the company's case in *Outlook* magazine, naïvely assuming that the "facts" would lead the people to rally to the company's support.

Luckily, the *Outlook*'s editor gave Pierre's preliminary draft to Elihu Root, formerly a Secretary of War under McKinley and Theodore Roosevelt. Root gently instructed Pierre in the facts of life: "The attitude of a very large element of our people is still such toward the great corporations that there is some possibility of stirring up a feeling that the War Department was championing the cause of the plain people as against 'Big Business.' " Ultimately, cool heads prevailed on both sides. The War Department realized that it needed Du Pont powder; Pierre accepted the fact that he must participate in a great patriotic crusade. The company turned to with its practiced celerity, throwing up plants, churning out powder, gathering profits that were less than on Allied contracts, but nevertheless contributed significantly to Du Pont's swelling surplus.

On May 1, 1919, shortly after the war's end, Pierre du Pont retired from the presidency of the company. He was satisfied that he had fulfilled the goals set when he and his cousins had taken control. "I am firmly of the opinion," he told the board of directors, "that we have now reached another turning point ... ; therefore it would seem wise to place responsibility for future development and management of the business on the next line of men." To his intense gratification, "the next line of men" included his younger brothers: Irénée, who succeeded to the presidency, and Lammot, who became first vice-president and chairman of the executive committee. Without children of his own, Pierre had assumed paternal responsibility for his brothers and sisters since their father's death. All of them had called him "Dad" since childhood, so his younger brothers served as surrogates for the sons he never had. With control of the company passed on, and with family ownership still firm, Pierre retired satisfied with a trust fulfilled, a legacy enriched, a heritage preserved. The great wealth that he himself had accumulated was secondary to these benisons.

Rich, efficient, run by a modern organization that had proved its mettle in wartime, the Du Pont Company remained solidly Du Pont. Pierre, his family obligations more than met, looked forward to retirement into the quiet, private life he preferred. A botanical garden at his estate and philanthropies for his beloved Delaware had already begun to absorb his attention.

As it turned out, Pierre's retirement plans had to be postponed. Suddenly, in 1920, General Motors teetered on the brink of bankruptcy. With both his family and his company investments at stake, Pierre reluctantly involved himself deeply in the auto company's affairs. He maneuvered a complete reorganization, assumed the presidency, and promoted the rise to power of Alfred P. Sloan. His collaboration with Sloan on the reorganization helped make General Motors what it remains today, the paragon of American corporate efficiency. Not until 1928 was Pierre du Pont able to retire to his flowers and his charities.

Alfred P. Sloan, Jr. (left), in 1937, with his successor,
William S. Knudsen

8

The Organization Man
Alfred P. Sloan

As a third-generation Ford man, I grew up with an intense, innate distaste for General Motors and all its products, especially Chevrolets. My father argued the case for Ford superiority with references to arcane technical deficiencies hidden in the Chevrolet innards. But of such things as vacuum-assisted gear shifts I knew nothing and didn't need to learn. Chevrolets were no good because they weren't Fords, and that was reason enough. It baffled me that my maternal grandfather, who otherwise seemed perfect, preferred the hated rival and always had one sitting, to my embarrassment, in his driveway.

Such childhood prejudices die hard. Political scientists tell us that people tend to vote the way their parents did, and I suspect the same sort of loyalty to one corporation or another affects buying patterns as well. Certainly they did in my case. When I grew old enough to become a consumer, I assiduously avoided GM products. No Frigidaire appliances for me, despite the fact that in the part of the country where I grew up, Frigidaire was the generic name for all refrigerators. As for cars, the idea of buying one from GM never occurred to me.

My first intimate acquaintance with General Motors products therefore came through occupational necessity, not consumer choice. In the 1950s the Pennsylvania Railroad dieselized, to the distress of an army of steam-locomotive sentimentalists for whom the Pennsylvania's classic engines had held a cherished place, but to the intense relief of operating railroaders like me, who had an all too painful acquaintance with the cantankerous inefficiencies of steam.

In the freight yards where I worked, the Pennsylvania installed diesels from three manufacturers: Baldwin, Alco, and General Motors. Each brand had its own peculiarities. The Baldwins, which were everybody's favorite, combined quick acceleration, good braking, and a lot of pulling power. They were said to have "a lot of heart." The Alcos were powerful but slow; "they'd pull the world if you could couple one up to it." The GM locomotives seemed to me to be just like Chevrolets. They did everything acceptably, but unspectacularly. They started slowly, were hard to stop, and were notoriously "slippery" when the rails were wet. Watching one of them spinning its wheels one rainy day, I called the engineer on the radio and asked him if the engine was out of sand. "I don't need sand," he answered, "I need a Baldwin. This bastard would slip if the *rails* were made out of sand."

I discovered, however, that my negative view toward GM's locomotives wasn't shared by the men who maintained them. Engine-house foremen told me sulfurously that the railroad should junk everything else and buy all General Motors products. "They're easy to work on," one foreman told me, "the parts are always in stock, and if you have a problem, GM will send a man out from LaGrange [Illinois, headquarters of GM's Electro-Motive Division] right away. Those people are organized." Indeed they were — so organized that they eventually drove their competitors clear out of the locomotive business and, but for the later entry of General Electric, would have had a monopoly of the field.

GM's financial resources alone suffice to make it a formidable competitor in any field it cares to enter. The largest corporation in the world, its 1977 income of $55 billion exceeded that of most countries. With assets of $26 billion, it can buy whatever technology it needs to enter any promising market and has often done so. GM got into the appliance business by buying the Guardian Refrigerator Company in 1918, into aircraft engines by acquiring the Allison Engineering Company in 1929, and into diesel locomotive manufacturing by absorbing Winton Engine and Electro-Motive Engineering in 1930. In each case, General Motors acquired patents and expertise that brought it into a young industry at the forefront of existing technology. Technology alone, however, doesn't guarantee success. Indeed, as Alfred P. Sloan, principal designer of General Motors' modern organization observed, "American industry has always drawn from a common pool of technology." As Whitney learned, and McCormick, Edison, and Ford after him, no American manufacturer can expect to enjoy more than a brief technological advantage over his competitors. Carnegie showed that industrial supremacy depends upon coupling technology to systematic organization. Pierre du Pont improved the mix, and Alfred Sloan brought the union to its most fertile consummation at General Motors.

What lay behind my engine-house foreman's observation of General Motors' superiority was the ability of the GM organization to translate technological development into a full-blown industry. A Dayton engineer named Alfred Mellowes created the original Guardian refrigerator by harnessing the heat-absorbing properties of vaporizing gas. This principle had intrigued inventors before Mellowes, but none had succeeded in turning it into a marketable product. Mellowes himself hadn't mounted much of a threat to the iceman when Billy Durant, then GM president, visited the shoestring Guardian operation in 1919. "This man's got an idea," observed Durant, after threading his way through the clutter; "the rest is a lot of junk. . . . I'll tell you what I'll do. I'll organize a company with one hundred thousand dollars new capital and give you people a quarter interest." Two years later Frigidaire (as Guardian was renamed) had run up losses of two and a half million dollars. Sloan turned the operation over to GM's Delco-Light Division. Delco-Light "had a fine sales force spread over large areas of the country, and some unused manufacturing capacity," as well as access to GM's research staff and capital. Four years later Frigidaire had more than half the booming mechanical refrigerator market. GM's capital, research facilities, manufacturing know-how, market research, and sales techniques had turned Mellowes's rudimentary idea into a household necessity.

When GM bought Winton Engine, the diesel locomotive hadn't yet become practical. The necessary research and testing, which Winton's limited budget had held to a snail's pace, rushed ahead, financed by GM's petty cash and driven forward by Charlie Kettering, the doyen of GM experimenters. For Kettering, the diesel challenge, one of his colleagues observed, "was just like the sound of a bell to a fire horse." For GM the diesel locomotive, once perfected, provided a product that opened a new market to exploitation by the company's manufacturing and sales techniques.

Realizing that diesel locomotives had more in common with automobiles than with steam engines (a fact that eluded some manufacturers to their dying day), GM discarded the traditional industry practice of building locomotives to custom specifications. It designed a standard model that could be mass-produced at low cost, built several demonstrators for railroads to try, and, taking a leaf from Henry Ford's book, told prospective customers, "You can have any model you want as long as it's this one." To the diesel's efficiency, GM added the whole panoply of customer enticements developed in the mass production and marketing of harvesters and automobiles: long-term finance, speedy delivery, interchangeable parts, and factory-trained maintenance men.

As time passed, GM offered more models, but kept them simple and cheap by building them from standard components. As locomotives aged, GM offered to take old models in trade or to rebuild them, even to rebuild competitors' products with genuine GM parts. Trade-ins were, of course, refurbished and resold.

Within twenty years these methods had revolutionized the locomotive industry and, to a degree, the railroad business as well. The once-crude Winton Diesel had grown into a profitable General Motors division. For the General Motors organization such a development wasn't revolutionary; it was a matter of routine. It was, in fact, Alfred Sloan's greatest pride that he had created an organization that could attack such challenges systematically. Sloan was the "Organization Man" par excellence, a fully evolved specimen of the modern executive for whom the organization, not the product, is the indispensable ingredient of success. Sloan wasn't the first manufacturer to recognize the necessity for organization, of course. Whitney's failure to profit from the cotton gin was largely a failure of organization; his subsequent success derived from his systematic conception of production. Each of the actors that I have introduced after him made lasting contribution to the organization of some aspect of American industry: McCormick to sales and distribution; Carnegie to cost analysis; Edison to applied science; Henry Ford to mass production; Pierre du Pont to market forecasting and diversification. Before Carnegie, however, organization was secondary, the means to cherished ends — making some particular product and maintaining family control.

In Carnegie a transition of emphasis from product to organization appeared. Unlike his predecessors, Carnegie was no mechanic and no expert on his firm's product. He knew how to get steel made, not how to make it. "My preference was always for manufacturing," he said, but his strength lay in his organization. "Take away everything else," he declared, "but leave me my organization and in ten years I'll be back on top."

Pierre du Pont's career plots the shift clearly, for he discovered that the organization he designed to perpetuate his firm's dominance of a single product could be adapted to control a diversified operation with equal efficiency. For the shy, retiring Pierre, the boardroom and the executive office formed more natural habitats than laboratories or factories. In his hands, organization charts, more comfortable to manipulate than tools or people, became the blueprints for survival in the increasingly complex world of twentieth-century American industry. Although certainly he was neither an inhumane nor an insensitive individual, Pierre's decision to exclude inept family members from Du Pont showed his real commitment. His admission of some outsiders evolved naturally into a feeling that no man was bigger than the organization, while the organization as a whole had capacities greater than the sum of its individual human parts. At Du Pont, top-level management became a universal art that subordinated the imperatives of research, manufacturing, and selling to the transcendent guiding principle of return on investment. Viewed narrowly, Pierre's handiwork can be seen as the logical outgrowth of businessmen's endless struggle to match production to shifting, uncontrollable market demands in a way that kept their assets busy at a profit. Whitney solved the problem by relying on the government as a customer, a solution not available to people like McCormick, who found himself perpetually bedeviled by having made too many machines or too few. Carnegie and Ford relied on efficiency, believing that prices could always be driven down to the point where demand revived. For these, as for many other American manufacturers, the assumption that the American economy would forever expand seemed validated by experience. It took a long time for most to realize that excess capacity was one of the driving forces behind the trust movement that ultimately absorbed Carnegie's firm, McCormick's, and hundreds of others. Pierre's vision, informed by his experience at the Johnson Company, was clearer: markets had to be calculated, not assumed; the business had to be shaped by statistical realities, not by romantic obsessions.

In a broader sense, the ascendancy of corporate organization men fits into the larger historical patterns of the time. American business, like American society, had become infinitely larger and more complex than in Whitney's day. As the variety of products proliferated, the trickle of innovation became a flood, and every aspect of manufacturing became subdivided and specialized. Business had to develop more complex organizations to function at all, let alone at a profit. At the same time, for government, an increasing population, swelled and diversified by the arrival of immigrants from dozens of countries and spread thinly across the continental vastness or packed tightly into cities, presented challenges never contemplated by the Founding Fathers.

In the late nineteenth century, a quest, sometimes even a mania, for order pervaded America, infecting some businessmen as well as political reformers, doctors, engineers, and farmers. The prospect of achieving stability through combination fascinated financiers, appealing to their logical minds as a way to bring system to competitive chaos. The sheer tidiness of trusts often led to merger for merger's sake, even in industries where combination made no sense. For every International Harvester that succeeded, there was a U.S. Cotton Duck that failed. In other cases, the merger process created "paper concerns," as Carnegie derided them, saddled with massive quantities of bonds and stocks on which no management could hope to pay interest and dividends. Nor were such mistakes limited to amateurs or small fry. J. P. Morgan put together U.S. Shipbuilding, which sank upon launching.

Management, in consultation with Frederick Taylor and others of the new breed of efficiency gurus, tried to raise efficiency through organizational tinkering. The results were mixed. The symmetry of organization and flow charts, so easily redrawn, often seemed to convert hope to reality in the office, while mutiny and confusion reigned on the shop floor.

Henry Ford, driven by a different mania, created yet another sort of industrial order. Fired by the excitement of turning his company into one vast conveyor belt, carrying raw materials from his mines to his plants in his ships and his railroad cars, Ford pushed through the complete vertical integration that worked well enough while prosperity prevailed but became an expensive albatross on his neck when the market glutted and sales declined. Ford's plan, like many others that proved wanting in hard times, stemmed from the traditional optimistic attitude of American businessmen, an attitude nurtured in the expansive climate of the nineteenth century. For a Carnegie, an Edison, a Ford, it was difficult to imagine that much could go wrong for long, and impossible to plan on such a pessimistic basis.

For Alfred Sloan, however, as for Pierre du Pont, the true test of an organization was its ability to prosper during slack times. They regarded recessions as inevitable, however bright the long-term outlook. The Depression of 1893 affected them both deeply; Pierre because of the Johnson Company's vicissitudes, Alfred because he encountered a dismal job market when he left MIT in 1895. He spent his first working years with the Hyatt Roller

Bearing Company as it skated along on the brink of bankruptcy. Even when prosperity returned, Sloan, in supplying bearings to myriad automobile manufacturers, saw how failure relentlessly stalked the weak and poorly organized. In the free-for-all early automotive market, Hyatt's customers and competitors went under frequently, their weaknesses exposed by a decline in the market, or exploited by a better organized rival.

In a series of transactions between 1916 and 1918, General Motors absorbed Hyatt; Sloan became a vice-president and a major shareholder in GM, making his wealth a hostage to the company's fortunes. "I found myself," he recalled, "with rather little cash and a devil of a lot of stock." He also found himself in the midst of an administrative chaos that was slackly tolerated by Billy Durant, the founder and chairman, who was another old-style optimist who planned only for success. Alarmed, Sloan pressed Durant for system, order, organization, preferably along lines laid out by Sloan himself. Durant responded with smiles, encouragement, and inaction. Then the market collapse of 1920 swept through the ramshackle GM structure. In its wake came Pierre du Pont and a Du Pont-trained salvage crew, determined to pick up the pieces, reorganize, and preserve the stockholders' investment. The arrival of the Delaware cavalry and its calm, high-collared, pince-nezed leader pleased no one more than Sloan. The Du Ponts had $67 million tied up in GM stock, a princely sum, to be sure, but the money had come from surplus war profits that the Du Ponts could find no better place to invest. They could have lost it all without damaging much but pride. Sloan, on the other hand, had a measure of desperation in his organizing zeal. "Everything I had in the world," he later recalled, "was in General Motors."

In Pierre du Pont, Sloan saw a savior. Pierre knew nothing about making automobiles, but he brought an unmatched reputation for business probity, massive financial clout to tide the company over its immediate crisis, and a determination to reorganize for stability and security. If anyone could bring system to the GM muddle, Sloan thought Du Pont could. The two men were kindred spirits, similar in temperament, both MIT-trained, and both men who based decisions on facts, not brainstorms.

Sloan had long found Durant a trial to work with. Durant, he admitted, was a "genius," but *genius* was no complimentary term in Sloan's lexicon, for it denoted men who gloried in the "kind of thinking" that relied on "hunches." Sloan himself "much preferred the slow process of getting all the available facts, analyzing them as completely as ... possible, and then deciding our course." He worked most comfortably with men who, when "confronted by a problem ... tackled it as [he] did [his] own, with engineering care to get the facts." Durant, on the other hand, said Sloan, "would proceed on a course of action guided solely, as far as I could tell, by some intuitive flash of brilliance. He never felt obliged to make an engineering hunt for facts." Durant, moreover, "could create but he could not administer," and his breezy, back-slapping manner and boundless optimism grated. Sloan was by nature a quiet, retiring, cautious character — often called "Silent Sloan" by his coterie.

Sloan was not only not, as he reflected, "a Durant man," but he did not think Durant the man for General Motors. The company "had become too big for a one-man show. It was ... far too complicated. The future required more than an individual's genius." To realize "the potential industrial force under the General Motors emblem" required not "boldness and daring," but "the most competent executive group that could be brought together."

Such a group meant first of all "a new president to take the place of Mr. Durant." Sloan knew just the man he wanted. "It was apparent," he later wrote, "that [Pierre S. du Pont] was the one individual ... who had the prestige and respect that could give confidence to the organization, to the public, and to the banks, and whose presence could arrest the demoralization that was taking place." Sloan, of course, was also aware of the "capability for business leadership [Pierre] had shown ... in the Du Pont Company." Sloan also found Pierre personally compatible; indeed, his description of Du Pont would have served for a description of himself: "tall, well built, and reticent," a man "who would not put himself forward."

Pierre, as we know, was reluctant to take over. He soon found in Sloan, however, an alter ego who had the knowledge of the automobile industry that he himself lacked. Sloan, moreover, was a man with a plan, the same plan of reorganization that Durant had dismissed. Couched in the organizational language that Pierre used like a mother tongue, Sloan's blueprint became the basis for General Motors' reconstruction; Sloan himself became Pierre's right-hand man, the operational head of the company, with the title of vice-president of operations. Together, in 1921, these two spare, taciturn MIT graduates set about the business of reshaping General Motors' helter-skelter collection of establishments into a smoothly functioning organization, tuned for systematic growth in a fluctuating marketplace. For Pierre du Pont the GM challenge capped an already masterful career; for Alfred Sloan it represented the opportunity he had worked for since boyhood.

Alfred P. Sloan was born in 1875, five years after Pierre du Pont. The son of a coffee and tea importer, Sloan grew up in comfortable, but not opulent, surroundings. A studious boy with a bent for mathematics and science, young Alfred became something of a child prodigy, finishing high school at the Brooklyn Polytechnic Institute a year ahead of his class. He passed the entrance examinations for MIT, but the school delayed his admission for a year because of his youth. Once admitted, he got himself back on schedule, becoming a "grind" who "worked every possible minute" and graduated after three years.

Even for a student as promising as Sloan, the depression year 1895 was an unpropitious time to look for a job. But through his father's friendship with John E. Searles, kingpin of the American Sugar Refining Company, Sloan found work as a draftsman at the Hyatt Roller Bearing Company in Newark, New Jersey. John Wesley Hyatt, Sloan's nominal superior, was an old-style, self-trained, lone-wolf inventor, a man Sloan described as "scientifically illiterate." Hyatt had not done badly for an illiterate. He had invented celluloid, the first practical plastic, hoping to make his fortune by substituting celluloid for ivory in billiard balls. A later invention, the roller bearing, had more potential for real money. Wherever metal turns upon metal, some sort of antifriction bearing is required. Since industrial America was a land of turning shafts, carrying increasingly heavier loads, the market potential for a device like the Hyatt roller bearing seemed unlimited.

Yet there were real problems involved in bringing the roller bearing to a marketable stage. They illustrate the increasing complexity and interlocking of scientific disciplines that beset late nineteenth-century manufacturers. Roller bearings depended on metallurgy to make a metal hard enough to bear loads without wearing, on petroleum chemistry to develop lubricants that would not break down when subjected to the bearings' heat, and on mechanical engineering to develop machines that would turn the bearings to precision tolerance in large volume and at low cost.

The real power at Hyatt, as at so many fledgling American manufacturing firms, lay not with the inventor, but with the man who put up the money, John Searles. Searles eventually wearied of the unending drain on his finances and withdrew his support. Sloan's father came to the rescue, put up $5,000 to keep the business alive, installed his son as president, and gave him six months to show a profit. Sloan cut costs and raised production by installing systematic controls and procedures at the Hyatt plant, now located between a junkyard and a city dump in Harrison, New Jersey. With the aid of a hustling sales manager who was a master of the drummer's ancient arts of wining, dining, and razzle-dazzling the customers, Hyatt cleared $12,000 at the end of the first six months and went on to bigger and better things.

As the turn of the century approached, Sloan realized that the fledgling automobile industry could become his most important customer. He had a product that every automobile manufacturer could use because every car rolled and every engine turned on some kind of bearing. Early automobile producers spent much of their time scrambling around looking for people to manufacture necessary components. A company like Hyatt, already turning out a needed product, was a godsend. Sloan and his sales manager followed developments in the automobile industry closely. Any new manufacturer was aggressively solicited for his business. Sloan, for example, first wrote Henry Ford in 1899, nine years before the first Model T was produced.

Among a welter of such fledgling component suppliers, Sloan's firm rose steadily to the top. Hyatt offered car makers an invaluable service, for Sloan's development organization could design bearings tailored to fit specific needs. In addition, Sloan's manufacturing organization established a reputation for punctual delivery of orders, vital for an industry where assembly waits until all the parts are on hand. Sloan kept up with rising demand by driving the work force hard, concentrating on efficiency, and plowing profits back into expanding capacity.

Business often took Sloan to Detroit, where he met most of the automobile industry pioneers, including Henry Ford, the Dodge brothers, Ransom E. Olds, the Fisher brothers, Charles Nash, and others. This rough-and-ready crew consisted largely of "shirt-sleeve mechanics" turned manufacturers. They gathered daily at the Hotel Ponchartrain bar, the automobile industry's watering hole, to exchange shop talk and rumors. Sloan never felt comfortable in such an environment ("A couple of cocktails [were] just about my limit"), but he endured it for the sake of personal contacts and keeping abreast of industry news. If you waited at the Ponchartrain bar, it was said, anybody you wanted to see in the automobile industry would turn up within two days.

Sloan admired these pioneers, but felt at ease with few of them. His contempt for the "scientifically illiterate," a rare disease in those days (since become an American epidemic), tinged his outlook and caused him to rank his peers according to the degree of science with which they approached their work. He respected Henry Leland because "quality was Leland's god" and because the old man, micrometer in hand, taught professional engineer Sloan the real meaning of precision by rejecting an order of Hyatt bearings. "Mr. Sloan," Leland told him, "Cadillacs are made to run, not just to sell." Thanks to Leland, who told him, "You must grind your bearings. Even though you make thousands, the first and the last should be precisely alike," Sloan acquired a "genuine conception of what mass production should really mean" even before Henry Ford made it the hallmark of the industry. When manufacturers began demanding parts machined to interchangeable precision, Hyatt, unlike many competitors, was ready and prospered accordingly.

Another kindred spirit for Sloan was Charles Stewart Mott, a mechanical engineer trained at Stevens Institute. Mott manufactured axles and, a Leland disciple, he learned to make them fully interchangeable. Naturally enough, Mott turned to another precision manufacturer for the necessary bearings. Soon, Sloan said, "Mott and Hyatt were interdependent to an extraordinary degree." This relationship required close cooperation between the two firms' chiefs, who established an easy rapport. "I liked to work with Mott," Sloan said. "His training had made him methodical" and endowed him with that quality Sloan cherished above all others, "engineering care [for] the facts."

Between 1905 and 1915, as automobile sales soared from a handful to over 800,000, Sloan and Mott prospered, their firms following parallel and often interlocking courses as volume suppliers of precision parts. Gradually the industry took a new shape. As dozens of manufacturers expired, the survivors concentrated in and around Detroit. Major car manufacturers began to draw their suppliers into closer corporate and geographic relationships. In 1913 Mott moved most of his production facilities from Utica, New York, to a new plant in Flint, Michigan, at the behest of his largest customer, Billy Durant. Mott financed the move by selling a share of his business to General Motors.

Sloan watched in alarm as Mott's firm was woven into Durant's corporate web. The emerging configuration of the industry seemed to menace his life's work, his father's fortune, and his own. "I had put my whole life's energy into Hyatt," he recalled; "everything I had earned was there in bricks, machinery, and materials." By driving profits back into expansion, Sloan had by 1916 transformed the shabby Harrison building into a 750,000-square-foot plant, turning out 40,000 bearings a day. The "works were highly organized . . . as nearly scientific in . . .

operations as a business could be." "An effective cost system" monitored efficiency; "chemists and metallurgists" kept the company abreast of scientific developments; "every step in the [manufacture] of raw material into antifriction bearings was checked by scientific methods." To serve the customers, Hyatt had "three sales divisions, each with its own engineering and sales staff." The Newark office "promoted the use of our bearings . . . in all classes of machinery." A Chicago outlet handled the tractor industry, and one in Detroit dealt with the company's mainstay, the automobile industry.

Despite all this efficiency, capacity, and diversity, Sloan feared for his firm's health. He was vulnerable to the expansion strategies of the two automobile giants, Ford and General Motors, which together supplied the bulk of Hyatt's business. Either or both might decide to dispense with Hyatt's services anytime, in which case, Sloan said, "our company would be in a desperate situation." It would be stuck with excess capacity, an idle plant, and, horror of horrors to a dedicated capitalist, unproductive capital.

The Ford Motor Company grew entirely through internal expansion, using its profits to establish its own parts manufacturing plants. Henry Ford had the capital by 1916 to do anything he pleased, including going into the bearing business overnight, on a scale that would not only supply his own needs, but also make him a devastating competitor for the remaining market. Ford showed no signs of such a move, but, given his vast resources and mercurial temperament, Ford's past behavior offered no reassurance of Sloan's future. One thing Sloan could be sure of: Ford wouldn't buy him out. When Henry did something, he did it from scratch his own way. Looking for future security, Sloan had to look elsewhere.

General Motors, on the other hand, following a course diametrically opposed to Ford's, bought up existing producers through exchanges of stock. Thus Durant, an even more unpredictable character than Ford, might deal Hyatt a crippling blow by buying out and building up a competitor. In 1916 as before, plenty of people, including bearing manufacturers, were ready to clean up by "selling to the trust." When Durant invited him to lunch and offered to buy him out, Sloan found that he himself was one of them. After some negotiation, they settled on a price of $13.5 million.

In his two autobiographical volumes, Sloan retrospectively explained his decision with ineffable logic as a Hobson's choice. Since he subsequently rose to chairman of the board of the world's most powerful corporation, it would be quixotic to call his decision wrong. It was, nevertheless, significant, symptomatic of the changing climate of American enterprise in the early twentieth century. Sloan himself was in the prime of life, rich, successful, and controlling owner of his company. The company itself was no gimcrack operation, thrown together in hopes of a quick sale to the trust, but rather a prosperous, efficient enterprise with an enviable record for quality and dependability.

It was a sign of the times that Sloan lacked the fierce pride of ownership that characterized so many of his predecessors. They had seen their firms as an extension of themselves. Had Sloan had a son to carry on, he might have acted differently, as also might the older Carnegie in 1900. But Andy would never have accepted a subordinate's role in United States Steel. Sloan, however, craved wealth and power and saw a chance to multiply both by joining a vastly larger organization. Identity and independence as a manufacturer seemed to him a small forfeit for such an opportunity. Many of Sloan's contemporaries faced the same choice: Charles Mott, the Fisher brothers, and Charles Kettering (inventor of the self-starter) chose to join GM. Henry Ford (who turned down an $8 million offer from Durant in 1908), Charles Nash, Walter Chrysler, and the Dodge brothers opted for independence and went their own ways, some to glory, some to oblivion.

Since Sloan's day many a successful entrepreneur has made the same choice, becoming part of a process that the economist Joseph Schumpeter saw as the harbinger of capitalism's doom. According to Schumpeter, and other ravens who followed him, capitalism depends on individual initiative, something inexorably stifled by corporate bureaucracies.

All his years at General Motors Sloan defended a contrary view, arguing that even the biggest corporation could be structured so as to encourage, not extinguish, individual effort. "General Motors," he declared, "was built on initiative." The corporation's resources, first of all, multiplied the possibility of individual satisfaction through achievement. "After all," Sloan said, "what any one individual can accomplish is not great, but through the power of organization the effect of a few may be multiplied almost indefinitely." As supporting evidence, Sloan cited the career of Charles Kettering. Working at first alone in a barn, Kettering invented the self-starter. Later, backed by GM's resources and aided by technical staffs at Du Pont and Standard Oil, Kettering developed quick-drying paints that enabled the company to offer cars in a variety of colors, perfected tetraethyl lead for gasoline that permitted high-combustion engines, synthesized Freon, the first practical refrigerant for home use, and perfected the diesel engine.

The second way, according to Sloan, GM preserved individual incentive was through promotion and stock bonuses. Both recognized individual contributions to the firm's success. It was, of course, Pierre du Pont who brought the bonus plan to GM. Sloan became an avid booster and expanded the plan over the years. Bonuses not only made company men of individuals "by encouraging executives to relate their own individual efforts to the welfare of the whole corporation," but also insured them against financial loss as a result of trading independence for corporate loyalty. "By placing its executives in the same relative position . . . that they would occupy if they were conducting . . . their own . . . business," intoned Sloan, "[the company] provides opportunity for accomplishment through the exercise of individual initiative and opportunity for economic progress commensurate with performance."

That the GM method worked Sloan thought irrefutable. In business, success furnishes the ultimate proof, and Sloan endorsed the views of Walter S. Carpenter, Jr., of Du Pont, who observed in the early 1960s that "the Du Pont Company and General Motors . . . the most prominent exponents of the bonus plan have been extraordinarily successful." They had excelled in the "assembling and retention of an organization of outstanding men."

There, in Carpenter's last statement, lurks evidence of a fundamental shift in American outlook, a shift symbolized by Sloan's career. It suggests how a nation that had long prided itself as a place where "everyman" could be "his own boss" could embrace a system where virtually everyone worked for someone else. It shows how a country of "independent yeomen, shopkeepers, and mechanics" could transform itself into a society of interdependent employees, bureaucrats, and corporation men, yet persuade itself that the new arrangements preserved, or even — to men like Sloan — strengthened the cherished American tradition of individualism.

Sloan believed that high salaries, bonuses, the chance to multiply one's individual efforts through the corporation's financial and mechanical leverage preserved individualism for executives. In the case of the workers, steady wages and increased leisure time more than compensated for the loss of independence and craftsman's pride. Perhaps he was right. On such meat the Caesars fed and grew mighty, and society today more closely reflects Sloan's perception than that of Jefferson, Ralph Waldo Emerson, Terence Powderly, and other apostles of self-reliance.

All this lay far in the future when Sloan agreed to sell to Durant; he somehow concluded that the massive GM organization offered a more satisfying repository for his ambitions than did the continuation of his own business. Durant, no fool, sensed Sloan's drive for power. He sweetened his proposition by offering Sloan the presidency of United Motors, a GM parts-manufacturing subsidiary, thus giving him the chance to run four companies instead of one.

So the year 1916 began Alfred Sloan's tempestuous four-year association with William Crapo Durant, a fabulous character in American business history. Unfortunately for Durant, posterity's portrait has largely been sketched by historians of business organization, who portray Durant as the bungler who made the mess that Sloan and Pierre du Pont had to clean up. But there was much more to Durant than that. He was a man of extraordinary vision. Like Henry Ford, he foresaw the automobile as a necessity for the masses at a time when other manufacturers considered it a rich man's plaything. Early in the game, Durant told his peers, "Gentlemen, you don't realize the purchasing power of the American people. I look forward to the time when we'll make and sell one million cars a year." \

Durant, in fact, had a more sophisticated presentiment of the American car market than did Ford, who refused to the bitter end to abandon his conception of the automobile as a simple utility vehicle. Americans, Durant believed, would buy all sorts of cars, from the spartan to the sumptuous, as their incomes permitted and their pretensions dictated. The automobile could be sold as a status symbol as well as for its usefulness, and Durant tried to build a manufacturing empire to supply every buyer's craving.

In his early years, Durant followed an orthodox, relatively conservative path of development. He had already accumulated much money and skill in becoming the country's largest carriage manufacturer, complete with specialized parts plants and a nationwide distribution network. In 1904, he bought the small, bankrupt Buick Motor Company in his home town of Flint, Michigan, and soon turned it into the country's largest car producer. Durant redesigned the car, built new assembly plants, attracted parts suppliers like sparkplug maker Albert Champion to Flint, and outsold Ford 9,000 cars to 6,000 in 1908.

In 1908, when the Model T took to the road, Ford rattled off to a seemingly insurmountable lead. Durant, boiling with frustration and impatience at seeing his competitor steal a march, threw caution aside. For Durant, the Ford method of growth seemed much too slow. He couldn't, or rather, wouldn't, wait for retained earnings to finance new plants. Instead, he decided to buy existing facilities. In 1908 he formed General Motors, combining Buick, Cadillac, and Oldsmobile. Ford's success had brought a bullish atmosphere to the industry, but he hadn't the least notion of letting outsiders in on the best thing going. In those circumstances, General Motors looked to frustrated investors like a heaven-sent opportunity. Durant had little trouble raising capital or finding sellers who would accept GM shares in payment. In its first two years, GM's profits rose from $29 million to $49 million.

Durant, confident that ever-expanding sales would always provide plenty of working capital, spent the money as fast as it came. In 1910, however, he found himself caught short when the market paused. Undaunted, he secured $13 million from a syndicate of bankers. The rescuers exacted a stiff price — $15 million in notes, plus $6 million worth of the company's stock as a "bonus." In addition, they demanded that Durant turn over his voting rights to a voting trust (of bankers, needless to say) for five years, and ousted him as president. Still unchastened, Durant joined Louis Chevrolet to form the Chevrolet Motor Car Company. Chevrolet, raised lean and efficient on a slim capital diet, produced a sporty car that sold well. On the strength of Chevrolet's performance, Durant found a new source of money in John J. Raskob, once Pierre du Pont's secretary, now risen to chairman of the Du Pont Company finance committee. Raskob, a poor boy made good, shared Durant's roseate view of the future of the American economy in general and of the automobile industry in particular. He invested in Chevrolet and persuaded Pierre to do the same.

With his pool of Chevrolet profits fortified by this freshet from the bountiful Du Pont fountains, Durant began quietly buying General Motors stock. His former banker friends unwittingly aided him by paying no dividends on GM stock, although their efficient interim management generated substantial profits. Such prudent parsimony exacted its price; the stock fell from $100 a share to $24. Then the five-year voting trust expired. Durant showed up at the next meeting and soon proved, to the bankers' dismay, that he and his Chevrolet Motor Company owned a majority of General Motors' stock. In the reorganization of the company, Pierre du Pont became chairman of GM's board, but, what with his marriage and a flood of Allied powder orders on his mind, Pierre left control of operations to Durant, who immediately resumed expansion.

Between 1915 and 1920, GM grew by leaps and bounds, corralling car builders and a herd of parts manufacturers. Buick, Oldsmobile, and Cadillac were joined by a clutch of lesser firms such as Cartercar, Marquette, Ewing, Randolph, Welch, and Oakland, and others long since gone to their rewards. Sloan's United Motors Company, which had been set up as a GM-controlled holding company to acquire parts manufacturers, bought out, in addition to Hyatt, New Departure (ball bearings), Remy Electric and Delco (lights, ignition parts), Harrison Radiator, Klaxon (horns), and others.

In a quandary, as we have seen, to find an outlet for their wartime surpluses, the Du Ponts in 1918 shoveled in another $25 million to fuel expansion, acquiring now a quarter interest. Raskob persuaded Pierre that the price of the stock was cheap, that dividends were good and would improve, and, not least, that GM would buy all its artificial leather, paint, and varnish from Du Pont. Durant also agreed to turn GM's financial management over to a committee to be appointed by the Du Ponts. In the event, Pierre chose Raskob as guardian of the Du Pont interest, which turned out to be like appointing a rat to guard the cheese. Raskob, for all Pierre's confidence in him, turned to putty in Durant's hands. Durant continued on his merry way, wheeling and dealing; Raskob followed along, paying the bills. Amid the exuberant and uncoordinated chaos only a few division chiefs kept their heads. Sloan methodically brought order to United Motors while forwarding his constant suggestions for overall reorganization to Durant. Harry Bassett ran a tight ship at Buick. Like Sloan, he introduced systematic cost control in production and tried to establish a rational marketing scheme.

The chaos that prevailed should not obscure the fact that Durant, too, had an overall plan, one so brilliant that it laid the foundation for the reorganized firm's subsequent rise to the top of the corporate heap. First, he assembled a full line of cars that catered to a variety of tastes and pocketbooks. Second, he diversified by manufacturing refrigerators, home lighting plants, and trucks in addition to automobiles. Third, he integrated by absorbing parts manufacturers to supply the car-building plants. His successors validated all these policies by continuing them.

Durant failed because he didn't create a strong enough central organization to coordinate the properties once acquired, analyze their performance, and shape up the laggards. He let most of the acquisitions operate as independently after they joined GM as before. Consequently Du Pont accountants discovered that only two of the automobile divisions (Buick and Oldsmobile) consistently made money, and, worse, most of them competed with one another. No market forecasting was undertaken; therefore no real production planning existed. Each plant simply built as many cars as it could, hoping to sell them all. GM, furthermore, had no purchasing policy or inventory control. Each division manager bought materials independently, sometimes from GM-owned parts makers, but often not. When Sloan and Du Pont took over, they found that the company's various divisions had inventories that totaled over $200 million. This tied up an amount of working capital almost double the Du Pont Company's total assets and, needless to say, contributed massively to GM's perpetual cash shortage. Outside of Cadillac and Buick, the GM car divisions had paid little attention to quality control. Many of the company's products had acquired a shoddy reputation. GM could survive these weaknesses only as long as an expanding market or optimistic investors kept the cash coming. In 1920 both sources dried up and Durant fell.

Whether Durant, given enough time, would have turned from mere combination to real consolidation is anybody's guess. His record at Buick and Chevrolet suggests that he knew how to run an efficient operation, and even Sloan admitted that Durant might have tightened up GM eventually. But sometime between 1904 and 1908, Durant seems to have undergone a fundamental change in outlook. Perhaps Ford's competition led him to abandon caution for haste and daring, reversing the progression toward conservatism that supposedly accompanies aging.

Psychologists have had a lot to say about the critical mid-years in men's lives, and some have suggested that most creative men do their best work either early or late, but rarely throughout their lives. If successful manufacturers can be considered creative, and my sample of them representative, then such men present an exception. By and large their originative, successful work continued through their middle years. Indeed, their careers suggest that the ability to mount a sustained effort over many years is a precondition to entrepreneurial success.

On the other hand, Durant was not the only industrialist for whom the middle years brought a sharp change, manifested by some irrevocable choice, bold move, or galvanizing of effort. Whitney was thirty-three (middle-aged for his time) when he gave up on the cotton gin and contracted for the entirely new task of making thousands of muskets. McCormick transplanted himself and his factory to Chicago at thirty-nine. Carnegie gave up his career flogging securities and, as he said, "put all [his] eggs in one [steel] basket" at thirty-eight. Edison, passing forty, turned away from electricity, which had occupied him from boyhood, sold his General Electric stock, and concentrated on developing the phonograph, motion pictures, and his iron ore separation scheme. Henry Ford was thirty-nine when he decided to break with his luxury-car minded backers and form a new company to "build a car for the great multitude." Sloan sold Hyatt to GM at forty-one. As we shall see, Henry Ford II was in his early forties when he supplanted his hired managers and took charge of his company, and Edwin Land introduced the Polaroid camera at thirty-eight.

So Durant's indefatigable daring and drive were not so unusual, but his policy of expanding first and organizing later undoubtedly led to his downfall. Sloan, with Pierre du Pont's solid backing, immediately set about reorganizing the company. Durant's tripartite plan — variety, diversification, and integration — remained company policy, but was subordinated to a more fundamental principle: "The primary object of the corporation," said Sloan later, ". . . was to make money, not just to make motor cars." Furthermore, Sloan argued, just making a profit wasn't enough to justify continuation of any operation:

The profit resulting from any business considered [alone] is no real measure of the merits of that particular business. An operation making $100,000 a year may be . . . very profitable [,] justifying expansion and . . . all the additional capital that it can profitably employ. On the other hand, a business making $10,000,000 a year may be . . . very unprofitable . . . not only not justifying further expansion but even justifying liquidation. . . . It is not, therefore, a matter of the amount of profit but of the relation of that profit to the . . . invested capital.

This positive declaration of the rate-of-return principle, a principle Durant had ignored, naturally struck a resonant chord in Pierre du Pont, for whom it had long been gospel. Their basic unity of thought cemented the working relationship between the two men. (Indeed, Sloan later declared that he and Pierre had only ever disagreed once on an issue relating to the company: John Raskob's acceptance in 1928 of the chairmanship of the Democratic National Committee, while still a GM officer.)

Sloan, as he had expected, had a most useful partner in his rebuilding campaign. Du Pont cash and credit with the Morgan house furnished working capital to carry the company over the market crisis of 1920–1921, and provided investment capital for expansion and modernization. A swarm of Du Pont accountants, led by Donaldson Brown, buzzed through the GM labyrinth, taking inventory, analyzing the profitability of current operations, installing standardized accounting practices everywhere. Du Pont engineers surveyed the company's plants, did efficiency studies, drew plans for reconstructing old facilities and building new ones, and supervised the work.

With the capital situation under control and statistics flowing, economy measures began. Purchasing was stopped until inventories ran down. Central controls were established to prevent any recurrence of scarcity or glut. Chevrolet became a GM division, while unprofitable lines like Scripps-Booth, Sheridan, and Oakland were consigned to the automobile Valhalla. Remaining divisions got orders to buy parts from GM subsidiaries or explain why they didn't.

Donaldson Brown adapted a Du Pont concept, "standard volume," to the automobile industry. Standard volume supplied a hypothetical statistical yardstick that showed the detailed costs and profits that should result from normal levels of production.

When compared to actual performance, this yardstick could tell who produced efficiently and who didn't. Personnel were shifted accordingly in a barrage of promotions, transfers, marching orders, and walking papers. Many of Durant's cronies departed as fresh talent, including Ford protégés Norval Hawkins and William Knudsen, arrived.

Sloan wanted to preserve the good qualities of GM's tradition of divisional independence, even while holding all operations subject to policies established by central authority. He further divided GM's multiple operations into divisions according to function — Chevrolet, Oldsmobile, research, parts, accessories, and so on. Each division operated semiautonomously according to the instructions of the executive committee. That body labored continuously to "determine the functioning of the various divisions constituting the Corporation's activities, not only in relation to one another, but in relation to the central authority."

Striking the appropriate balance between centralization and decentralization involved a lot of trial-and-error. There was constant reshuffling of organization charts on the basis of statistical results, a complex process that goes on to this day, but mercifully need not be dissected here. After all, as Sloan himself said, "The language of organization has always suffered some want of words to express the true facts and circumstances of human interaction." Suffice it to say that Donaldson Brown's yardstick did indicate when and where the rate-of-return goals were met and where they weren't. A little centralization here and a little decentralization there toned up the structure accordingly.

Once adequately equipped to judge results, Sloan went about improving them. He told Charlie Kettering's research team to improve the cars and ordered divisions to develop quality controls to make sure they stayed improved. He reorganized the product line so that each division produced for a particular price level without competing with the others. The bottom level he left, for the time being, to Ford, since Henry had such a hammerlock on it. As Sloan said, "No conceivable amount of capital short of the United States Treasury could have sustained the losses required to take [Ford's] volume away from him at his own game."

(Ultimately, the availability of used cars, the Depression, rising consumer tastes for automotive luxury, and Ford's own obstinacy did the job for them, thus sparing GM the expense.)

With better quality in the works and product lines established, Sloan, borrowing another tool from the Du Pont kit, installed market forecasting. As the company learned to evaluate the four principal variables that affected demand — growth, seasonal variation, general business conditions, and competition — it translated market forecasting and predicted rates of return into policy that determined prices, production, employment, inventory levels, and capital investment. Once institutionalized in statistical bureaus, market forecasting supplied the finishing touch to the GM organizational structure and philosophy. Completed in the late twenties, the GM structure, Sloan later recorded, "has remained essentially unchanged since," and the policies it represents "have become the general practice in American business."

So this immensely powerful engine of production was not enough. Sloan coupled it to a refurbished dealer network and a panoply of techniques designed to stimulate sales. Annual model changes featuring this or that gimmick, planned, Sloan admitted, "to make you dissatisfied with your current car so you will buy a new one," liberal trade-ins, GM-sponsored financing, advertising ballyhoo, searchlights, parades, banquets, balloons, indeed the whole carnival of modern hard sell, all were adapted to push GM's products into the market. And pushed they were, in ever-increasing number until 1929.

In 1922, Sloan's first full year in operational control, GM sold 457,000 cars and trucks and netted $61 million. In 1923 the figures rose to 800,000 vehicles and $80 million profit. In May of that year Pierre du Pont declared that the corporation had achieved "stability," turned over the presidency to Sloan, retired "to his enormous hothouses at Longwood Gardens, [to] pluck orchids and figs, to sit in the evening on his broad plaza and watch his $500,000 fountain swish and spurt in beams of many-colored lights," to listen to his $250,000 organ, and to pursue his philanthropic campaign to improve his native state until he died, childless, in 1954.

As president of GM, Sloan more than fulfilled Pierre's expectations. Cars rolled out and money poured in. In 1929, GM sold 1.9 million cars and trucks, netted $248 million after taxes for a 16.5 percent return on assets. These results, however, came during the boom of the 1920s, the kind of climate where even Durant had made money. The Depression provided the acid test for Sloan's organization methods. Not until 1939 did sales return to the 1929 level; in 1932 they fell to less than a third of 1929. GM, nevertheless, made a profit and paid a dividend every year because, as Sloan said, "We had learned to react quickly" to a changing market and adjust production, employment, and inventories immediately "through [its] system of financial and operating controls." Through depression and war, therefore, and on into an era of increased government presence in its affairs, Sloan's organization kept plowing ahead, "making money and not just making motor cars."

To Sloan himself, perhaps the ultimate proof of his achievement was the fact that the organization continued to thrive after he departed. The GM presidency passed to a series of men whose names few of the public ever knew and fewer still can remember. It cannot be said of Sloan that he cared nothing for individuals. After retirement from the presidency in 1946 he became a philanthropist, donating much of his fortune to cancer research. But certainly in business he thought the organization more important than any one man. Reflecting on his life's work, he observed that "it is imperative for the health of the organization that it always tends to rise above subjectivity." He had perhaps earned the right to the small boast that in the structure he had built, "one of the ... great strengths is that it was designed to be an objective organization, [not] the type that gets lost in the subjectivity of personalities."

Sloan thought himself a creative man, as many of his gray-flannel- and double-knit-leisure-suited successors in business bureaucracies have since thought themselves. Designing something as ephemeral as an organization or, worse yet, some minuscule part for an assembly-line-produced gewgaw may seem poor stuff in a creative tradition that included such handcrafted gems as the ax handle and the clipper ship. Sloan, however, faced a problem that, to his mind, taxed human creativity to the utmost: how to enlist for GM's benefit the same sustained, driving effort, rooted in self-interest and self-respect, that men gave their own businesses. That he succeeded in the face of the company's massive bureaucratic structure, diffuse absentee ownership, and minute subdivision of tasks, he regarded as a creative triumph: the organization chart as work of art. Whatever one thinks of the consequences, Sloan and others like him succeeded where Schumpeter thought they would fail. The modern corporation bureaucratized the entrepreneurial function without destroying it, at least so far.

Sloan, it seems, tried to play his role so that when it ended and he slipped through the curtains, no one ever again would occupy center stage. It is perhaps just as well that he did not entirely succeed. We need organizations that produce, and they may well require organization men to run them, but it would be a dull firmament that had no stars. Fortunately, they still rise now and again, and Henry Ford's grandson is one of them.

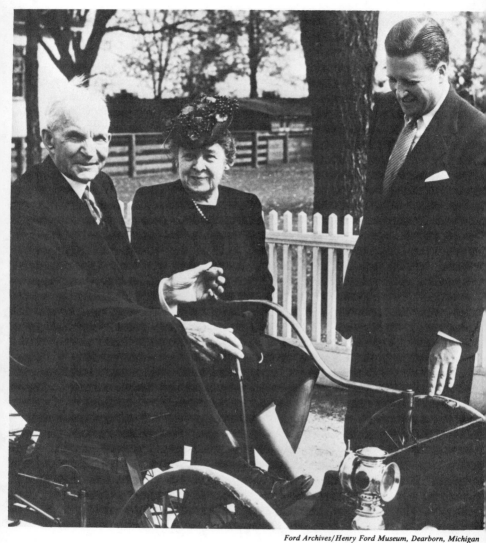

*The old order passes: Henry and Clara Ford with grandson
Henry Ford II at Greenfield Village, 1946.*

9

Superstar of the Worldwide Car Henry Ford II

SPEAKING of his generation, the generation that fought the Civil War, Justice Oliver Wendell Holmes remarked, "Through our great good fortune, in our youth, our hearts were touched with fire." In Holmes and many of his contemporaries, the flame of individualism, a legacy of generations of Americans before them, burned brightly on. In people there lurked much evil, and in nature much hostility, but in mankind's goodwill and common sense reposed the strength to master both. The vehicle of progress remained what it had always been, individuals. Often they could and should work in concert, as Progressive reformers did, deriving through unity and nobility of purpose a power greater than the sum of their separate abilities, but never thereby creating organizations with goals or ethical systems not found in the people themselves.

It was a bold faith and, perhaps excepting a trust in some supreme, benevolent power, the most noble faith of which man is capable. It was, moreover, a difficult creed to maintain in an era when proliferating bureaucracies subordinated personality to the collective needs of the nation-state and the giant corporation, engines that seemed to develop purposes and directions of their own. It was, however, a creed protected by the hothouse climate of national power, magnified to near-omnipotence by the American rescue of the Allied cause in World War I, and by the national prosperity that endured until 1929.

The hearts of my generation, in our youth, were touched with cold, the cold of fears that lapped over us in waves. First the fear of want and hunger that permeated the Great Depression, touching not only those who had no work today, but also those whose jobs might vanish tomorrow. The anguish and despair with which our parents contemplated the possibility that the American system had broken down beyond repair communicated itself subtly to a generation that knew nothing of the Depression's causes and all too much about its effects.

Then came the terror of Pearl Harbor and the months that followed. Looking back, it seems silly that we ever imagined that Japan and Germany, with most of the rest of the world arrayed against them, could possibly win the war. But I remember when Japanese invaders were expected momentarily on the Pacific Coast and when torpedoed oil tankers burned within sight of the Atlantic shore. I remember the anguish of Bataan and Corregidor, and the exultation of Guadalcanal and El Alamein. For a time at least it seemed we might lose the fight, the men who went off to it (including my father, two uncles, several cousins — virtually every male member of my family between eighteen and forty-five), and with them, our whole way of life.

Peace brought further traumas: the fear of lapsing back into the Depression; the emergence of the powerful, implacable, treacherous Soviet enemy; and the dread, literally, to end all dreads, the looming certainty of atomic holocaust. All in all, it didn't look too good for mankind. As for the individual's power to affect these cosmic disasters, why, it seemed to shrink with each tiding. Big Problems demanded Big Antidotes that only Big Government could supply: for depressions, the Full Employment Act of 1946; for the Russian bomb, bigger bombs and plenty of 'em; for segregationist Arkansas governor Orval Faubus, the 101st Airborne Division; for the Cold War, the Berlin Airlift, the Marshall Plan, "Containment," NATO, SEATO, "Brinksmanship." I had a firsthand experience with the last one, a real taste of anomie incarnate. In 1958 my unit of the 82nd Airborne Division was briefed for an assault (ultimately aborted) on Lebanon, a place few of us had heard of and none cared about. "Any questions?" ended the battery commander, jabbing his swagger stick into the sand table. "Sir," asked one "crack trooper" (as Henry Luce invariably called us in *Time*), "who the hell is the enemy?" "Never mind that bullshit," was the reply. "That's not your problem. We'll tell you who to kill." It was ten years later, in college, when it dawned on me he didn't know the answer any more than we did.

For me, college darkened the whole prospect. Outside the ivy walls there was Cuba, and then Viet Nam. Inside I was introduced to a Greek chorus of mandarins and savants who proclaimed (with footnotes) the inevitable rise of the impersonal mass in some form or other, and the concomitant decline of the individual, the certainty of whose downfall was exceeded only by his inherent bestiality. I was catechized by *Canticle for Liebowitz*, plowed under on *Animal Farm*, enshrouded in *Darkness at Noon*, abused by *The Power Elite*, lost in *The Lonely Crowd*, blown away by those titanic trumpeters of Götterdämmerung — Hegel, Marx, Weber, and Schumpeter. In graduate school I pondered the "Invisible Hand" of Adam Smith and the *Visible Hand* of Al Chandler, both these hands indiscriminately turning Matthew Josephson's *Robber Barons* and Alan Nevins's "Industrial Statesmen" into grist for the mills that churned out William Whyte's *Organization Man* as River Rouge turned out Model T's.

"Man," as Mick Jagger says, "what a mess. I was shattered." My grandmother's assurance that I and everyone else had come into the world trailing clouds of glory crumbled under the massed assault of gloom and doom. True, life went on, and true, for me it got better — fellowships, friends, lovely Baltimore evenings at Memorial Stadium watching the Orioles at play. The first years in graduate school seemed to me the best I had ever known. Listening to my friends discourse on the evils of the present system and the beauties of the socialist nirvana to come, I sometimes felt like paraphrasing William Black, a British novelist who toured the English countryside with Carnegie, listening to Andy's tirades about the monarchy and its abuses. "We had such a discourse on . . . freedom and . . . purity and . . . incorruptibility," Black recalled, that we longed . . . to fly away and be at rest in that happy land. Why should we be lingering here in slavery? . . . And as we listened the land of promise grew more and more fair, more and more dismal and desperate became the results of [our] government. We couldn't see any of [these evils] it is true; for the Wiltshire hawthorne bushes are thick, and around us were only pleasant meadows and rippling streams, but they were there somewhere; and we wondered that the birds, in such a condition of affairs could sing so carelessly.

But watching the unfolding Nixonian obscenity, the spreading inferno in Viet Nam, and the burning of Baltimore's inner city leached away most of my optimism. For a time I considered self-exile to England, where eccentricity, if not individualism, still seemed to be cherished, or withdrawal into professorial sanctuary, where the grim present could be anesthetized by romanticizing the past. Poverty, however, precluded flight to England and the vibrant presentism of the University of Michigan's undergraduates cut off retreat to the rear. Gradually, optimism returned, fed by calmer counsel, like Walt Kelly's Albert Alligator, telling his friends, "Man can't live his whole life worrying about ten seconds of boom and whango," and Pogo Possum, pulling up in flight from the cry, "Run for the hills; the dam is bust!" to ask, "Wait a minute; is the swamp even *got* a dam?" and reinforced by memories of unsophisticated but shrewd observations of former colleagues. Once, for example, while I was still on the railroad, a picturesque conductor named "Dirty Neck" Burke heard me fretting about the menace of the Congo, with its feuding chieftains, Kasavubu and Lumumba. "I'll worry about them guys," observed Burke (who never read Walter Lippmann unless he appeared in *Racing Form*), "when I hear they can swim five thousand miles."

Life isn't that simple, of course, but neither is it as simple as the "Domino Theory," "I have in my hand a list of Communists. . . ," "We gave China away," or "Make the World Safe for Democracy." I found it more congenial to be soothed by optimistic capsules than to be traumatized by gloomy ones. (It's also worth remembering that simple slogans, not arcane theorizing, have galvanized mass movements. Consider, for instance, the impact of "Christ is risen!"; "There is but one God and his name is Allah!"; "Workers of the world, unite. You have nothing to lose but your chains!"; "Ein Reich! Ein Volk! Ein Führer!"; "Never Again!"; "Hell no, we won't go!"; and "Four More Years!")

Ultimately, I concluded that the epitaph for the individual, bawled so widely in my formative years, was premature. He, and now increasingly she, is yet alive, hopeful, and influential. Even among giant corporations, those bastions of depersonalization, whose bureaucratization of the entrepreneur's function Joseph Schumpeter diagnosed as capitalism's fatal disease, idiosyncrasy still raises its warty head now and then, and personality sometimes prevails. Indeed, in the ability of the occasional strong character to convert bureaucracy to an instrument of his personal will, capitalism finds, for better or worse, a source of regeneration. Numerous examples are at hand and some of them — Thomas Watson's IBM, Sol Linowitz's Xerox, Edwin Land's Polaroid — have had a dynamic impact on American society and its economy. Moreover, each of them grew and prospered in the face of preexisting, efficient, bureaucratized competitors.

The story of Henry Ford II's ability to shape the Ford Motor Company into an instrument of his personal will, however, presents the most astounding such case in the history of American business. The Ford Motor Company is not just large; it is by any standards enormous. Consistently one of the half-dozen largest manufacturing firms in the world, Ford in 1977 ranked third among U.S. industrial corporations in sales ($38 billion), fourth in assets ($19 billion) and net profits ($1.7 billion). The second largest American car producer, it also operates a global manufacturing, assembling, and marketing empire in more than fifty countries worldwide, selling more vehicles outside North America than any other U.S. firm. In addition, the company is moderately diversified (electronics, aerospace) and retains the fully integrated structure created by its founder. River Rouge remains the only American automobile plant where raw materials come in one end and cars roll out the other. The firm makes enough of its own steel and glass to rank among major American producers of both.

Ford Motor Company obviously could not exist without a complex managerial bureaucracy to coordinate its intricate operations. If ever a firm's structure presented an insuperable obstacle to individual domination, Ford would seem to have been a prime candidate. In fact, the contrary situation has prevailed through most of the company's history. Despite the obviously necessary delegation of much authority to subordinates, through the 1960s and 1970s it was clear to industry observers and to company employees, from vice-presidents in Dearborn to the plant manager in Upper Hutt, New Zealand, that the boss was Chairman Henry. Ford knew his own mind and power, and never hesitated to interpose both, even against the advice of his managers, their staffs, and the sophisticated network of computers the company used constantly. He was known to bring a Lincolnesque ending ("Seven ayes, one nay; the nay has it") to executive committee meetings by inquiring, "Whose name is on the building?"

Ford played a constant, dominant role in the company's affairs, not only in broad policy making, but also at lower organizational levels, frequently intervening in personnel decisions down to the third level of management. The company's policy and products thus reflected Ford's personal view of business's social responsibilities to the community, his philosophy of international trade, and his opinion on what kinds of car the public would buy. Ford served as first chairman of the National Alliance of Businessmen, which tried to find industrial jobs for the hard-core unemployed, and he prodded his company to set an example in this area for all American industry. His cash, willpower, and persuasiveness powered the Detroit Renaissance. His company throve in the European market and probed for profitable openings in the underdeveloped world using structures and tactics developed from studies that he personally instigated and approved. No new model entered the Ford line without his personal imprimatur. He once gave direct orders to Ford Division

General Manager Donald Frey to abandon plans for a seven-passenger limousine, bypassing the three officers between him and Frey on the organization chart. As Arjay Miller, one of a legion of Ford Motor Company ex-presidents, once observed, "The first thing you have to understand about the company is that Henry Ford is the boss. . . . He was always the boss from the first day I came in [1946], and he always will be the boss until he decides to retire."

In addition to being boss of his company, Ford was a conspicuous celebrity. Opinionated, outspoken, leading a pyrotechnic personal life, he seldom was out of the news for long. He was the only American businessman of his time whose name recurred on "ten best-known American" lists and other such gauges of notoriety and the only head of a *Fortune*'s "Top 500" that most Americans could identify. His friends included not only the moguls of the automotive world in the U.S. and abroad, but also race-car drivers, beautiful women, and a New York City police reporter. He had close ties with three of America's most prominent black leaders: Whitney Young of the Urban League, whose father got a $300-a-month job as an electrical engineer from the original Henry Ford at a time when few blacks could find such jobs anywhere; Carl Stokes, former mayor of Cleveland, ex-assembly line worker; and Coleman Young, mayor of Detroit, partner with Ford in the city's resurgence, and former organizer for the United Auto Workers during the union's most violent period of confrontation with Henry's grandfather and his "Enforcer," Harry Bennett.

Chairman Henry's achievements loom even larger in light of the circumstances in which his leadership of the company began. In the fall of 1945, when Henry II's mother and grandmother joined forces to persuade his legendary grandfather to turn over the reins, the Ford Motor Company was sliding rapidly down the razor blade of business life. It seemed only a matter of time — and not long at that — until the Ford name joined the long list of family firms that passed from the American business scene. Bankruptcy or, more likely, sale to a competitor seemed inevitable.

The problem was not an inability to make cars — enough old hands like Meade Bricker remained to keep the line going — or sell them — you could sell anything in the car-starved, cash-flush market of postwar America — but rather a question of not knowing what it cost to make them. In fact, no one at Ford knew what it cost to do anything or even whether the company's massive wartime contracts had yielded a profit or loss.

The company had no cost-accounting capability whatever. Three decades before, as Model T production rose and unit costs fell, Charlie Sorenson had shown Henry I his calculations that showed economies of scale. "That's enough, Charlie," said Ford. "Don't show me any more figures; I've got the smell of the thing now." Thereafter, Ford concentrated on design and "running full" in the Carnegie manner. He despised accounting (a seedy offshoot of the banking conspiracy), wouldn't use accountants, and wouldn't let anyone else bring them in either. Once while Henry was out of town, his son Edsel authorized construction of a new office building with the fourth floor set aside for an accounting department. When Henry returned and heard the news, he left without comment, but sent a nocturnal raiding party that cleared the floor of the offending desks, telephones, and office machinery. Next morning Ford told his son, "Edsel, if you really need more [office] room, you'll find plenty of it on the fourth floor." For the old man, dividing the number of cars produced into the year's total expenditures was cost accounting enough; consequently, in 1945, the firm was run the same way as the pre-Carnegie iron trade, as a "lump business."

For a long time it didn't matter; as long as new plants and bank balances kept going up, income obviously exceeded expenses. Plenty of great fortunes had been made — by English textile manufacturers, and by the early Du Ponts, for example — in blissful ignorance of costs. Henry Ford's was not the first, though it was surely the greatest and probably the last. When the time arrived — during the declining market of 1920 and thereafter — when such information became important, the elder Ford simply didn't care. Like his friend Edison and other contemporary industrialists, he was not intrigued by money per se and certainly not motivated by it.

Ford also had not a whisper of market forecasting ability. Old Henry didn't believe much in statistics and scoffed outright at the notion of past data as an indication of future truth: the idea was a hoax on the face of it. (It's tough for me, who listened to Robert McNamara's "body counts" and the projections he made from them, not to warm to the old codger at that.) Besides, if someone had somehow divined accurate cost data and market predictions, the company couldn't have used them. Above the shop floor the lines of authority disappeared into a chaos of untitled executives with no clear-cut responsibilities and with positions that often resulted not from ability, but from personal relationships with Harry Bennett.

Ford's free-form arrangements worked fine in the halcyon days of the Model T, but they failed to withstand the competitive onslaught of General Motors, kept in constant fighting trim by Sloan's statistical guidelines. In the increasing chaos of the 1930s and 40s, only the company's enormous cash reserves and the residual goodwill of dealers and the loyalty of die-hard customers (many of them attached to the V-8, which Chevrolet didn't offer until 1955) kept the firm afloat until young Henry arrived at the top. The steady decline of the company's cash reserves and its fading third place in sales provided graphic evidence of past decay and grim omens for the future.

Confronting this mess, Henry Ford II had paper credentials that could only charitably have been called so much as modest. From a childhood spent playing with locomotives and automobiles on his grandfather's estate, he had gone on to an undistinguished academic career at private schools and at Yale. In college he switched from engineering to sociology when the former proved "too tough," but failed to graduate even from the easier curriculum because he was caught turning in a custom-written term paper. Back in Dearborn, he went to work for the company, learning the business as a "grease monkey in the experimental garage and a checker in the dynamometer room." In

1941 he entered the navy, where he filled inconsequential stateside posts.

When his father died in 1943, he was released from the navy and returned to the company, where, like almost everyone else in the Ford executive ranks, he had no defined duties or authority. Between his return in 1943 and his assumption of the presidency in 1945, Ford later described himself as having been "green and searching for answers." He found some, mostly bad: the company was a mess and Bennett would have to go before much could be done about it. He did, however, discover one man he could trust, John Bugas, and Bugas helped him find a few more. But together they numbered a small crew to try to overhaul such a foundering hulk.

Henry II did have certain other intangible assets, as he soon proved. He had his heritage in the automobile business; he had been raised in it and had never considered any other career. Detroit, where car-building is often called "a disease, not a profession," doesn't think any amount of technical skill or bureaucratic finesse will avail a man unless he had a dose of gasoline in his blood, and this young Henry certainly had. He also had a goal — perhaps a vision would have been a more apt description under the circumstances — of returning his company to its former preeminent position in the industry, while keeping it a family firm. He had the ability to assess realistically his own capacities. These included a talent for assuming and exercising authority surprising in a young man whose most responsible experience had been as undergraduate manager of the Yale crew. He also radiated a strong personal charisma that came in handy when recruiting a new team.

As soon as Henry became president, he fired Harry Bennett and his cronies. To begin the salvage process he rounded up what trustworthy old hands he could find at Ford. Then he recruited Earl Newsom, a public relations specialist, and public opinion poller Elmo Roper to begin repairing the company's image, tarnished by years of anti-Semitism and antiunion goonery. But none of these could tackle the most pressing problem: installing a cost-accounting system, locating the hemorrhages, and applying tourniquets before the company bled to death. Something had to be done in a hurry, for the company was losing $10 million a month through the first half of 1946. And always, across town, there was the intimidating presence of General Motors — rich, efficient, powerful, capable of swallowing the market if Ford should falter.

In this menacing competitor, however, Ford found the instrument of his company's resurrection in the person of Ernest R. Breech, president of Bendix Aviation, a GM subsidiary. Bright, ambitious, thoroughly versed in the GM method, Breech had been shunted from the main line to the top of GM onto the side track at Bendix by, ironically enough, ex-Ford man William Knudsen, who (according to Sloan) thought Breech a "financial man" and not a "car man." It took several visits and a liberal application of the Ford charm to lure Breech from his perch on a high branch of the GM corporate tree, but in the end, he succumbed. His task — restoring order and doing so profitably — required so thoroughgoing a reorganization as to nearly undo him, as Breech admitted to his biographer. Driving to work one morning in 1946, a month after he took the job, he was suddenly struck by the magnitude of the shambles and pulled off the road to gather his wits: "For the first time in my life I was overwhelmed. Not afraid, but very disturbed. Our problem seemed almost insuperable. Things were in a mess. It would take years to get them under control." More specifically, he diagnosed Ford's ills as "rundown plants, obsolete products, almost nonexistent financial control, an inadequate engineering staff, and just sufficient cash [flow] to meet daily [needs]." (He might have added to the list the worst labor relations in the industry and a poor public image.)

Breech's prescription was about what one would have expected from a GM man (and, not coincidentally, included a list of the contributions to American industry made by several of the principal characters in this book):

What we went after was precisely what it will take for any firm to be competitive in the rich but hard-fought market of today and tomor-

row . . . above all . . . competent management, flexible and big enough
to respond swiftly to changing market conditions [Sloan, Pierre du-
Pont]; research and engineering adequate to meet the enormous
strains of modern product competition [Edison, Whitney]; plants and
machinery efficient enough to compete with the best in the industry
[Henry Ford I, Carnegie]; and a financial control system which supplies some forecasting [Sloan], that keeps operations efficient, and is
geared to produce peak profits [Du Pont].

Few Ford employees were prepared to administer (or swallow
easily) this massive dose, so Breech raided the ranks of his former employer. GM, with as much depth at every position as the
Michigan football team down the road in Ann Arbor, had talent
to waste and wasted plenty of it. Dangling the prospect of mean-
ingful responsibilities and swift promotion, Breech lured hundreds of supervisers from GM to Ford. Not all of them worked
out, but many had the time of their lives. One of them subsequently observed that he "had more downright fun and progressed further in his first six months with Ford than he had in 16
years" with a GM division.

Ford himself contributed to the recruiting program, reversing
a long-standing company policy of not recruiting college graduates (another of old Henry's fetishes that had been manifested in
company policy). He also hired the so-called Whiz Kids, a group
of ten former air force statistical analysts who sold themselves as
a package in the postwar job market. The Whiz Kids included
Tex Thornton, who later put together the Litton Industries con-
glomerate; Arjay Miller (later dean of Stanford's business
school) and Robert McNamara (John Kennedy's Secretary of
Defense), who rose to the Ford presidency; and J. Edward
Lundy, who became a Ford executive vice-president.

The galaxy of new talent encountered reactions ranging from
entrenched resistance to cooperative bewilderment at the new
methods. When they asked the controller's office what the financial projections were for six months ahead, they might as well
have asked for a projection of lunar eclipses. Willing but unable,
the controller replied, as the Pentagon apparently replied to Sec-

retary of Defense McNamara twenty years later, "What do you want them to be?" Gradually, however, the new management turned the company around. Henry Ford II made peace with the labor unions; Newsom rebuilt the company's public image; Breech's system analyzed costs, and the company assaulted them by revamping and expanding its obsolete plant, spending money with a dedication Carnegie would have relished — $4 billion between 1945 and 1962; the basic Ford was redesigned and reengineered, while new models expanded the line to broaden the base of competition.

By the end of 1946, Ford was making money and went on to make more, a total of $5.5 billion during Breech's tenure, which lasted until 1960. General Motors remained far ahead in total sales, but Ford regained second position and even managed to outsell Chevrolet once in a while. Mistakes were made along the way, and some of them — like the Edsel, which chewed up two or three hundred million dollars — were humdingers. The GM decentralized, divisional structure turned out to be inappropriate at Ford and subsequently was revamped into a functional arrangement — product development, manufacturing, and marketing. On the whole, however, Breech did everything asked of him. In the eyes of many, he literally saved the company. One observer declared:

When the history of the Ford Motor Company is finally written, it should be noted in bold type that Ford was saved from imminent oblivion or at least a complete change of ownership by Mr. Ernest R. Breech. . . . In my opinion this rescue operation under forced draft while in competition with the most successful company in the world, ranks with Alfred Sloan's structuring [of] General Motors as the outstanding corporate achievement of the twentieth century.

Earl Newsom put it more succinctly, "There would be no Ford Motor Company today if it hadn't been for Ernie Breech."

No man, of course, is indispensable, not even Breech; he wasn't the only talented, frustrated executive who could have been induced to leave GM and bring its methods with him. The second Henry, nevertheless, owed him a great deal, which he acknowledged in print, in salaries, stock options, and business deals that made Breech a millionaire many times over, and by naming a Ford ore ship after him. Breech left Ford in 1960 (of his own free will, he and Henry claim; forced out, according to Detroit's underground telegraph) and went on to a successful career reorganizing TWA while grappling with Howard Hughes, a tycoon who made Henry Ford II look like Herbert Hoover by comparison.

In 1960, with his company prospering, solidly organized, and well stocked with executives capable of assuming control, Henry Ford II might well have been expected to retreat from the man-killing regimen demanded of active automobile executives. (Skeptics are invited to spend a week in the Ford World Headquarters parking lot, logging people in and out. Don't forget to show up on Saturday and Sunday; the automobile industry pays its executives well, but from those who have much, much is expected.) He could have been many things instead: avuncular board chairman, philanthropist, art collector, jet set playboy, adviser to presidents, sponsor of urban redevelopment, for all but the first of which he demonstrated a proclivity. He did, in fact, take the opposite course, reclaiming the reins from his hired help and taking firm hold of the company's operations.

Ford regarded the Breech years as more than a period of renaissance for his company; in effect, he himself accepted them as a period of apprenticeship in its management. By 1960, he had learned enough. "I've graduated, Ernie," he reportedly told Breech, who commented at the time, "Henry doesn't need me anymore." Ford, no ball of fire in college ("I was flunking engineering," he remembered, "and they said sociology was easy so I transferred, but I flunked that too"), became an apt pupil in Dearborn. "He listened," Breech said, "he took advice, and he learned. He may not have been a great student at Yale, but he certainly was a great student of how to become an executive and he became one."

After taking over, Ford ran the company with an eye-catching flamboyance, personally making decisions about products and people with a celerity that might sometimes have been arbitrary, capricious, or even cruel, but that often left competitors in the dust. Ford made and unmade top executives with lightning speed. Some — Miller, McNamara — left with their shields; others — Jack Reith, Bunkie Knudsen, Lee Iacocca — departed upon them. Ford may have acted out of vanity: Knudsen and Iacocca projected strong images of their own, while J. Edward Lundy, who spoke with a powerful voice inside the organization but was a nonentity to the public, survived more than thirty years. Or he may simply have been protecting the family position at the top while his son Edsel, born in 1949, learned the business. (His appointment in 1978 of his younger brother, William Clay Ford, as prince regent supported the family-continuity hypothesis.)

Whatever his reasons, Chairman Henry's personnel policies, while producing casualties and tension in the ranks, created enticing possibilities for advancement as well. Ford executives down the line often reflected the attitude of junior British navy officers in the days of sail, who used to drink to "long, bloody wars; oceans of gore; promotions galore." As one Ford aspirant told me:

The exciting thing about this company is that if you come up with an idea, no matter how big, you know the money can be found, and you know who the man is that has to be convinced. In a situation like that you can dream any kind of dream. At GM, it's hopeless. Everything has to be passed up the line through a dozen committees, but the credit doesn't pass back down.

Mavericks did actually seem to survive more often at Ford than its competitors. GM produced few if any Iacoccas, brazenly hustling the head man with bright ideas like the Mustang; the last one, John Delorean, quit in frustration in 1972. On the other hand several emerged at Ford, including William Bourke, who vaulted from Ford Asia-Pacific to Ford of Europe to a Dearborn vice-presidency in five years.

Ford's decisive vote on which cars to make could lead to mistakes, as the Edsel undeniably proved, but could also expedite a success like the Mustang, which leapt from drawing board to

showroom to an insurmountable sales lead before GM could get
its committees together to mount a competitive model. Henry
claimed to have a feel for what the American public would buy
(the ultimate attribute of a consummate "car man") and a string
of winners — Mustang, Maverick, Pinto, Cougar, Capri, Granada, Fiesta, Fairmont — suggests he was not entirely wrong.
The company had particular success with cars and trucks that
expressed individualistic flair, while the great mass market for
conservative sedans remained Chevrolet's happiest hunting
ground, suggesting that buyers gravitated to the company that
reflected their own self-image. If so, the very quirks of the current Henry's personality, like his grandfather's before him, by
resonating with the traditional American admiration for stubborn independence, became salable commodities.

Certainly his penchant for speed and motor racing, another
inherited trait and a widespread American enthusiasm, contributed to strategies that widened the market for Ford automobiles.
The V-8 engine had long made Fords top dog in American stock
car racing, a position usurped after the war by the Hudson Hor-
net and others. Ford didn't like losing, and he responded to Lee
Iacocca's pitch that racing could sell cars. In the 1960s Ford
fielded factory teams in several racing categories and developed
engines that won at Indianapolis and on the European Grand
Prix circuit. An inveterate reader of racing magazines, Henry
knew that the Daytona Five Hundred and the Twenty-Four
Hours of Le Mans represented the top of the greasy pole in
American stock car and European road racing respectively. He
wanted to win both and told his engineers to design equipment
that would do the job. So they did that. In 1963, Fords took the
first five places at Daytona. Le Mans came harder, but failure in
1964 and '65 was followed by four successive wins that gave the
company enormous publicity and the boss the chance to hold
court in the grand marshal's box, posing for pictures in a Ford
jacket and holding the trophy aloft. Having won the big prizes,
Ford withdrew to a lower profile, but Ford engines in Wolf-
Fords, Coyote-Fords, Lotus-Fords, and other hybrids continued

*The grandson with his own racing car: Henry Ford II
squints into the Le Mans glare, June, 1967.*

to win a lot of races around the world through technical collaboration between the company and racing-car designers.

Less spectacular, but equally influential in the long run, was Chairman Henry's role in revamping the company's overseas operations into their current multinational structure. Throughout the 1950s, and increasingly after 1960, the firm's international strategies reflected Henry's philosophy of global economics.

Ford Motor Company earned its first export dollar in 1903 and remained active outside the United States thereafter. The evolution of the company's overseas facilities was a complex one, but the results can be summarized simply. By 1960 three companies, Ford of Canada (which owned subsidiaries in the British Commonwealth countries outside Great Britain itself), Ford of England, and Ford of Germany, existed as self-sufficient, essentially autonomous divisions, each producing its own line of cars, occasionally drawing on Dearborn for technological assistance, and submitting, sometimes reluctantly, to its coordination of export markets outside the three companies' defined domains. International sales had historically contributed an important share of the company's total business: 9 percent (by units sold), 1911–1920; 12 percent, 1921–1930; and 24 percent in each succeeding decade through 1960, as well as a significant share of its profits — 20 percent in 1962, for example.

Despite this record, Ford soon felt that his company's international structure was inadequate for the future. It consisted, in his words, of "a collection of individual national organizations." Efficient as they might be in their own bailiwicks, such organizations had horizons too limited to deal with "the day [that] might not be far off when organizations even of the scope of North America and Europe will prove too limiting." Furthermore, the national companies' facilities, concentrated in the industrialized countries of the world, could not hope to penetrate the potential markets of the underdeveloped world, where the people, "deeply committed to fast industrialization" demanded local manufacture or assembly as a prerequisite for doing business. "Whether we like it or not," Ford declared in 1961, "Africa, Latin America, and Asia are going all-out into the industrial age. . . . If we want to share in those markets, rich and vast as they will someday surely be . . . we are going to have to go in with our tools and know-how and help them get the things they want."

In these statements and others, Ford revealed that he was more than a parochial American industrialist; he was an internationalist who saw the whole world as a potential market for Ford products. Widely traveled in the service of the company (he made trips to Europe in 1948 and 1952, and frequently thereafter traveled around the world to the company's facilities), he broadened his perspective as an alternate delegate to the United Nations in the early 1950s. Robert McNamara, speaking not only of his experiences with Ford at the company but also as head of the World Bank, declared, "There's no doubt that he's one of the best informed businessmen in the U.S. on the rest of the world."

Like his grandfather's, Ford's world view envisioned a global market for automobiles; not a market in which American manufacturers could plunder less fortunate peoples, but rather one in which American industry stood to benefit from worldwide industrial prosperity. In the 1920s the elder Ford had said, "We ought to wish for every nation as large a degree of self-support as possible. Instead of wishing to keep them dependent upon us for what we manufacture, we should wish them to learn to manufacture themselves and build up a solidly founded civilization." Forty years later, his grandson called upon American firms "to go in with our tools and know-how and help them get the things they want." He had already publicly advocated free trade in an industrializing world: "I believe this country should step forth boldly and lead the world toward freer trade. . . . We need competition the world over to keep us on our toes and sharpen our wits. The keener the competition, the better it will be for us. . . . People cannot keep on buying from us unless we buy from them, and unless international trade can go on, our business will stagnate here at home."

In the 1960s Ford transformed the structure of his overseas affiliates according to his philosophy by creating local manufacturing facilities. Specifically, this resulted first in the coordination of Ford of England and Ford of Germany by Ford of Europe, and a unified product line to optimize the advantages of the emerging European free trade communities; and second, in the creation of Ford Asia-Pacific (FASPAC) to develop and produce vehicles for the southeast Asian market including, if possible, Japan. Both organizations embodied a heavy dependence on a policy (called "complementation" by Ford Asia-Pacific) of cross-hauling components from specialized parts plants in various countries to strategically located assembly plants. Both organizations resulted from plans prepared by the Ford staff at Henry Ford II's instigation. He accepted the plans not because they offered the only alternatives (both General Motors and the Japanese manufacturers employ a different method), but because they combined the prospect of profit with a company structure consonant with his personal beliefs. Indeed, they embodied his grandfather's conveyor belt concept, blown into global dimensions.

In implementing the plans for global organizations, the company benefited from steps already taken by its chairman. In 1948, Ford had instructed his overseas subsidiaries to sell worldwide in any market they could find. During the 1950s he began buying up the affiliates' stock, much of which had been sold to local investors during the 1920s. By 1962 the parent company owned 75 percent of Ford of Canada, 99 percent of Ford of Germany, and 100 percent of Ford of England. In 1961, already sure of unquestioned control of the subsidiaries, he moved further toward an integrated international structure, stepping up overseas investment so that for the first time it exceeded domestic capital expenditure, and informing his subordinates that: "to further the growth of our world-wide operations, each purchasing activity of the Company or an affiliated company should consider . . . sources . . . not only in its country but also . . . in other countries." To break down local resistance to the new policies, Ford dispatched American executives to key posts abroad. In 1962, for example, Americans headed eight of the twelve European sales, assembly, and manufacturing companies.

In Europe, Ford of England and Ford of Germany were in effect super overseas operating divisions by 1966, still functioning highly autonomously although plugged into the Dearborn staff for technical assistance. Each company produced a wide range of vehicles that not only duplicated and competed, but also used no common parts. Each company, nevertheless, made money and gave Ford Motor a foot in each of the European free trade camps, the Common Market and the European Free Trade Association (EFTA). Even so, Ford found this arrangement wasteful and inadequate. He accepted a staff plan of reorganization and authorized Ford of Europe to coordinate the integration of the European companies into a single unit, producing a single line of cars assembled from common parts flowing from all over the region. "Implicit in this change," he said, "was a growing recognition that the entire Company needed to think more and more in world-wide terms and that the foreign subsidiaries no longer could be thought of as a collection of individual national organizations. This was particularly true of Europe, where eventual expansion of the common market seemed certain to require a strongly integrated approach."

In the years after 1967, Ford of Europe moved steadily toward a goal of a product line built of internationally interchangeable parts. In doing so it adhered to the original plan's assumptions: that the European vehicle market would expand, that the Common Market would survive and incorporate Britain and the rest of EFTA, and that European consumers would accept cars that had no local national identity. Manufacturing, at the same time, became more decentralized with the construction of single-product plants such as a transmission plant in Bordeaux, France. Parts flow from these works to an expanding network of assembly plants in Europe; the plants ship engines and transmissions to Asia and the United States and supply, for example, major components for the American Pinto, fulfilling Ford's contention that "the entire web of components and end products [will] become increasingly multi-national."

Such a complex restructuring of going concerns, of course, met many obstacles such as national pride, the integration of metric and English systems of measurement, shortages of components resulting from labor disputes (particularly in Britain), and product defects (especially in quality-conscious Germany); and the structure had to be modified accordingly. The company persevered with its original plan, however, and maintained its position, first achieved in 1965, of leading the world in sales by U.S. companies outside North America. Overall results seem to have justified Ford's determination to create a single European company despite the objections of many of his subordinates. For example, Sir Patrick Hennessy, who headed Ford of Britain, strongly resisted the plan, but later admitted, "He [Ford] was right and I was wrong."

Ford's gamble on the Common Market's viability and Britain's entry into it paid big dividends. At a time when many American firms, frightened by the decaying British economy or the specter of its semisocialist government, left the United Kingdom or curtailed operations there, Ford not only stayed, but poured in tens of millions of dollars in additional investment. The resulting expanded capacity increased the company's ability to compete in the British market and provided a source for components priced in cheap pounds, many of which went into cars sold for ever-dearer Deutschmarks, guilders, and other appreciating continental currencies.

In an equally bold risk, Ford decided that Spanish political stability would survive Franco's succession and spent a billion dollars there. The company in effect bet that Spain's relatively low labor costs, its undeveloped but potentially large domestic market, and its probable access to the Common Market would recoup the investment. Ford gambled that thousands of Spaniards would abandon their casual Mediterranean lifestyle to work like hell on the assembly line and that enough Spanish entrepreneurs could be found to set up supplier industries and dealerships. Spaniards repaid the Company's investment with production and profits, and Henry Ford II himself with a tumultuous, flower-strewn welcoming parade when he arrived on a tour of inspection.

The company's European operations have, in recent years, contributed to the success of its American sales. Reversing the original process, in which Dearborn designed cars for manufacture in Europe, and reflecting Ford's personal preference for European cars, Ford of Europe developed a series of cars that achieved instant success in North America — the Capri, the Granada, and most recently the Fiesta. Chairman Henry clearly belonged to that group of Americans designated by French journalist-politician Jean-Jacques Servan-Schreiber as the only people who fully comprehended the potential of the Common Market.

In Asia, Ford confronted a very different set of circumstances. Outside of Australia and New Zealand, where the company had long-established and profitable subsidiaries, the region's huge population constituted an enormous potential market, but its low income levels translated into weak effective demand. Ford, in common with a long line of British and American businessmen who dreamed of selling every Chinese a bowler hat, a bicycle, or a Coca-Cola, seemed fascinated with the potential of the Asian market. Its relative poverty, however, precluded the establishment of self-sufficient national companies on the Ford of England model. Unfortunately for American producers, this sort of commitment to local manufacturing was just what the government of many of the region's emerging states demanded. Ford Asia-Pacific's answer was the "Complementation Plan," presented to Henry Ford II in February, 1971. ("That's not a plan," he derided, when presented with the original version. "It's an idea. Bring it back when it's a plan.") In this scheme, the company combined its existing Asian facilities with a set of local manufacturing plants constructed around the region, each producing parts consonant with the level of local technology and labor skill and shipping them to assembly plants throughout the area, much as Ford of Europe did. The more sophisticated components were drawn from the company's sources in Australia, New Zealand, and England until local markets and technical capacities could justify local manufacture.

Complementation offered attractive benefits to some local governments: large capital expenditures ($40 million for a body plant in the Philippines); increased employment, both in Ford plants and home-owned supplier companies; the training of local supervisory and labor forces; and the chance to generate export earnings by shipping components abroad (Ford, as the company tells prospective host countries, is Britain's largest single generator of export earnings). Ford himself approved the plan, both because it offered some chance to operate profitably at an early stage of regional development, and because it squared with his view of the appropriate American role in developing industrialization in the underdeveloped world, a role he thinks free enterprise can play better than any government program.

The plan moved forward slowly, beset by the difficulties inherent in a region of so many different languages, cultures, tastes, business conditions, and governments. Dealing with these problems required massive staff work. The FASPAC handbook on "Regulatory Issues," for example, which outlines government regulations relevant to Ford Motor, runs to some sixty pages and is revised almost daily. Labor relations required an industrial relations staff to "translate . . . the company's United Auto Workers Agreement in the United States into all the languages and customs of Asia." Advertising had to be not only multilingual, but also tailored to local tastes and the available media. The Japanese, for example, responded to advertisements featuring luxury cars and Caucasian models adorned with designer clothes and dripping with jewelry. The Taiwan Chinese, on the other hand, regarded such displays as insulting; to beguile them the company's staff prepared layouts of small cars and Oriental models wearing traditional garb. Market forecasting, so essential to success, particularly in a developing market, demanded novel approaches in a region where the company often supplied statistics on population and vehicle ownership to the local governments rather than vice versa.

Finally, producing vehicles demanded complex coordination, even for the simplest prototype. Ford's Fiera, designed to be the "Model T" of Asia, consisted basically of "a motorized tray on wheels" to which a variety of body parts (square, because rounded sheet metal parts cost more and require greater skills to produce than angular ones) could be bolted to create trucks, utility cars, or vans. Despite its simplicity, the Fiera embodied components from around the world. As assembled in Thailand (a relatively advanced country for the region), for example, it included an engine from Taiwan, axles from Mexico, a steering gear from Japan, a transmission from France, and other parts from Australia, New Zealand, Canada, Germany, Britain, and local suppliers in Thailand.

With these methods Ford established a modest presence on the periphery of the two potentially significant Asian markets, China and Japan. Politics blocked access to both: to China completely and to Japan except for a trickle of luxury vehicles like Thunderbirds and Continentals acquired by the wealthy as status symbols. Both situations vexed Chairman Henry. He always favored free trade with China (with all countries for that matter) and didn't mind telling John Foster Dulles so. The Japanese government's fiercely protectionist policy, he said, "burns me up. . . . I can't go into Japan. We can't build, we can't sell, we can't service, we can't do a damn thing over there. . . . I'd be in there tomorrow if the Japanese would let me. I'd be manufacturing cars and I'd give [them] a run for their money." The American government "ought to have the guts to stand up to unfair competition. The Australians had the guts to do something about it. [The Australians told the Japanese that if they wanted to sell cars there, they'd have to manufacture them there.] Why can't we?"

It was a mark of the man's confidence in himself and his organization that he was sure he could compete with the Japanese on their own ground. Perhaps he could have, for surely he did remarkable things. His determination and his ability to choose the right man at the right time brought one of America's venerable manufacturing companies back from the brink of oblivion equipped with techniques of management, production, and sales refined by generations of manufacturers from Whitney to Sloan. By taking personal charge of his revivified firm and dominating its complex bureaucracy, Ford turned a giant corporation into an enormously potent instrument of his own will. By translating his philosophy of international business and economics into company policies, he made the Ford Motor Company a global empire.

Whether that empire will pass to his son time will tell. But Henry Ford II's own career showed that even in an age when business, government, and labor seemed to spawn ever-larger units and power ran to bureaucracies and committees, one man could still make his mark and be measured by it. Whether this can be construed as the vaguely defined "individualism" that Americans nostalgically cherish as part of their heritage is, I suppose, a matter of outlook. Certainly the late twentieth century boasts few Henry Ford II's to serve as the caretakers of a national mythology, but the operative question seems to be not how many are there, but how many do there have to be? Statistically, few nineteenth-century Americans actually made the trek from rags to riches, but Carnegie's spectacular career demonstrated that it could be done. Millions of Americans, basking in the reflected glow of Andy's well-publicized triumphs, could see the modest improvements in their own lives and their children's as part of the same glorious, uniquely American progress toward a brighter world. Learning English, finding a job, puzzling out the labyrinth of a strange city, bringing in the first crop on a homestead farm, buying a home, sending a child off to college — in retrospect these accomplishments may seem small potatoes compared to the opulence squandered in Carnegie castles and Frick mansions. And the meanness, squalor, and drudgery of everyday life in industrializing America make it seem that most ordinary people lived on a dung heap, from which a handful of plutocrats quarried diamonds. But for people of the time — most of them, at least — their small successes were interlinked with the greater ones, and millions of people who never heard of Herbert Spencer, let alone read him, could feel, with Carnegie, that all was well because all got better.

Henry Ford II, surrounded by flashy cars, escorting beautiful women, able and willing to tell anyone he pleased to go to hell, provided the veritable incarnation of modern American machismo. This independence of spirit many of his workers admired ("He's a mean son-of-a-bitch, but he's a man," they told me in several languages around the world) and emulated, sometimes by throwing a monkeywrench into the Ford works.

For better or worse, Henry Ford II's image — in fairness to the man it was neither entirely accurate nor wholly of his own making — comported with the surviving tradition of personal independence. In that tradition, people keep trying to make it and some of them, like Edwin Land, make it big.

Edwin Land (left), addressing a gathering

10

The Philosopher Scientist Edwin Land

L IKE many an academic, I'm a frustrated novelist. I even wrote a novel once; the manuscript and a set of rejections squat on the shelf in front of me. My problem is plots. I have trouble concocting reasonable ones; mine wander from the pedestrian to the wildly improbable.

Here, for example, is one such excursion from the mundane to the implausible. I'll make the hero the son of a prosperous Jewish scrap dealer in Connecticut, thus subtly establishing a background blended of ethnicity, social mobility, and Yankee ingenuity. As a boy my hero, as boys so often do, grew up in awe of his father. This makes for a banal plot situation, truly, but one that lets me establish motivation by saying that my hero, at an early age, decides to outstrip his father's achievements.

The father, in classic American style, wants to launch his son on a loftier trajectory than his own, so sends the lad off to a fancy prep school, far removed from the family scrap yard. At prep school the young man becomes something of a prodigy in science, but just to prove he's not one of those weird prodigies, I'll also make him an athlete. In fact, I'll make him a track man, which shows he's competitive but nonviolent, and that he prefers individual achievement to submersion in team efforts.

After prep school comes college, and since I can send my hero anywhere I want, I'll send him to — O Bastion of Genius, O Citadel of Knowledge — where else? — Harvard.

Now for a twist in the plot. During a school vacation the boy goes to New York. Wandering through Times Square, as all good tourists must, he finds himself blinded by the glaring lights of the Great White Way. Dazzled by the myriad bulbs flashing away on billboards and theatre marquees, and fearful that in his blindness he may be run over by an automobile, our hero decides there must be some way to cut down all that glare without diminishing the brilliance of the spectacle that radiated it. Instantly he perceives his chance for fortune.

I once read in a "how to" book for writers that you're allowed one explanation by coincidence per story, so I guess I'll use mine here. The boy grew up in a town where scientific books were scarce, but coincidentally he had come into possession of one, R. W. Wood's *Physical Optics*. He had thus become absorbed with light and its behavior and could see the coruscating brilliance of Times Square as a problem in physics, not just a spectacular pain in the eye. Even as a coincidence this is a bit far-fetched, but I have, after all, the citable precedent of the boy Thomas Edison, finding inspiration in the pages of Richard Parker's *Natural and Experimental Philosophy*.

Pursuing his vision, the young man drops out of Harvard and moves to New York, where, supported by indulgent parents, he conducts experiments in a makeshift laboratory set up in his Fifty-fifth Street room. When these jury-rigged facilities prove inadequate, he avails himself of a well-equipped laboratory at the Columbia University physics department, gaining unauthorized access by sneaking in through an unlocked window. On these nocturnal prowls he enjoys the assistance of a young female companion, who, to add a dash of classic romance, subsequently becomes his partner in a marriage that endures a lifetime.

After three years of this, the young man returns to Harvard. At that august institution, the powers-that-be soon realize they have a genius on their hands and, despite the fact that he is technically only a sophomore, turn over to him and his bride the laboratory and materials needed to carry on their work. Three additional

years of labor at last bring results. One semester short of graduation, our hero leaves college forever, sets up his own business
backed by family capital, and patents a process for reducing
glare.

Soon giant corporations beat a path to his door: Kodak buys
light filters for its cameras; American Optical signs him up to
manufacture glare-free sunglasses. The barons of Wall Street,
ever on the alert for profitable places to put idle capital, get wind
of the young genius and his tiny company. They come, they see,
they are conquered. They supply a million dollars in fresh capital; moreover, the young man (now twenty-eight) so impresses
these hard-bitten money moguls (I'll give them names like
Rockefeller, Kuhn-Loeb, Harriman, and Warburg, just to make
them recognizable) that they give him the cash on terms that
leave him in complete control of the company, free to do anything he wants so long as he remains in its service ten years.

To make this part of the story even more incredible, I'll have it
span the worst years of the Great Depression by having my hero
go back to Harvard in 1929, drop out of school again and enter
business in 1932, get his first big contracts in 1935, and conquer
Wall Street in 1937.

Freshly funded, the company moves from its basement headquarters in Cambridge to a succession of larger factories and laboratories. During the Second World War the firm prospers,
devising this and that bit of optical equipment for the military.
Near the end of the war the hero has yet another vision, this one
of a product that few people need but that almost everyone, as
our genius foresees, will turn out to want. It is a product that no
one, including our hero, knows how to make; but he, like Edison
before him, has a knack for knowing that a thing *can* be done. In
due time this vision becomes a reality. On the wings of it, and a
succession of others that spring from his fecund mind, our pro-
tagonist rises from being an obscure scientist to a figure of world
prominence, gazetted with medals and honorary degrees at home
and abroad, becoming in the process one of the half-dozen richest men in America. His company, an extension of his genius,

follows an equally meteoric path, spreading around the world while its securities become a "glamour stock," one of the highest of the high fliers.

It's a good story, but I have a feeling it wouldn't sell as fiction. In reality, of course, it's the story of Edwin Land, founder and presiding genius of the Polaroid Corporation, and, in the form of newspaper and magazine articles, not to mention the company's products, it has sold quite well indeed. As an "incarnation of the American dream" (as Land's biographer called it) it's not in a class with Carnegie's story, for Land rose, not from rags, but from respectability to riches. It's a remarkable tale, nevertheless, not so much because of the man's flashes of brilliance, but rather because of his ability to translate his visions into industrial realities and sell them to his subordinates, his stockholders, and the buying public. To a degree remarkable in a corporate, bureaucratic age, Land has dominated the Polaroid Corporation, making it the embodiment of his personal will. His dominance was symbolized by the titles — chairman (chief executive officer), president (chief operating officer), and director of research — that he held from the company's founding until 1975. He then relinquished the presidency, with its control of day-to-day affairs, to William McCune, an old associate, but retained his other posts and has given no hint of retiring. As the head of a firm doing a billion-dollar-a-year business, Land obviously has to rely on a staff of professional managers, and the day has long passed when he knew every employee personally; nevertheless, every product Polaroid makes, or has ever made, reflects a vision of its founder and research that he personally conducted or supervised.

Land is a hard man to write about, a man of obsessions, including a ferocious dedication to his own privacy. He once declined to supply a *New York Times* reporter with the names of his married daughters, though they were obviously a matter of public record. Mark Olshaker, his biographer, got no closer to an interview with Land than a few sessions with Polaroid's director of publicity. Although Land has continuously made news since World War II, he was notoriously unwilling to give press conferences, submitting to one in 1947 and then one more twenty-four years later in 1971.

As a sop to the investment community, Land occasionally and grudgingly granted an audience to a reporter from the *New York Times, Forbes,* or *Fortune,* but the results scarcely justify the effort involved. Asked to elaborate on his methods, his point of view, or his processes, Land responded circuitously, in terms of individual eccentricity:

I find it very important to work intensively for long hours when I am beginning to see solutions to a problem. At such times *atavistic competences* [italics mine] seem to come welling up.

philosophical treacle:

We are ultimately as concerned about the success or failure of the society as we are about the success of our own enterprise. Indeed, we are convinced that we [these are imperial "we's," no doubt] cannot succeed . . . unless our society is successful.

or technical opacities:

This departure from what we expect on the basis of colorimetry is not a small effect but is complete . . . the factors in color vision hitherto regarded as determinative are significant only in a certain special case. What . . . misled us . . . is the accidental universality of this special case.

Heavy stuff, all that. Doubtless it was clear enough in Land's mind, but hardly a contribution to any layman's guide to business success. Not that Land was incapable of brevity, but his frequent one-liners didn't help much either. Asked once what problems he had encountered developing the SX-70 camera, Land answered, "There are no problems in science, only opportunities." Pressed by a *Fortune* reporter to explain Polaroid's success, described by the reporter as "one of the great miracles of business, fully documented and widely publicized, but still awesome to contemplate," Land replied winsomely, "Virtue and a good product are invincible!"

His stockholders fared little better at extracting information, despite the fact that at the annual shareholders' meeting (his only regular public appearance), they theoretically had a clear shot at him. Land dominated the meetings, tantalizing the faithful with vague but glowing allusions to miracles to come, occasionally bewitching them by levitating one like the OneStep instant color camera, or an instant home movie system. These unveilings were conducted with all the subtleties of television late-show commercials; they featured fanfares, dancing girls, babies, dogs, and demonstrations by Land himself. The audience was then divided into groups and herded away to try their own luck with the new gadgetry. After blazing away at the babies, the dancers, the dogs, and each other (but not at Land; shooting him, even with his own cameras, was strongly discouraged), the multitude reassembled.

Thus softened up, the stockholders usually abided the balance of the meeting with becoming docility. The occasional obstreperous outburst got a cold reception from Land, who, though he called his stockholders his "partners," clearly thought they should remain of the silent variety. Pressed for specifics about future products, Land might retort that he had no obligation to give any and hold this ground until loyal followers shouted the dissident down. At the 1977 meeting, after rhapsodizing about the wondrous achievement of the instant movie system (Polavision) with its "rather miraculous cassette," Land confronted one antidisestablishmentarian who wanted more than the song-and-dance act. The extravaganza aside, the "partner" declared, all that really counted was what the new system would do for "the bottom line" of the balance sheet. "The only thing that counts is the bottom line?" Land sneered. "What a presumptuous thing to say. The bottom line," he declared with finality, "is in heaven."

Indeed, given Polaroid's uneven dividend record and the stock's fluctuating market value ($24 to $60 per share in the first three months of 1979, for example), it may often have appeared to some Polaroid stockholders that they had more hope of a celestial than an earthly reward, despite their company's glamour status. For a stockholder to ask his firm's chief executive about the profit potential of some new product is not in itself unusual. It's a prerogative exercised routinely at annual corporate clambakes, though in fact stockholders have little recourse regardless of the reply. But Land's brand of tartness *was* rare; stockholders expect, and usually get, some soothing, if uninformative, response. Land could not only rebuke such impertinence and get away with it; most of his "partners" saw his aloofness as part of his charisma, an aura powerful enough to cement stockholder loyalty against the mundane centrifugal forces of disappointing earnings.

Land could not only serve "Pie in the sky, by and by," but his partners also ate it up. "Polaroid and . . . Dr. Edwin Land [the title by virtue of his honorary degrees]," wrote a *New York Times* market analyst in 1973, "continue to dazzle Americans, who clearly regard him as a latter-day Henry Ford." Considering the "uneven . . . earnings over the years," the column went on, some stockholders were obviously attracted because the "founder is an original," not "because of the results."

The Polaroid Corporation is, of course, much more than a carnival and its founder something more than a charismatic crank. From its million-dollar funding in 1937, the firm grew in thirty years to be the 230th largest American industrial corporation (in terms of sales), and to have an even better standing in assets (180th), net income (140th), and net income as a percentage of sales (53rd, but only 348th in net income as a percentage of stockholders' equity).

To achieve such growth, Land had to be much more than visionary genius, snake-oil merchant, and propounder of sonorous platitudes. Singly or together these are not unusual qualities. Even Land's ability to resist bedazzlement in Times Square and see at once a technical solution (plastic or glass with a molecular structure that eliminates glare), while extraordinary, was certainly not unprecedented. In fact, the validity of an inventor's "visionary flash" is a principle accepted in law as far back as George Westinghouse. What distinguished Land was his combination of inventive genius and personal charisma with a hard-headed business sense that included a shrewd grasp of the market, a conservative approach to business finance, and an ability to select and inspire talented subordinates. In these qualities and his exercise of them there emerged the fascinating interplay of Land's innate personality and the values and traditions of American society.

However much he came across as a cornball in expressing his convictions, Land, like Carnegie, Edison, Ford, and others before him, genuinely believed that his firm's success depended on and contributed to the success of his society. Nor did he see any contradiction between business and aesthetics. "I am first of all an artistic person," he said in 1975:

> I'm interested in love and affection and sharing and making beauty part of everyday life. . . . I'm lucky enough to . . . earn my living by contributing to a warmer and richer world. . . . And if I use all my scientific, professional abilities in doing that, I think that makes for a good life.

And not just a good life for him, but potentially for everyone, everywhere. Land, like most scientists and like generations of Americans, scientists and otherwise, saw science as the key to unlock the chains of misery and ugliness. "It bothers us at Polaroid," he said in 1972, "to see a world that could be ever so much more tender and beautiful if the full potential of science were realized."

Like Henry Ford, who argued that if you "do good" in business, "the money will fall into your hands; you can't get out of it," Land insisted that profit is an inevitable end result of good work, not the reason for it. "If anything characterized [Polaroid and drove] the analysts wild," he exulted, it was the fact that "we grow and grow and grow, not on the basis of bottom line but on the basis of faith that if you do your job well [,] the last thing you have to worry about is money, just as if you live right, you'll be happy." Land thus advocated a belief in the harmony and symbiosis among work, virtue, profit, beauty, technology, and progress that, if not unique to Americans, has characterized them to an extraordinary degree throughout their history and has so often served businessmen as motive and justification.

Land saw utility and beauty as synonymous, and often described such mundanities as cameras and film cassettes as "miraculous" and "beautifully self-contained." Moreover, they opened vistas of art and communication for mass enjoyment. As Ford could visualize the Model T, in all its utilitarian ugliness, as opening to "the great multitude . . . the blessing of hours of pleasure in God's great open spaces," so Land could see his cameras removing "all mechanical obstacles between . . . people . . . and the exercising of a new art" and opening "a domain . . . in which friends can share the deep satisfaction of creating together and in which strangers while photographing together can explore the pleasant periphery of friendship."

Beneath Land's idealism, however, there lurked a hard-won awareness that all these glorious benefits depended upon market acceptance. That acceptance, he learned, does not come automatically, however much potential beauty some gadget may have in the eye of its creator. In the late 1930s, having mastered the art of manufacturing glare-reducing glass, Land stalked a quarry much bigger than the limited market presented by camera filters and sunglasses. The virtues of applying the Polaroid system to automobile headlights and windshields, thus reducing glare and the bloody crashes it produced, seemed so obvious to Land that he could not imagine the automobile industry declining to avail itself of such a boon. Decline it did, however, citing expense and complexity, a Detroit anthem that has become all too familiar over the years.

With that chance gone a-glimmering, Land cast about for some other product with mass market potential. He came up with the "Vectograph" system of motion pictures, the so-called 3-D movies, successfully demonstrated at the 1939 New York World's Fair. While there wasn't as much profit potential in cardboard Polaroid glasses as there was in automobile headlights, it was, nevertheless, a juicy enough possibility to make visions of sugarplums dance in anyone's head. After an interruption for World War II, Polaroid pressed on with the Vectograph, and for a time millions of Americans, little cardboard glasses perched on their heads, leaped and squirmed about in darkened moviehouses, dodging spears and darts flung and spat at them by Hollywood aborigines. In the early 1950s the fad died, of its own absurdity, trashy movies, and competition from that emerging giant, television. Polaroid, like the makers of hula hoops later, suddenly found itself stuck with warehouses full of the silly things.

Twice, then, the firm had come to a dead end, both times by relying on another industry as the market for its products. "We learned," one of Land's lieutenants later recalled, "that the best way [was] to sell as directly to the consumer as possible." Fortunately, by the time the 3-D movie craze subsided, Land was already producing by the million a product that could be sold just that way, the instant camera.

The instant camera had resulted from another of Land's flashes. On vacation with his wife and three-year-old daughter, Jennifer, in New Mexico in 1943, Land took a picture of the little girl, who at once demanded to see the result. It was Times Square all over again. Why not a combination camera-developer that would need only to be aimed and shot before disgorging a fully developed color picture? Snapshots while you wait; who could resist such a marvel? Almost no one, Land thought, for his vision ignited a "fantasy" that the instant camera would "be as widely used as the telephone," and could "have the same impact as the telephone on the way people live."

Almost at once, Land sensed he could make such a camera, though he knew it would take time: "By the time Jennifer and I returned from our walk," he said, "I had solved all the problems except for the ones it [took] from 1943 to 1972 to solve. Within an hour," he added, "the camera, the film and the physical chemistry became so clear" that he could rush to a friend and describe in detail "a dry camera which would give a picture immediately after exposure." Such a creation required compressing the whole apparatus of darkrooms — tanks full of chemicals, rinsing baths, enlargers, and printers — into a process that could be crammed into the innards of a small, inexpensive camera. Assuming all this could be done, the product then had to be flogged into a market dominated by Eastman Kodak, an old, established, technically proficient, productively efficient firm with resources that dwarfed pygmy Polaroid's.

None of these obstacles deflected Land. If he could imagine the camera, he could make it: "All that we at Polaroid had learned about . . . polarizers and plastics, and . . . viscous liquids, and . . . microscopic crystals . . . was preparation for [that] day when I suddenly knew how to make a one-step photographic process." And, if he could make, it, he could sell it. After all, "Virtue and a good product are invincible." What Kodak might or might not do was irrelevant. Within six months, Land had worked out the essential technical details of the developing process and had begun to erect the battlement of patents necessary to defend his handiwork against marauding competitors. Land like many an inventor predecessor, might have made his fortune by selling his patents, thus avoiding the vexations of manufacturing and distribution, but for him, making and selling the camera were not "problems" to be foisted off on some more able firm, but "opportunities" that Land himself could exploit.

When World War II ended, and with it most of the lucrative military contracts that had assured the firm's prosperity, Land had renounced the precarious role of peacetime military contractor. Instead, he bet everything on the instant camera, gambling that he could win a race between product development and bankruptcy. It was a close call. By 1947 business had declined to less than a tenth of the wartime level, while research expenses had skyrocketed, producing three consecutive years of heavy losses. On February 21, 1947, however, Land dazzled the Optical Society of America by demonstrating his instant camera. A subsequent appearance at the 1948 convention of the Photographic Society of America stole the show, garnered reams of free publicity, and whetted the public's appetite. Finally, on November 26, 1948, the Polaroid Land Camera, Model 95, went on sale at the Jordan Marsh department store in Boston.

The first camera was a far cry from Land's ideal of a compact, one-step, color picture machine. It was large, heavy (five pounds), and relatively expensive ($89.95); it required manual setting of shutter speed and lens opening, needed considerable practice to get passable results, took a minute to develop its film, and turned out pictures printed in sepia tones reminiscent of a bygone era. The public, nevertheless, loved it; it took months for production to catch up with demand.

As Land had predicted, the new camera created its own un-challenged market. It catered to Americans' love of gadgetry, their craving for instant gratification, and their orientation to-ward things visual, a penchant long nurtured by movies, news-reels, picture magazines,and soon to be intensified by television. It also unleashed a whole new cottage industry, home pornogra-phy, permitting the libidinous to memorialize their fantasies without fear of exposure by prurient druggists or tale-bearing film developers.

As the years passed, Polaroid expanded its original market by cutting prices, which put the camera in reach of ever-larger seg-ments of the public, and by improving quality, which rendered previous models obsolete. The two strategies were not always in-corporated into a single camera model. Within eighteen months black-and-white film replaced the original sepia; in 1954, the Highlander model ($60) appeared; in 1960, ten-second devel-oping film; in 1963, color film and the Automatic 100 to shoot it ($130–$160); in 1965, the Swinger ($14); in 1967, the Colorpack series ($50–$180); in 1968, the Big Swinger ($20) and the Color-pack II ($30). The firm thus reached up and down in the market, seeking customers among both serious photographers and the le-gions of artistically unwashed. The trick was to get the camera into people's hands. If that could be done, success was assured because the big profits, both in terms of volume and markup, were in the sale of the film. Indeed, so remunerative was the film business that it justified selling the camera at cost and, in fact, might have justified giving it away.

Carrying on the simultaneous activities of research, manufac-turing millions of cameras and hundreds of millions of film packets, and distributing the products into the mass consumer market entailed a burden of responsibilities that not even Land's energy could transcend. The combined operation, moreover, re-quired vast masses of capital. Land, in the tradition of financially conservative manufacturers before him — Carnegie, Pierre du Pont, Ford — thought borrowed capital a shortcut to loss of control or ruin. Consequently, Polaroid has never borrowed a dime; it financed its growth with retained profits and the proceeds from the sale of additional stock. Land surmounted the myriad problems by spinning off some to outside manufacturers and delegating other responsibilities within the company. He himself concentrated on research in physics, chemistry, and optics. To William McCune he assigned the job of making proposed products an engineering reality. "Land told us what we were going to make," one employee remembered. "Bill McCune showed us how to make everything." The responsibility for creating a sales and distribution system went to J. Harold Booth, a former vice-president at Bell and Howell, whom Land made executive vice-president of Polaroid.

The actual manufacture of the cameras was subcontracted to Bell and Howell, a manufacturer of motion picture equipment, and U.S. Time, producer of Timex watches. Land's archcompetitor, Kodak, was willing enough to make lenses and film to Polaroid specifications. By 1960 these arrangements had succeeded so well that Polaroid products were on sale in forty-five countries around the world and penetrating new markets almost daily. The company's stock had a total market value of over a billion dollars; the share price of $250 or more was better than ninety times annual earnings, indicating what investors thought of future prospects. Through the 1960s, Land fueled this optimism by periodically dropping hints of better things to come, not only in photography, where his predictions were generally fulfilled sooner or later, but also in exotic areas such as photocopying and color television, which to date (1979) have come to nothing.

As prosperity replaced anxiety, Land acquired wealth and fame suitable to the plots of Horatio Alger, collecting honorary degrees (fourteen), medals and awards (thirty-seven, including the Presidential Medal of Freedom), and prestigious appointments (to the faculties of Harvard and MIT, to the President's Science Advisory Committee, and to the President's Foreign Intelligence Advisory Board, among others). All this accumulated bijouterie of success vindicated Land's faith in his abilities as a technician and organizer, but eminently more gratifying was the validation of his whole philosophy of life. Land always conceived of himself as a philosopher/scientist and thought the two roles intertwined and strengthened one another like the strands of a cable.

Land's creed had several distinct components. Underpinning all his work was his faith in mankind's ability to solve its problems rationally. "If you [can] state a problem — any problem — and if it is important enough," he declared categorically, "then the problem can be solved." At first glance this proposition suggests that Land must have been a humbug, a zealot, or a case of arrested development. American society, let alone the rest of the world, festers with important problems readily enough stated but fiercely resistant to solutions. On reflection, however, Land's axiom emerges as one of the stars by which Americans have always steered. By and large, most Americans *have* believed that society's ills can be diagnosed and solved. This attitude has been enshrined in the Constitution, institutionalized in the public education system, transmogrified into the phalanxes of government agencies that send hither swarms of officers to harass our people and eat out their substance, and burlesqued by packs of social scientists roving the land, interviewing pimps and professors, and plugging wires into hired copulators.

For the rationally minded, there are no unknowables, only unknowns, nothing insoluble, only things unsolved. Failure proves only that the diagnosis, the prescription, or both were wrong. Better luck next time. Certainly Land's philosophy took failure readily in stride. "Lots of companies put a great premium on avoiding . . . mistakes," he observed, but at Polaroid, they "put a great premium on being able to make mistakes" because "an essential aspect of creativity is not being afraid to fail. . . . By calling their activities hypotheses and experiments . . . scientists made it possible to fail repeatedly until in the end they got the results they wanted." Land thus was a latter-day Edisonian and doubtless would have seen no paradox in the fact that Edison, who once said, "Results? I've gotten plenty of results. I know several thousand things that won't work," was awarded more patents (1,093) than any other individual in history. Land, whose research team tried more than 5,000 compounds before coming up with one that worked as a dye-developer in instant color film, secured over 500 patents himself, second only to Edison.

Land saw the interrelationship between his personal achievements, the scientific breakthroughs of his research teams, and the growth of the Polaroid Corporation as microcosms of the historical process at large. "There are two opposing theories of history," he declared. "Either you believe that . . . individual greatness does exist and can be nurtured and developed, that such great individuals can be part of a cooperative community [Polaroid, America, the world] while they continue to be their happy, flourishing, contributing selves — or else you believe that there is some mystical, cyclical, overriding, predetermined, cultural law — a historical determinism."

Philosophers, historians, scientists, and people generally have pondered these options for centuries and debate them still. Land thought that the choice between these historical philosophies "divides . . . the world . . . into two parties. They are not Democratic or Republican, or capitalist or communist," but one group that says that "Beethoven was a necessary, inevitable and predictable racial consequence of his predecessors," and another that argues that if Beethoven had never lived, "the history of music would have been entirely different." For Land, the choice seemed clear-cut. With Thomas Carlyle, he believed unequivocally that "Great Men make history" and do so not in interaction with ineluctable, predictable forces, but in interplay with chance and chaos: "For the most part there will be no change [in society] and there must be no change, but what real changes do occur are entirely the result of accidents called individuals."

Science, Land thought, validated his philosophy: "The great contribution of science is to say that [deterministic historical] theory is nonsense." "In retrospect," he observed, society *seems* to have been "continuous in its progress," thus giving the illusion of having followed a predetermined path. Deluded by these mirages in the past, a Karl Marx or a Herbert Spencer could articulate a philosophy that made the future inevitable and foreseeable. For Land, however, such false logic yielded only

absurdity. Actually, "in prospect society is completely un predictable." And there, in the very unpredictability and seeming
disorder of society, lay its fascination and its challenge to the individual, and to individual scientists especially: "Science demonstrate[s] that a person can regard the world as chaos, but can find
in himself a method of perceiving ... small arrangements of
order." If so, he can, by adding his own discovery to "the order
that previous scientists have generated" — a process described
by Sir Isaac Newton as seeing far by "standing on the shoulders
of giants" — "make things that are exciting and thrilling to
make." And these sensations are something much more than the
titillations of successful gadgeteering, because the scientist's
creations can make "deeply spiritual contributions to himself
and to his friends." Better yet, to all mankind: "The scientist
comes to the world and says, 'I do not understand the divine
source, but I know, in a way that I don't understand, that out of
chaos, I can make order, out of loneliness I can make friendship,
out of ugliness I can make beauty!' "

Land himself thought that he had accomplished all this, and
his sense of having contributed to spirituality, order, friendship,
and beauty bolstered his pride more than all the baubles, ban-
gles, wampum, and glory he accumulated. Of course, what applied to him may not hold for everybody. (Okay, you're a bird,
but suppose you're a worm?) His understanding of history may
have been flawed, as his understanding of color vision once was,
in that "the factors ... regarded as determinative are significant
only in a certain special case," his own. If so, he may once again
have been "misled" by the "accidental universality of this special
case." Accidental universalities, however, may serve well enough
to steer a course by. For centuries sailors navigated with pinpoint
accuracy using the Ptolemaic system of the universe, for all that
it was wrong. Certainly Land's philosophy sustained him
through thick and thin, and he never needed it more than in the
early 1970s, when the struggle to develop the SX-70, the ultimate
in instant color cameras, turned out to be a struggle for Polaroid's survival.

The SX-70 represented the camera of Land's original dream.

Its electronic wizardry sensed light conditions and distance to the subject, then took care of all the necessary adjustments to the focus, lens opening, and shutter speed. Once the little red button was pushed, a motor, powered by a battery contained in the film pack, shoved out the picture, which then developed in full color right before your eyes and even had a protective plastic coating. No fuss, no muss, no garbage, no bother. No need to puzzle over a lot of complex instructions and then waste a lot of expensive film to find out that you didn't understand them. Just open the camera, shove in the film, close the camera, and blaze away. No wonder Land's pet name for the SX-70 was "Aladdin."

As a *fait accompli,* the camera seemed simple enough. In development, however, it was a technological nightmare, demanding simultaneous pathbreaking in chemistry, optics, and electronics. In vintage Land fashion he initiated the project by telling his staff what he wanted the camera to do, then complicated the whole business by demanding that Aladdin's genie fit in a very small bottle, to compete with Kodak's immensely successful pocket camera, the Instamatic. "Land gave my boss a block of wood," one design engineer recalled, "and told him that's how large the camera could be. . . . So in a sense you could say that Dr. Land's tailor determined the size of the SX-70."

The project took eight years and carried Polaroid into areas it had previously avoided. Because, as Land said, "these cameras and film are technologically unique, involving new science at each point of manufacture," Polaroid decided that for the first time it must do its own manufacturing. Not only did this mean designing and building film and camera plants, but it also involved going into the chemical business to assure an adequate supply of film components. In the long run, this integration of design and manufacture might vastly increase Polaroid's profits, but first a massive investment had to be made in plant and equipment. These expenses, added to a research budget that outran all expectations, put a massive strain on the company's finances. Altogether the SX-70 project gobbled up half a billion dollars before it returned a penny.

Finally, at the 1972 annual meeting, Land mounted the stage

and announced, "Photography will never be the same." The new camera, he declared, produced pictures in color that was "astounding, having qualities for which we have no names." He thereupon pulled an SX-70 from his pocket and fired off five pictures in ten seconds, to the tumultuous approval of the assembled faithful, who basked in the glow of riches certain to come. Land had done it again.

It was an auspicious beginning, to be sure, but big profits were to be delayed yet a while. Beset by production breakdowns, film spoilage, and a declining economy, Polaroid's sales and profits fell through 1973 and 1974. In January, 1974, *Fortune* published an article called "Can Polaroid Win That Half-Billion Dollar Bet? How Polaroid Bet Its Future on the SX-70." A year later things looked grim. Still learning how to run its new plants, Polaroid labored with the triple burden of high costs, low production, and erratic product quality. In November, 1974, the firm took the unprecedented and embarrassing step of laying off a thousand employees; in January, 1975, it deferred scheduled pay raises "to conserve [its] resources." Suppliers canceled contracts as Polaroid canceled orders. For a time it looked as though 1975 might be the company's first deficit year since 1948.

In addition to these woes, a new menace loomed on the horizon. In March, 1974, Kodak announced that it was developing its own instant camera. Given Kodak's resources (still ten times greater than Polaroid's), its expertise, and its aggressive marketing techniques, it promised formidable competition that might be in the field by the time Polaroid got its kinks worked out and demand revived. Through it all, while some of his executives confided to *Fortune*'s reporter that the company's fate hung in the balance, Land himself radiated serenity and confidence. Asked by a *Forbes* reporter about Polaroid's troubles with the SX-70, Land retorted, "What problems? Those problems are largely problems in the press." In fact, a little trouble was a good thing for a big company. Take, for example, the vexing tendency of the SX-70's battery to leak onto the film: "I think the battery saved us," Land said, "because without the troubles with it, we would have been spoiled and . . . growing too fast. It was a happy accident, a cloud with a very silver lining."

By April, 1976, when Kodak unveiled its own instant camera, Polaroid's clouds, silver-lined and otherwise, had thinned under the sunshine of resumed profits. Increased efficiency, revived consumer demand, and cheaper models of the camera all contributed to the surge, which continued through 1976, when Polaroid sold over six million cameras, a new company record. In the years since, although Kodak has expanded its share of the instant camera market to one third, it has absorbed huge losses ($75 million in 1977), while Polaroid was selling more cameras than ever and making money at it. In the instant camera field, Kodak seemed to have met its match. Analyzing the crucial Christmas sales of 1977, when Polaroid's OneStep met Kodak's Handle head-on in competition for the low-priced market, *Fortune* trumpeted, "Polaroid's OneStep Is Stopping Kodak Cold." By holding its share of the market, Polaroid justified William McCune's optimism, expressed in 1975, about Kodak's impending entry into the market: "We expect competition," he said, "and have been planning for it." Meanwhile, by Christmas, 1977, Land, who thought "optimism is a moral duty," had introduced the Polavision instant movie system, thus creating another market where no competition existed.

As Land turned seventy in 1979, and the string of miraculous surprises obviously neared its end, speculation focused on Land's successor and the future of his company. Land had no sons, and no man seemed likely to be able to take his place. Asked by *Fortune* about his successor, "Land launched into a description of such a paragon of talent, intelligence, and virtue that even he paused, laughed, and said, 'We're making him down in the laboratory.' " In fact, he'll doubtless turn out to have been produced down in the bureaucracy. Polaroid after Land, like Kodak after George Eastman, will pass from the ranks of the personal firms into the cadre of corporate bureaucratic giants.

As an industrialist, Land saw himself in the classic mold of the Schumpeterian entrepreneur, whose function was "to make a new kind of product." But industry had a further responsibility, "the production of a worthwhile, highly rewarding, highly creative, inspiring daily job for every one of a hundred million Americans." In 1945, when Polaroid was a young company, Land declared his intention of creating "products that are genuinely unique and useful, excellent in quality, made well and efficiently, [to] present an attractive value to the public and an attractive profit to the Company." His second goal was to provide "a worthwhile working life for each member of the Company — a working life that calls out the member's best talents and skills — in which he or she shares the responsibilities and the rewards."

The first task proved easier than the second, especially after Polaroid entered mass production. The assembly line presented problems of boredom and worker morale that not even Land's genius could resolve. Land, of course, thought it could and would be done, by some new actor emerging to play the lead role in what Land once called "high technological drama."

Land was right; we do have a choice of historical philosophies. We can opt for determinism and say we'll never see his like again. Or we can say maybe we won't, but who knows what human possibilities may lie ahead. In determinism there is only waiting; in possibility at least there is hope.

11

Of Things Past and Things to Come

I ONCE taught a course in American history to a class of United Auto Workers shop stewards. In terms of age and sex, and of religious, ethnic, and regional backgrounds, this group was the most random sample of American workers I have ever run across, with the exception of a bunch I encountered while waiting out a traffic jam on a Detroit freeway. A more contentious lot I never met; virtually every historical figure or topic I raised — Lincoln, F.D.R., John Kennedy, Lyndon Johnson, slavery, the New Deal, Viet Nam, the "War on Poverty" — touched off a furious debate, with opinions crushed into venomous metaphors and delivered by voices accustomed to making themselves heard over assembly lines. Compared to these biweekly imbroglios, the class I taught at Jackson State Penitentiary was a Quaker meeting.

Only once, when I asked the shop stewards whether they agreed with "Engine Charlie" Wilson's statement that "what's good for General Motors is good for the country," did the class declare a unanimous position. To these worthies, who spent a good part of their lives in a running fracas with car company management, Wilson's statement was so obviously true that talking about it would have wasted class time. When I said I could present a contrary opinion that some people, at least, firmly held, I was greeted first with open disbelief, then with guffaws, and finally with an accolade delivered by the senior member of the class: "For a professor, you're the goddamnedest agitator I ever saw, but you won't get us going with that one."

Finding a strong conservative element in such a group didn't exactly astonish me, for, as I knew from my own experience, an optimist could be defined as someone who expects to uncover a genuine radical in the American trade union hierarchy. I must admit, however, that the unity of opinion and depth of sentiment *did* come as a surprise. These people weren't fools; indeed, they labored (literally and figuratively) under far fewer illusions about American business than did most of my supposedly better-informed academic colleagues, including those given to fusillades of radical rhetoric.

What the class disclosed, of course, was the durable commonality of assumptions shared by American business and labor. From Eli Whitney through Henry Ford II and at all points between, American businessmen generally believed that their individual efforts redounded to the benefit of their society and, by implication at least, to the good of mankind as a whole. While this attitude sometimes served as an excuse for malevolent business conduct, ranging from the outrageous to the criminally abusive, most entrepreneurs thought the progress of American society, powered by the business system, validated their rationale and justified their actions. Manufacturers, whose tangible products contributed visibly to the rising standard of living, particularly conceived of themselves as agents of progress. On the whole, their fellow citizens, workers included, agreed.

As American society grew more complex and more engaged with the rest of the world, American businessmen and their organizations followed a parallel development. Tracing the route of American enterprise from Eli Whitney, who found the southern United States incomprehensible and felt at ease only in his New Haven water mill, surrounded by his fellow Yankees, to Henry Ford II, at home anywhere in the world, confidently guiding his global imperium, one continually intersects the trail of all America's past and finds it converging with the track left by the broad caravan of world history.

In a society and a world grown so complicated, beset with problems so vexing, the efficacy of the individual as a prime mover for good has seemed to diminish, and with it the American tendency to see businessmen as savants and their organizations as fonts from which healing waters may flow. With the exception of Henry Ford II and the occasional businessman who occupies a cabinet post, few of them are ever consulted, as Carnegie, Edison, Rockefeller, and the original Henry Ford so often were, for opinions on politics, famine, war, finance, and phrenology. In their stead we have the aperçus of rock stars, media mandarins, professorial pundits, and bureaucratic boffins.

At the same time, private business has suffered a decline in its estimated potential for contributing to the general welfare, both here and abroad. Bristling nationalism and wary internationalism have supplanted capitalistic chauvinism in many societies around the world; Americans who once looked to Carnegie's steel and Rockefeller's oil and Ford's automobiles for assurances of continued prosperity and tranquility now increasingly fasten their hopes on government or alliances of governments, while eying business and the men who run it as likely sources of grief.

Though I'm not so naïve as to think that unfettered liberty of individual actions inevitably leads to the best of all possible worlds, nor fool enough to believe that any tangle, no matter how knotty, in the skein of mankind's affairs can be unraveled by a single genius working alone, neither do I think that the record dictates a complete withdrawal from the rough stockades of individualism into the gray battlements of centralized planning, by whatever political philosophy defined.

People must certainly work together, but unless the inspiration and guiding spirit flow from some individual, the result is unlikely to better the visions of the least common denominator and may in fact turn out to be nothing at all. "Ten thousand committees," Eric Sevareid observed, "could never produce the Sistine ceiling. How many they prevent we shall never know." There is yet hope for the individual, even for individual businessmen, whose impact on those things that decent people everywhere cherish may be more salubrious than current opinion would have it. Sevareid, reflecting on a lifetime's experience as an eyewitness to some of history's most cataclysmic events, concluded that "among the underpinnings of the world's interdependence, which we have desired, and which is unavoidable, the underpinning of business may be the most solid of all and the least offensive." And this is so because "business is flexible enough to take and to give, to advance and retreat. It does not want people's souls, as do the intellectuals; it does not want their obedience, as does the military; it only wants their money, the cheapest of all commodities."

Sevareid's contemporary, Theodore H. White, offered a similar testimony, similarly wound onto his "spool of inner rhetoric" after a career that positioned him at one nexus of history after another: "Most liberals do not like to think of themselves as being linked historically with the traders because the drive force of trade is profit, a dirty word to moralists everywhere."

Nevertheless, White admitted,

It came to me slowly . . . that the values that liberals cherish flourish better in the trader's world than in the Pharaonic world. Art and music can flourish in both worlds. But learning and religion, letters, poetry and science thrive better in the trader's. . . . There are no other ways of governing men; one either lures them forward by hope of gain and selfish betterment, or one drives them forward by bayonet, club and fear of the knuckle breakers.

For White, the success of the Marshall Plan furnished the proof that justified advancing from the hypothetical to the axiomatic what Sevareid called "our basic premise [which] has been, these many years, that peace, democracy and material gain are not only good each in itself, but interdependent." The Marshall Plan, White argued, worked because

It had linked gain with freedom, had assumed that the movement of minds and the movement of peoples must go with the movement of goods and of merchants. In the noblest terms, it had enlisted the good will of free peoples against the discipline of orderly peoples. In the crudest terms, it had enlisted greed against terror.

These are, of course, but two opinions, though surely two with a better claim than most. Neither the two alone, nor any number of concurrences, is likely to convert dedicated opponents, and certainly no amount of optimism should loosen constraints against the abuses of greed, "hope of gain and selfish betterment." But history, as I have learned it in libraries, classrooms, and archives, and experienced it in railroad yards, truck stops, steel mills, and chemical plants, tells me that Sevareid and White are right, things *have* worked that way in the past. Common sense tells me that, barring some sea change in human nature, they're likely to work that way in the future. Pursuing gain, power, security in the elusive American marketplace, Whitney, McCormick, and the rest of my cast of characters came forward to solve problems of the past. Not all that resulted was good, but their labors eased, in America at least, the ageless yoke of cold, hunger, and want.

But it must be noted, as I have tried to show throughout this book, that while an individual may supply the catalyst, the inspiration, the guiding force, the discipline to solve problems and get things done and may indelibly stamp a personal flair into an organization or a product, success doesn't come from working alone. Indeed, each of my cast acted as a conductor, not as a soloist. Each was characterized by an extraordinary ability to create and inspire an organization — at least for a time — with the joy of cooperative effort, a spirit on which corporate capitalism depends just as much as would any variety of socialism. These men's charisma took many forms, from the exuberant Edison, flinging his top hat into a pan of oil, letting out a war whoop, and donning his greasy overalls, to the custom-tailored "Silent Sloan," who could ask a subordinate, "Have you ever heard me raise my voice about anything?"

The sheer variety of these men's styles, as well as their disparate origins, are themselves typical of the American experience. Their businesses have also benefited from a characteristic American trait: the ability to apply easygoing leadership to a fractious rank and file, creating organizations that drive ahead with verve and efficiency. Foreign observers, watching American troops in training, could never understand how they ever won battles. Similarly, an outsider who eavesdropped in an auto workers' bar on Eight Mile Road in Detroit or read the diatribes in a union newspaper might well expect to hear momentarily that the toilers had arisen, slaughtered the bosses like swine, torn down the factories brick by brick, and smashed the machines. But it hasn't happened yet, and I doubt it ever will.

Who or what comes next no one can say. Historian Livesay, like the poet Yeats, can only wonder

> *What rough beast, its hour come round at last,*
> *Slouches towards Bethlehem to be born?*

A Note on Sources

THIS book distills my own educational experiences, formal and informal. As the text indicates, it owes as much to the fifteen years I spent in railroad yards, steel mills, and truck stops as it does to the similar period I've spent leafing through the papers of American businessmen and the articles and books written about them. My own work, however, would have been impossible without the labors of other historians and biographers.

Three works in particular persuaded me that a book like this one could say something worthwhile about America: Carl Degler's *Out of Our Past* (New York, 1972), in my opinion the best one-volume essay extant on American history; Richard Hofstadter's *Age of Reform* (New York, 1948), many of its arguments now dated, but still a masterful demonstration of how individual lives can illuminate broader themes; and Robert Heilbroner's *Worldly Philosophers* (New York, 1972), in which biographical sketches elucidate complex minds and arcane theories comprehensibly and amusingly.

The literature of American history has reached intimidating dimensions, despite the fact that all of us who shuffle through the past are constantly reimpressed with how little we know about it. Every historical figure, every major theme, every peripheral comment in this book could be the subject of an extensive bibliography. One could, for example, while away many a shining hour exploring the debate about how much Eli Whitney actually contributed to the development of the American machine tool industry. What follows here, then, is not a comprehensive list of the sources I used, but rather a starting point — a list of relevant works, widely available, many of them containing notes and bibliographies that will carry interested readers as deep into the past as they care to journey.

HISTORY OF THE AMERICAN ECONOMY: Since American economic history tries to explain how one society has beaten the odds, becoming a luxury economy in a subsistence world, it should attract more attention than it does. Its neglect by students and the general public owes something to the literature, much of it a swampland of abstruse and conflicting theory, mind-numbing jargon, and numerological magic shows, all obscuring the fact that the underlying processes are simple enough, however complex their manifestations. There are, happily, some glowing exceptions. The uninitiated can begin with Robert Heilbroner's *Making of Economic Society* (Englewood Cliffs, N.J., 1975), which conveys the reader from the ancient world of farmers and herdsmen, armed with sticks and stones, through to the modern world of multinational corporations equipped with computers and telecommunications. Like all Heilbroner's books, this one explains and entertains as it goes along.

W. Elliot Brownlee's *Dynamics of Ascent* (New York, 1978) is a fine textbook requiring no background in business or economics.

HISTORY OF AMERICAN BUSINESS: Relatively young as specialized areas of history go, this subject remains the province of a small number of practitioners. Fortunately, two of them have produced masterworks that cover a lot of ground and contain encyclopedic references. Thomas C. Cochran's *Business in American Life: A History* (New York, 1972) relates American business practice to the larger environment. Alfred D. Chandler, Jr.'s *Visible Hand* (Cambridge, Mass., 1977) traces the genealogy of American business management. For the period it describes, Glenn Porter's *Rise of Big Business in the United States, 1860-1910* (New York, 1973) provides, in a style that incorporates grace and humor, a summary of the facts and what historians have made of them. All three of these works embody analytical structures of elegant simplicity that bring order to and establish causal relationships among a welter of details.

CHAPTER 2: ELI WHITNEY: Jeannette Mirsky and Alan Nevins, *The World of Eli Whitney* (New York, 1952) is a comprehensive biography containing a brief but useful summary of the history of machinery prior to Whitney. A shorter version is Constance Green, *Eli Whitney and the Birth of American Technology* (Boston, 1956). Much of the history of technology suffers from being written by and for technologists, but a helpful exception is Nathan Rosenberg, *Technology and American Economic Growth* (New York, 1972), which includes a discussion of the impact of patent laws on the rate of technological diffusion. H. J. Habbakuk, *British and American Technology in the*

Nineteenth Century (Cambridge, 1962) examines the greater rapidity with which Americans adapted labor-saving machinery. Habbakuk also raises the question of whether Britain ultimately suffered from its early lead in technology, a question Americans might ponder with respect to their own fate in the twentieth century. Finally, an excellent essay on Whitney and his relevance to the American economy is in Jonathan Hughes's *Vital Few* (New York, 1973), which also contains chapters on Edison, Carnegie, and Ford.

CHAPTER 3: CYRUS HALL MCCORMICK: The definitive biography is William T. Hutchinson, *Cyrus Hall McCormick* (New York, 1930 and 1935), 2 vols. Useful, if sometimes self-serving, details can be found in Cyrus Hall McCormick III, *The Century of the Reaper* (New York, 1933). The emergence of International Harvester is examined in U.S. Bureau of Corporations, *International Harvester* (Washington, D.C., 1913), which contains elaborate information on the premerger McCormick empire. The significance of McCormick's distribution methods is discussed in Chandler, *The Visible Hand*. Agriculture in the American breadbasket is the subject of Fred A. Shannon's *Farmer's Last Frontier: Agriculture, 1860–1897* (New York, 1957) and Gilbert C. Fite's *Farmer's Frontier, 1865–1900*. Few history books, however, can match the evocative impact of novels such as Willa Cather, *My Ántonia* (New York, 1962), or Ole Rölvaag, *Giants in the Earth* (New York, 1956).

CHAPTER 4: ANDREW CARNEGIE: Carnegie is one of a handful of American manufacturers subjected to a full-scale biography by a modern scholar. Joseph F. Wall, *Andrew Carnegie* (New York, 1970), is painstaking, thorough, and touches all aspects of Carnegie's many-faceted life. Less factually accurate, but more reflective of Carnegie's personality is Burton Hendrick, *The Life of Andrew Carnegie* (New York, 1932). Harold C. Livesay, *Andrew Carnegie and the Rise of Big Business* (Boston, 1975), concentrates on Carnegie's development as a manager and his contribution to modern American manufacturing management methods. An overview of America's economy in the time of Whitney, McCormick, and Carnegie can be found in George Rogers Taylor, *The Transportation Revolution, 1815–1860* (New York, 1968), and Edward C. Kirkland, *Industry Comes of Age* (New York, 1967). Alfred D. Chandler, Jr., ed., *The Railroads: The Nation's First Big Business* (New York, 1965), traces the railroad's pioneering role in management. Edward C. Kirkland, *Dream and Thought in the Busi-*

ness Community, 1860–1900 (New York, 1964), highlights the self-image fancied by Carnegie and some of his mogul contemporaries. Carnegie himself held forth on his favorite theme in *The Autobiography of Andrew Carnegie* (Boston, 1920), a fascinating book, but one not overwed to accuracy.

CHAPTER 5: THOMAS A. EDISON: There have been several Edison biographies, and more are on the way now that Edison's papers are in one place and available. Matthew Josephson, long one of America's premier biographers, produced an entertaining volume in *Edison* (New York, 1959), one that benefited from Josephson's lifetime of study and writing about Edison's era, its knights and knaves. More recent, less original, but brief and well written is Ronald W. Clark, *Edison: The Man Who Made the Future* (New York, 1977). Edison's inventions, the extent of their originality, their relationship to the emerging world of commercial electricity and the machines it ran is a story as complex as the wiring for New York City. The best for the nonmasochist is to stick to Harold C. Passer, *The Electrical Manufacturers, 1875–1900* (Cambridge, Mass., 1953). A collection of original Edisonian observations is Dagobert D. Runes, ed., *The Diary and Sundry Observations of Thomas Alva Edison* (New York, 1948).

CHAPTER 6: HENRY FORD: Ford ranks with the most-written-about Americans. Happily, Roger Burlingame, *Henry Ford* (New York, 1970), is one of the best brief biographies ever written about anyone. In addition, there is a massive, detailed opus that includes the history of the company: Alan Nevins et al., *Ford* (New York, 1954, 1957, and 1963), 3 vols. The Nevins team made extensive use of the Ford archives, but may have been a bit too admiring in their analysis. No such accusation could be made of Keith Sward, whose *Legend of Henry Ford* (New York, 1948) remains the most acerbic interpretation. Many of Ford's contemporaries wrote their own observations, but the most valuable is Charles Sorenson, *My Forty Years with Ford* (London, 1957). Ford has also enjoyed the attentions of a psychological biographer, Anne Jardim. The result, *The First Henry Ford: A Study in Personality and Business Leadership* (Cambridge, Mass., 1970), is an interesting if inconclusive attempt to lasso a will-o'-the-wisp. The popular view of Ford is the subject of an essay in Sigmund Diamond, *The Reputation of American Businessmen* (New York, 1955), and rated two full-scale books in addition: David Lewis, *The*

Public Image of Henry Ford (Ann Arbor, Mich., 1977), and Reynold M. Wik, *Henry Ford and Grass Roots America* (Ann Arbor, Mich., 1972). Both books contain rollicking good stories about Tin Lizzie and her creator. Lewis, in addition, furnishes a detailed, serious (if somewhat uncritical) account of the Ford public relations effort, including the disastrous anti-Semitic campaign. Most histories of the automobile industry are Gasoline Alley stuff, but Alfred D. Chandler, Jr., ed., *Giant Enterprise: Ford, General Motors, and the Automobile Industry*, summarizes major developments for the "Big Two" through 1941.

CHAPTER 7: PIERRE S. DU PONT: The basic source for Pierre du Pont's career is Alfred D. Chandler, Jr., and Stephen Salsbury, *Pierre S. du Pont and the Making of the Modern Corporation* (New York, 1971), an exhaustive work based on extensive research in the papers of Pierre and other Du Ponts. The Du Pont family squabbles and the career of one of the major combatants are in Marquis James, *Alfred I. du Pont, The Family Rebel* (Indianapolis, Ind., 1941). There are several histories of the Du Pont Company, none of them first-class. Bessie G. du Pont, *E. I. du Pont de Nemours and Company: A History, 1802-1902* (Boston, 1920), features the personal viewpoint of its author, Alfred I. du Pont's first wife. William S. Dutton, *Du Pont: One Hundred and Forty Years* (New York, 1942) is better, but dated and pedestrian.

CHAPTER 8: ALFRED P. SLOAN: Details of Sloan's accession to the General Motors presidency, his reforms, and their impact on American industry are in Chandler, *Giant Enterprise,* and Chandler and Salsbury, *Pierre S. du Pont.* An intensive study of General Motors under Durant and its subsequent reorganization is in Alfred D. Chandler, Jr., *Strategy and Structure* (Garden City, N.Y., 1966). Lawrence H. Seltzer, *A Financial History of the American Automobile Industry* (Boston, 1928), and Arthur Pound, *The Turning Wheel* (Garden City, N.Y., 1934), also contain useful information on the early days of GM. Sloan told his own story twice, in *Adventures of a White Collar Man* (New York, 1941) and *My Years with General Motors* (Garden City, N.Y., 1964). The latter, as might be expected, is the better of the two. In it Sloan, in semiretirement, reflected on the meaning of his fifty years as an organization builder.

CHAPTER 9: HENRY FORD II: Volume III of Nevins et al., *Ford: Decline and Rebirth,* discusses Henry Ford II's accession to power, his dismissal of Harry Bennett, and the early years of the company's reorganization. Ernest Breech, chief architect of the new structure, is the subject of Mel J. Hickerson, *Ernie Breech* (New York, 1969). Booton Herndon, *Ford: An Unconventional Biography of the Men and Their Times* (New York, 1969), is a journalistic but imaginative comparison of the two men and their companies, based on extensive interviews with Henry Ford II, some members of his family, and Ford executives. Since 1946, Henry II and his company have been the subject of a series of articles in *Fortune* magazine, as well as other business journals. In addition, a perusal of *The New York Times Index* since World War II reveals how much, how often, and in how many contexts Henry II has made news. Other members of the Ford hierarchy — Arjay Miller, Robert McNamara, Lee Iacocca, Bunkie Knudsen — have also enjoyed their share of the journalistic limelight. Mira Wilkins and Frank E. Hill, *American Business Abroad: Ford on Six Continents* (New York, 1964), tells the story of Ford overseas through the early 1960s; Wilkins, *The Emergence of Multinational Enterprise* and *The Maturing of Multinational Enterprise* (Cambridge, Mass., 1970 and 1974), put the Ford experience in the broader context of American overseas manufacturing operations. For the period since 1960, I have relied on my own research in company documents and interviews with Ford personnel in the United States and abroad.

CHAPTER 10: EDWIN LAND: Mark Olshaker, *The Instant Image: Edwin Land and the Polaroid Experience* (New York, 1978), is the only biography, but Land's career, like Henry Ford II's, can be followed in the pages of *Fortune, The New York Times,* and similar sources. The Polaroid Corporation *Annual Reports* also make worthwhile reading as they record the company's success, speculate on its future, and include specimens of Land's unmistakable prose.

CHAPTER 11: The White quotations are from Theodore H. White, *In Search of History* (New York, 1978); Eric Sevareid's from *Not So Wild a Dream* (New York, 1976).

Index